German

A ROUGH GUIDE
PHRASEBOOK

Compiled
by Lexus

Credits

Compiled by Lexus with Horst Kopleck

Lexus Series Editor:	Sally Davies
Rough Guides Phrase Book Editor:	Jonathan Buckley
Rough Guides Series Editor:	Mark Ellingham

This first edition published in 1995 by Rough Guides Ltd, 1 Mercer Street, London WC2H 9QJ.

Distributed by the Penguin Group.

Penguin Books Ltd, 27 Wrights Lane, London W8 5TZ
Penguin Books USA Inc., 375 Hudson Street, New York 10014, USA
Penguin Books Australia Ltd, 487 Maroondah Highway, PO Box 257, Ringwood, Victoria 3134, Australia
Penguin Books Canada Ltd, Alcorn Avenue, Toronto, Ontario, Canada M4V 1E4
Penguin Book (NZ) Ltd, 182–190 Wairau Road, Auckland 10, New Zealand

Typeset in Rough Serif and Rough Sans to an original design by Henry Iles.
Printed by Cox & Wyman Ltd, Reading.

British Library Cataloguing in Publication Data
A catalogue for this book is available from the British Library.

ISBN 1-85828-146-6

CONTENTS

INTRODUCTION

The Rough Guide German phrasebook is a highly practical
introduction to the contemporary language. Laid out in clear A-Z
style, it uses key-word referencing to lead you straight to the
words and phrases you want – so if you need to book a room,
just look up 'room'. The Rough Guide gets straight to the point
in every situation, in bars and shops, on trains and buses, and in
hotels and banks.

The main part of the Rough Guide is a double dictionary: English-
German then German-English. Before that, there's a page
explaining the pronunciation system we've used, then a section
called **The Basics**, which sets out the fundamental rules of the
language, with plenty of practical examples. You'll also find here
other essentials like numbers, dates and telling the time.

Forming the heart of the guide, the **English-German** section
gives easy-to-use transliterations of the German words wherever
pronunciation might be a problem, and to get you involved quickly
in two-way communication, the Rough Guide includes dialogues
featuring typical responses on key topics – such as renting a car
and asking directions. Feature boxes fill you in on cultural pitfalls
as well as the simple mechanics of how to make a phone call,
what to do in an emergency, where to change money, and more.
Throughout this section, cross-references enable you to pinpoint
key facts and phrases, while asterisked words indicate where
further information can be found in the Basics.

In the **German-English** dictionary, we've given not just the
phrases you're likely to hear, but also all the signs, labels,
instructions and other basic words you might come across in print
or in public places.

Finally the Rough Guide rounds off with an extensive **Menu
Reader**, giving a run-down of food and drink terms that you'll
find indispensable whether you're eating out, stopping for a quick
drink, or browsing through a local food market.

Gute Reise!
have a good trip!

PRONUNCIATION

In this phrase book, the German has been written in a system of imitated pronunciation so that it can be read as though it were English. Bear in mind the notes on pronunciation given below:

ay	as in m**ay**
e	as in g**e**t
g	always hard as in **g**oat
ī	as the 'i' sound in m**i**ght
J	like the 's' sound in plea**s**ure
KH	as in the Scottish way of saying lo**ch**
oo	as in b**oo**k
oo	as in mons**oo**n
ōō	like the 'ew' in f**ew** but without any 'y' sound
ow	as in c**ow**
uh	like the 'e' in butt**e**r
ur	as in f**ur** but without any 'r' sound

The common German sound 'ei', as in Einstein, is written either with a 'y' or as 'ine'/'ite'/'ile' etc as in **fine/kite/while**.

ABBREVIATIONS

acc	accusative
adj	adjective
dat	dative
f	feminine
gen	genitive
m	masculine
n	neuter
nom	nominative
pl	plural
sing	singular

NOTES

In the English-German section, when two forms of the verb are given in phrases such as 'can you ...?' **kannst du/können Sie ...?** the first is the familiar form and the second the polite form (see the entry for **you**).

An asterisk (*) next to a word means that you should refer to the Basics section for further information.

The Basics

NOUNS

All German nouns begin with a capital letter. They have one of three genders – masculine, feminine or neuter. Usually, the gender of a noun will have to be learnt together with the word itself. Certain noun endings, however, are reliable indicators of gender. For example:

Masculine nouns: ending in -or

der Motor
dair m**oh**tohr
the engine

der Professor
dair prof**e**ssohr
the professor

Feminine nouns: ending in -ei, -heit, -in, -keit, -ung

die Polizei
dee pohlits-**ī**
the police

die Abtei
dee ap-t**y**
the abbey

die Freiheit
dee fr**y**-hite
freedom

die Gesundheit
dee gez**oo**nt-hite
health

die Engländerin
dee **e**ng-lenderin
the Englishwoman

die Schauspielerin
dee sh**ow**-shpeelerin
the actress

die Telefonistin
dee telefohn**i**stin
the telephonist

die Flüssigkeit
dee fl**oo**ssish-kite
the liquid

die Geschwindigkeit
dee geshv**i**ndish-kite
the speed

die Reservierung
dee rezairv**ee**roong
the reservation

die Verbindung
dee fairb**i**ndoong
the connection

Neuter nouns: ending in -chen, -ment

das Mädchen
dass m**ay**tshen
the girl

das Verkehrszeichen
dass fairk**ai**rss-tsyshen
the road sign

das Kompliment
dass komplim**e**nt
the compliment

das Medikament
dass medikam**e**nt
the medicine

Plurals

There are a certain number of general rules about the formation of plurals, but the plural of most German nouns, like their gender, will have to be learnt individually.

Many German nouns form their plural by adding -e, -n or -en.

der Berg	die Berge
dair bairk	dee b**air**g-uh
the mountain	the mountains

die Reise	die Reisen
dee **rize**-uh	dee **ry**zen
the journey	the journeys

die Mahlzeit	die Mahlzeiten
dee m**ah**ltsite	dee m**ah**ltsyten
the meal	the meals

Many nouns of foreign origin, though not all, form their plural by adding -s.

das Auto	die Autos
dass **ow**to	dee **ow**tohss
the car	the cars

but:

der Computer	die Computer
dair 'computer'	dee 'computer'
the computer	the computers

Some nouns do not change at all in the plural. Others add -er. This is often, but not always, combined with a change of vowel: a number of nouns which contain an a, an o or a u have an umlaut (ä, ö or ü) in their plural form.

der Wagen	die Wagen
dair v**ah**gen	dee v**ah**gen
the car	the cars

der Apfel	die Äpfel
dair **a**pfel	dee **e**pfel
the apple	the apples

der Koch	die Köche
dair koKH	dee k**ur**sh-uh
the cook	the cooks

das Tuch	die Tücher
dass tooKH	dee t**oo**sher
the cloth	the cloths

The following list of regular noun endings should prove useful:

noun ending	gender	plural
-ar	m	-are
-är	m	-äre
-chen	n	-chen
-eur	m	-eure
-ich	m	-iche
-heit	f	-heiten
-in	f	-innen
-ium	n	-ien
-keit	f	-keiten
-ling	m	-linge
-ment	n	-mente
-nis	n	-nisse
-or	m	-oren
-schaft	f	-schaften
-ung	f	-ungen

ARTICLES AND CASES

German has three genders, masculine (m), feminine (f) and neuter (n). Each gender has its own article.

For masculine nouns, the definite article ('the' in

English) is der and the
indefinite article ('a' in
English) ein:

der Mann	ein Mann
dair man	ine man
the man	a man

For feminine nouns, the
definite article is die and the
indefinite article eine:

die Frau	eine Frau
dee frow	**ine**-uh frow
the woman	a woman

For neuter nouns, the definite
article is das and the
indefinite article ein:

das Kind	ein Kind
dass kint	ine kint
the child	a child

The plural form of the
definite article, regardless of
the gender of a noun, is die:

die Männer	die Frauen
dee menner	dee frowen
the men	the women

die Kinder
dee kinder
the children

There are four cases:
nominative, accusative,
genitive and dative. The form
of the definite and indefinite
articles changes in line with
the case being used, as shown
in the following tables:

The Definite Article

	m	f	n	pl
nom	der	die	das	die
acc	den	die	das	die
gen	des	der	des	der
dat	dem	der	dem	den

The Indefinite Article

	m	f	n
nom	ein	eine	ein
acc	einen	eine	ein
gen	eines	einer	eines
dat	einem	einer	einem

The nominative is the case
used for words when they are
the subject of the sentence:

der Wagen fährt schnell
dair **vah**gen fairt shnell
the car goes fast

The accusative is the case
used for words when they are
the object of the sentence:

ich habe den Wagen gestern
gekauft
ish **hah**b-uh dayn **vah**gen
gestern gek**ow**ft
I bought the car yesterday

The genitive is the case used
to show possession:

der Preis des Wagens war
sehr hoch
dair price dess **vah**genss var
zair hohкн
the price of the car was
very high

GRAMMAR

The dative is the case used to show motion towards a person or an object:

> er ging dem Wagen entgegen
> air ging daym **vah**gen
> ent**gay**gen
> ḥe walked towards the car

PREPOSITIONS

Most German prepositions take either the accusative or the dative or both.

The accusative is used after the following prepositions:

bis	biss	until
durch	doorsh	through
für	foor	for
gegen	**gay**gen	against
ohne	**oh**n-uh	without
um	oom	around

> wir gehen durch die Stadt
> veer **gay**en doorsh dee shtatt
> we walk through the town

> ohne die Kinder
> **oh**n-uh dee kinder
> without the children

The dative is used after the following prepositions:

aus	owss	out of
außer	**ow**sser	except
bei	by	at, near
gegenüber	gaygen-**oo**ber	opposite
mit		with
nach	naKH	to
seit	zite	since
von	fon	from
zu	tsoo	to, at

> mit den Kindern
> mit dayn kindern
> with the children

> seit dem letzten Jahr
> zite daym **le**tsten yar
> since last year

The following prepositions can either take the accusative or the dative:

an		on, to
auf	owf	on
hinter		behind
in		in
neben	**nay**ben	beside
über	**oo**ber	over, across
unter	**oo**nter	under
vor	fohr	before, in front of
zwischen	tsvishen	between

The accusative is used whenever motion is shown, whereas the dative indicates position:

> ich stelle die Vase auf den Tisch
> ish sht**ell**-uh dee **vah**z-uh owf dayn tish
> I put the vase on the table

> die Vase steht auf dem Tisch
> dee **vah**z-uh shtayt owf daym tish
> the vase is on the table

wir fahren über den Fluß
veer fahren **oo**ber dayn flooss
we are crossing the river

die Brücke über dem Fluß
dee br**oo**ck-uh **oo**ber daym flooss
the bridge across the river

ADJECTIVES AND ADVERBS

In German, there is no special ending to distinguish an adverb from an adjective (as '-ly' in English). The adverb is the same as the basic form of the adjective.

das Wetter ist schön
dass v**e**tter ist shurn
the weather is beautiful

sie singt schön
zee zingt shurn
she sings beautifully

When an adjective is used on its own, ie not in front of a noun, it appears in its basic form, without an ending:

die Straße ist naß
dee shtr**ah**ss-uh ist nass
the road is wet

es ist zu spät
ess ist ts**oo** shpayt
it is too late

If, however, an adjective appears in front of a noun, it needs an ending in order to agree with the noun:

die nasse Straße
dee n**a**ss-uh shtrahss-uh
the wet road

ein später Zug
ine shp**ay**ter ts**oo**k
a late train

The adjective's ending further depends on whether it is used after a definite article (der, die, das) or after an indefinite article (ein, eine). As can be seen from the following tables, the endings vary according to gender and case of the noun.

Endings After Definite Articles

	m	f	n	pl
nom	-e	-e	-e	-en
acc	-en	-e	-e	-en
gen	-en	-en	-en	-en
dat	-en	-en	-en	-en

Endings After Indefinite Articles

	m	f	n
nom	-er	-e	-es
acc	-en	-e	-es
gen	-en	-en	-en
dat	-en	-en	-en

das große Hotel
dass gr**oh**ss-uh hotel
the big hotel

ein großes Hotel
ine gr**oh**ssess hot**e**l
a big hotel

die großen Hotels
dee gr**oh**ssen hot**e**lss
the big hotels

wir wohnen in dem großen Hotel
veer v**oh**nen in daym gr**oh**ssen hot**e**l
we are staying in the big hotel

die Zimmer eines großen Hotels
dee ts**i**mmer **ine**-ess gr**oh**ssen hot**e**lss
the rooms of a big hotel

Comparatives and Superlatives

The comparative form of an adjective or adverb is used to express that something is bigger, better, more interesting etc than something else. In German, as for a number of English adjectives, this is shown by adding -er.

klein	kleiner
kline	kl**i**ner
small	smaller
schön	schöner
shurn	sh**ur**ner
beautiful	more beautiful

The superlative form of an adjective or adverb is used to express that something is the biggest, the best, the most interesting etc of all. In German, this is shown by adding -ste.

billig	der/die/das billigste
b**i**llish	dair/dee/dass b**i**llishst-uh
cheap	the cheapest
weich	der/die/das weichste
vysh	dair/dee/dass v**y**shst-uh
soft	the softest

Note that if adjectives contain an a, o or u, these will frequently change to ä, ö or ü in comparative and superlative forms:

lang	länger
lang	l**e**nger
long	longer

der/die/das längste
dair/dee/dass l**e**ngst-uh
the longest

groß	größer
grohss	gr**ur**sser
big, tall	bigger, taller

der/die/das größte
dair/dee/dass gr**ur**sst-uh
the biggest, the tallest

dumm	dümmer
doomm	d**oo**mmer
stupid	more stupid

der/die/das dümmste
dair/dee/dass d**oo**mmst-uh
the most stupid

Some comparative and superlative forms are irregular completely:

gut	besser
goot	besser
good	better

der/die/das beste
dair/dee/dass best-uh
the best

hoch	höher
hohKH	hurher
high	higher

der/die/das höchste
dair/dee/dass hurkst-uh
the highest

viel	mehr
feel	mair
much	more

der/die/das meiste
dair/dee/dass myst-uh
the most

The word for 'than' is als:

er ist größer als ich
air ist grurser alss ish
he is taller than me

Possessive Adjectives

Possessive adjectives are words like 'my', 'your', 'our' etc. In German, they have to agree with the gender and number of the noun they refer to:

	m	f	n	pl
my	mein	meine	mein	meine
	mine	mine-uh	mine	mine-uh
your (sing, familiar)	dein	deine	dein	deine
	dine	dine-uh	dine	dine-uh
(sing, polite)	Ihr	Ihre	Ihr	Ihre
	eer	eer-uh	eer	eer-uh
his	sein	seine	sein	seine
	zine	zine-uh	zine	zine-uh
her	ihr	ihre	ihr	ihre
	eer	eer-uh	eer	eer-uh
our	unser	unsere	unser	unsere
	oonzer	oonzer-uh	oonzer	oonzer-uh
your (pl, familiar)	euer	eure	euer	eure
	oyer	oyr-uh	oyer	oyr-uh
(pl, polite)	Ihr	Ihre	Ihr	Ihre
	eer	eer-uh	eer	eer-uh
their	ihr	ihre	ihr	ihre
	eer	eer-uh	eer	eer-uh

GRAMMAR

hast du deine Fahrkarte?
hast doo dine-uh fahrkart-uh
have you got your ticket?

das ist mein Hotel
dass ist mine hotel
this is my hotel

sind unsere Koffer schon hier?
zint oonzer-uh koffer shohn heer
have our suitcases arrived yet?

PERSONAL PRONOUNS

Subject Pronouns

I		ich	ish
you	(sing, familiar)	du[1]	doo
	(sing, polite)	Sie[2]	zee
he		er	air
she		sie	zee
it		es	ess
we		wir	veer
you	(pl, familiar)	ihr[3]	eer
	(pl, polite)	Sie[2]	zee
they		sie	zee

[1] du is used when speaking to one person and is the familiar form generally used when speaking to family, friends and children

[2] Sie is the polite form of address in the singular as well as the plural; it takes the third person plural of verbs

[3] ihr is the familiar form used when speaking to more than one person

Note that, when talking to strangers, unless they are children, you should always use Sie, never du or ihr.

It is important to remember that the German for 'it' is not automatically es but always depends on the noun which 'it' refers to. If the noun is masculine, use er; if it is feminine, use sie; only if the noun is neuter is es the pronoun to use.

ist der Zug schon da? – da kommt er
ist dair tsook shohn da – da kommt air
has the train arrived yet? – there it comes

wo ist die Zeitung? – da liegt sie
vo ist dee tsytoong – da leekt zee
where's the paper? – there it is

was macht das Kind? – es spielt
vass maKHt dass kint – ess shpeelt
what's the child doing? – he / she is playing

Direct Object Pronouns

These occur if you are using the pronoun as an object.

me	**mich**	mish
you (sing, familiar)	**dich**	dish
(sing, polite)	**Sie**	zee
him	**ihn**	een
her	**sie**	zee
it	**es**	ess
us	**uns**	oonss
you (pl, familiar)	**euch**	oysh
(pl, polite)	**Sie**	zee
them	**sie**	zee

ich habe sie gesehen
ish h**ah**b-uh zee gez**ay**en
I have seen her/them

kann ich dich morgen anrufen?
kann ish dish m**o**rgen **a**nr**oo**fen
can I phone you tomorrow?

ich möchte euch einladen
ish m**ur**sht-uh oysh **ine**-lahden
I would like to invite you

Indirect Object Pronouns

If you are using an object pronoun to mean 'to me', 'to you' etc (although 'to' might not always be necessary in English), you use the following:

(to) me	**mir**	meer
(to) you		
(sing, familiar)	**dir**	deer
(sing, polite)	**Ihnen**	**ee**nen
(to) him	**ihm**	eem
(to) her	**ihr**	eer
(to) it	**ihm**	eem
(to) us	**uns**	oonss
(to) you		
(pl, familiar)	**euch**	oysh
(pl, polite)	**Ihnen**	**ee**nen
(to) them	**ihnen**	**ee**nen

sie hat es mir gegeben
zee hat ess meer geg**ay**ben
she has given it to me

ich habe es ihm gesagt
ish h**ah**b-uh ess eem gez**ah**kt
I told him

er hat ihnen einen Brief geschrieben
air hat **ee**nen **ine**-en breef geshr**ee**ben
he has written them a letter

Reflexive Pronouns

These are used with reflexive verbs like **sich waschen** 'to wash (oneself)', **sich umdrehen** 'to turn around':

myself	**mich**	mish
yourself (familiar)	**dich**	dish
(polite)	**sich**	zish
himself	**sich**	zish
herself	**sich**	zish
itself	**sich**	zish
ourselves	**uns**	oonss
yourselves		
(familiar)	**euch**	oysh
(polite)	**sich**	zish
themselves	**sich**	zish

wir haben uns gut unterhalten		Sie irren sich
veer h**ah**ben oonss goot oonterh**al**ten		zee **ee**rren zish
we enjoyed ourselves		you are mistaken
		ich habe mich geärgert
		ish h**ah**b-uh mish ge-**air**gert
		I was annoyed

Possessive Pronouns

Possessive adjectives are words like 'mine', 'yours', 'ours' etc. In German, they have to agree with the gender and number of the noun they refer to:

	m	f	n	pl
mine	meiner	meine	meins	meine
	m**i**ner	m**i**ne-uh	m**i**ne-ss	m**i**ne-uh
yours (sing, familiar)	deiner	deine	deins	deine
	d**i**ner	d**i**ne-uh	d**i**ne-ss	d**i**ne-uh
(sing, polite)	Ihrer	Ihre	Ihres	Ihre
	eerer	**ee**r-uh	**ee**ress	**ee**r-uh
his	seiner	seine	seins	seine
	z**i**ner	z**i**ne-uh	zine-ss	z**i**ne-uh
hers	ihrer	ihre	ihres	ihre
	eerer	**ee**r-uh	**ee**ress	**ee**r-uh
ours	unserer	unsere	unseres	unsere
	oonzerer	**oo**nzer-uh	**oo**nzer-ess	**oo**nzer-uh
yours (pl, familiar)	eurer	eure	eures	eure
	oyrer	**oy**r-uh	**oy**ress	**oy**r-uh
(pl, polite)	Ihrer	Ihre	Ihres	Ihre
	eerer	**ee**r-uh	**ee**ress	**ee**r-uh
theirs	ihrer	ihre	ihres	ihre
	eerer	**ee**r-uh	**ee**ress	**ee**r-uh

das sind meine	möchten Sie Wein? – wir haben unseren schon bestellt
dass zint m**i**ne-uh	m**ur**shten zee vine – veer h**ah**ben **oo**nzeren shohn besht**e**llt
these are mine	would you like some wine? – we've already ordered ours
ist das mein Glas oder Ihres?	
ist dass mine glahss **o**der **ee**ress	
is that glass mine or yours?	

VERBS

The basic form of German verbs (the infinitive) usually ends in -en, occasionally in -ln or -rn.

gehen	to go, to walk
schlafen	to sleep
angeln	to fish

Present Tense

The present tense corresponds to 'I leave' and 'I am leaving' in English. To form the present tense in German, remove the verb ending (-en or -n) and add the endings to the stem of the verb, as shown in the tables below (the 'stem' of a verb is the past without the final '-en', '-eln' or '-ern'):

		machen (to do)		reden (to talk)	
		maKH-en		rayd-en	
I		ich	mach-e	ich	red-e
you	(sing, familiar)	du	mach-st	du	red-est
	(sing, polite)	Sie	mach-en	Sie	red-en
he/she/it		er/sie/es	mach-t	er/sie/es	red-et
we		wir	mach-en	wir	red-en
you	(pl, familiar)	ihr	mach-t	ihr	red-et
	(pl, polite)	Sie	mach-en	Sie	red-en
they		sie	mach-en	sie	red-en

See the section on **SUBJECT PRONOUNS** page 10 for the use of the different words for 'you'.

Note that verbs ending in -t or -d, as reden above, insert an additional -e- to form some of their tenses.

Some common verbs are irregular:

haben	hahben	to have	sein	zine	to be
ich	habe	hahb-uh	ich	bin	
du	hast		du	bist	
Sie	haben	hahben	Sie	sind	zint
er/sie/es	hat		er/sie/es	ist	
wir	haben		wir	sind	
ihr	habt	hapt	ihr	seid	zite
Sie	haben		Sie	sind	
sie	haben		sie	sind	

dürfen	d**oo**rfen	to be allowed to	fahren	f**a**hren	to go, drive
ich	darf		ich	fahre	f**a**hr-uh
du	darfst		du	fährst	f**air**st
Sie	dürfen	d**oo**rfen	Sie	fahren	f**a**hren
er/sie/es	darf		er/sie/es	fährt	fairt
wir	dürfen		wir	fahren	
ihr	dürft	d**oo**rft	ihr	fahrt	
Sie	dürfen		Sie	fahren	
sie	dürfen		sie	fahren	

können	k**ur**nen	to be able to	mögen	m**ur**gen	to like
ich	kann		ich	mag	mahk
du	kannst		du	magst	m**a**h**k**st
Sie	können	k**ur**nen	Sie	mögen	m**ur**gen
er/sie/es	kann		er/sie/es	mag	
wir	können		wir	mögen	
ihr	könnt	kurnt	ihr	mögt	murkt
Sie	können		Sie	mögen	
sie	können		sie	mögen	

müssen	m**oo**ssen	to have to	sehen	z**ay**en	to see
ich	muß	mooss	ich	sehe	z**ay**-uh
du	mußt	moosst	du	siehst	zeest
Sie	müssen	m**oo**ssen	Sie	sehen	z**ay**en
er/sie/es	muß		er/sie/es	sieht	zeet
wir	müssen		wir	sehen	
ihr	müßt	m**oo**sst	ihr	seht	zayt
Sie	müssen		Sie	sehen	
sie	müssen		sie	sehen	

werden	vairden	to become	wollen	vollen	to want
ich	werde	vaird-uh	ich	will	vill
du	wirst	veerst	du	willst	villst
Sie	werden	vairden	Sie	wollen	vollen
er/sie/es	wird	veert	er/sie/es	will	
wir	werden		wir	wollen	
ihr	werdet	vairdet	ihr	wollt	vollt
Sie	werden		Sie	wollen	
sie	werden		sie	wollen	

Past Tense

To describe an action that has taken place in the past, both the imperfect and perfect tense can be used.

Imperfect

The imperfect describes events which have occurred once in the past or which were repeated, habitual or took place over a period of time. To form the imperfect, the following verb endings are used:

machen (to do)		reden (to talk)	
ich	mach-te	ich	red-ete
du	mach-test	du	red-etest
Sie	mach-ten	Sie	red-eten
er/sie/es	mach-te	er/sie/es	red-ete
wir	mach-ten	wir	red-eten
ihr	mach-tet	ihr	red-etet
Sie	mach-ten	Sie	red-eten
sie	mach-ten	sie	red-eten

als ich Student war, lebte ich in Köln
alss ish shtoodent var laypt-uh ish in kurln
when I was a student, I used to live in Cologne

wie war das Wetter in den Alpen?
vee var dass vetter in dayn alpen
what was the weather like in the Alps?

Both haben and sein are irregular in the imperfect tense:

haben	hahben	to have		sein	zine	to be
ich	hatte	hatt-uh		ich	war	var
du	hattest			du	warst	varst
Sie	hatten			Sie	waren	vahren
er/sie/es	hatte			er/sie/es	war	
wir	hatten			wir	waren	
ihr	hattet			ihr	wart	vart
Sie	hatten			Sie	waren	
sie	hatten			sie	waren	

Perfect

The most common way of referring to the past is the perfect tense. The perfect is formed with the present tense of either haben or sein (see page 13) followed by the past participle of the verb. The past participle is formed by taking the stem of the verb and adding a prefix and ending as follows:

mach-en to do ge-mach-t done
red-en to talk ge-red-et talked

Most verbs take haben to form the perfect tense:

er hat es gemacht
air hat ess gemaKHt
he has done it, he did it

wir haben davon geredet
veer hahben dafon geraydet
we (have) talked about it

Some verbs take sein, mostly verbs of motion. Some of these are:

fahren to go, to drive
  ich bin gefahren
fallen to fall
  ich bin gefallen
fliegen to fly
  ich bin geflogen
gehen to go
  ich bin gegangen
kommen to come
  ich bin gekommen
sein to be
  ich bin gewesen
sterben to die
  ich bin gestorben
werden to become
  ich bin geworden

er ist nach London gefahren
air ist naKH london gefahren
he went to London

letztes Jahr sind wir in
München gewesen
letstess yar zint veer in
moonshen gevayzen
last year we were in Munich

Some common verbs have irregular past tenses. The following list shows the infinitive, the third person singular of the imperfect tense and the past participle.

Some Common Irregular Verbs

beginnen	to begin	begann	begonnen
bleiben	to stay	blieb	geblieben
bringen	to bring	brachte	gebracht
dürfen	to be allowed to	durfte	gedurft
essen	to eat	aß	gegessen
fahren	to go, to drive	fuhr	gefahren
finden	to find	fand	gefunden
fliegen	to fly	flog	geflogen
geben	to give	gab	gegeben
gehen	to go	ging	gegangen
haben	to have	hatte	gehabt
kennen	to know	kannte	gekannt
kommen	to come	kam	gekommen
können	to be able to	konnte	gekonnt
lassen	to let, to allow	ließ	gelassen
lesen	to read	las	gelesen
liegen	to lie	lag	gelegen
müssen	to have to	mußte	gemußt
nehmen	to take	nahm	genommen
schreiben	to write	schrieb	geschrieben
sehen	to see	sah	gesehen
sein	to be	war	gewesen
sitzen	to sit	saß	gesessen
sterben	to die	starb	gestorben
trinken	to drink	trank	getrunken
verlieren	to lose	verlor	verloren
werden	to become	wurde	geworden
wissen	to know	wußte	gewußt

Future

The future tense in German is formed by the verb **werden** and the infinitive of the verb concerned:

ich	werde	kommen	I will come etc
du	wirst	kommen	
Sie	werden	kommen	
er/sie/es	wird	kommen	
wir	werden	kommen	
ihr	werdet	kommen	
Sie	werden	kommen	
sie	werden	kommen	

er wird es nicht schaffen
air veert ess nisht shaffen
he's not going to manage it

was werden Sie morgen machen?
vass vairden zee morgen maKHen
what are you going to do tomorrow?

er wird morgen kommen
air veert morgen kommen
he'll come tomorrow

Note that German, like English, frequently uses the present tense for the future:

was machen Sie morgen?
vass maKHen zee morgen
what are you doing tomorrow?

er kommt morgen
air kommt morgen
he's coming tomorrow

Negatives

To make a sentence negative, German uses the word **nicht**:

ich verstehe
ish fairshtay-uh
I understand

ich verstehe nicht
ish fairshtay-uh nisht
I don't understand

If you want to say 'no' or 'not any' with nouns, use the word **kein** or **keine**:

ich habe kein Geld
ish hahb-uh kine gelt
I have no money

er hat keine Geduld
air hat kine-uh gedoolt
he hasn't got any patience

Imperatives

The imperative is used to express a command (such as 'come here!', 'let's go' etc).

Generally, the imperative forms are similar to those of the infinitive. In fact, just adding Sie to the infinitive gives the polite form of the imperative:

warten
to wait   **warten Sie!**
varten zee
wait!

The familiar form (singular) is identical with the infinitive without the final -n, or, in some cases, without the final -en:

warte! but: **komm!**
vart-uh   komm
wait!   come (here)!

The corresponding plural form adds a -t to the singular:

wartet!   **kommt!**
vartet   kommt
wait!   come (here)!

QUESTIONS

To form a question, the word order of subject and verb in the sentence change:

Sie sprechen Deutsch
zee shprechen doytch
you speak German

sprechen Sie Deutsch?
shprechen zee doytch
do you speak German?

Word order is also inverted in other cases, especially when a question word is used:

wann schließt das Museum?
van shleesst dass moozayoom
when does the museum close?

ist mein Gepäck schon angekommen?
ist mine gepeck shohn angekommen?
has my luggage arrived yet?

DATES

Dates are expressed with ordinal numbers (see below):

der erste Juli
dair airst-uh yoolee
the first of July

am ersten Juli
am airsten yoolee
on the first of July

der zwanzigste März
dair tsvantsishst-uh mairts
the twentieth of March

am zwanzigsten März
am tsvantsishsten mairts
on the twentieth of March

At the beginning of letters, the following form should be used:

Frankfurt, den 20. März
Frankfurt, March 20

TIME

what time is it? wie spät ist es?
vee shpayt ist ess
one o'clock ein Uhr ine OOr
two o'clock zwei Uhr tsvy OOr
it's one o'clock es ist ein Uhr
ess ist ine OOr
it's two o'clock es ist zwei Uhr
ess ist tsvy OOr
it's ten o'clock es ist zehn Uhr
ess ist tsayn OOr
five past one fünf nach eins
fOOnf naKH ine-ss
ten past two zehn nach zwei
tsayn nahKH tsvy
quarter past one Viertel nach
eins feertel nahKH ine-ss
quarter past two Viertel nach
zwei feertel naKH tsvy
*half past ten halb elf halp elf
twenty to ten zwanzig vor zehn
tsvantsish for tsayn
quarter to two Viertel vor zwei
feertel for tsvy
at half past four um halb fünf
oom halp fOOnf
at eight o'clock um acht Uhr
oom aKHt OOr
14.00 14 Uhr feertsayn OOr
17.30 siebzehn Uhr dreißig
zeeptsayn OOr dryssish
2 a.m. 2 Uhr morgens tsvy OOr
morgens
2 p.m. 2 Uhr nachmittags tsvy
OOr nahKHmittahks
10 a.m. 10 Uhr vormittags
tsayn OOr formittahks
10 p.m. 10 Uhr abends tsayn

OOr ahbents
noon Mittag mittahk
midnight Mitternacht
mitternaKHt

an hour eine Stunde **ine**-uh
shtoond-uh
a/one minute eine Minute **ine**-
uh minOOt-uh
two minutes zwei Minuten tsvy
minOOten
a second eine Sekunde **ine**-uh
zekoond-uh
a quarter of an hour eine
Viertelstunde **ine**-uh
feertelshtoond-uh
half an hour eine halbe
Stunde **ine**-uh halb-uh
shtoond-uh
three quarters of an hour eine
Dreiviertelstunde **ine**-uh
dryfeertel-shtoond-uh

*Note the difference here.
German for 'half past ten/
three/five' etc is, literally,
'half eleven/four/six' etc.

NUMBERS

0	null nooll
1	eins ine-ss
2	zwei tsvy
3	drei dry
4	vier feer
5	fünf fOOnf
6	sechs zeks
7	sieben zeeben
8	acht aKHt
9	neun noyn
10	zehn tsayn

11	elf elf
12	zwölf tsvurlf
13	dreizehn dry-tsayn
14	vierzehn veer-tsayn
15	fünfzehn foonft-tsayn
16	sechzehn zesh-tsayn
17	siebzehn zeep-tsayn
18	achtzehn aKH-tsayn
19	neunzehn noynt-tsayn
20	zwanzig tsvantsish
21	einundzwanzig **ine**-oont-tsvantsish
22	zweiundzwanzig tsvy-oont-tsvantsish
23	dreiundzwanzig dry-oont-tsvantsish
30	dreißig dryssish
31	einunddreißig **ine**-oont-dryssish
40	vierzig feertsish
50	fünfzig foonftsish
60	sechzig zeshtsish
70	siebzig zeeptsish
80	achtzig aKHtsish
90	neunzig noyntsish
100	hundert hoondert
110	hundertzehn hoondert-tsayn
200	zweihundert tsvy-hoondert
300	dreihundert dry-hoondert
1,000	tausend towzent
2,000	zweitausend tsvy-towzent
10,000	zehntausend tsayn-towzent

50,000	fünfzigtausend foonftsish-towzent
100,000	hunderttausend hoondert-towzent
1,000,000	eine Million **ine**-uh mill-yohn

Ordinal numbers are formed by adding -te or -ste if the number ends in -ig. For example, fünfte foonft-uh (fifth), **zwanzigste** tsvantsishst-uh (twentieth).

1st	erste **air**st-uh
2nd	zweite tsvite-uh
3rd	dritte dritt-uh
4th	vierte feert-uh
5th	fünfte foonft-uh
6th	sechste zekst-uh
7th	siebte zeept-uh
8th	achte **a**KHt-uh
9th	neunte noynt-uh
10th	zehnte tsaynt-uh

In German, thousands are written with a full-stop. A comma is used for decimals.

German	English
10.000	10,000
2,83	2.83

22

CONVERSION TABLES

1 centimetre = 0.39 inches   1 inch = 2.54 cm

1 metre = 39.37 inches =   1 foot = 30.48 cm
    1.09 yards
                              1 yard = 0.91 m

1 kilometre = 0.62 miles =
    5/8 mile   1 mile = 1.61 km

km	1	2	3	4	5	10	20	30	40	50	100
miles	0.6	1.2	1.9	2.5	3.1	6.2	12.4	18.6	24.8	31.0	62.1

miles	1	2	3	4	5	10	20	30	40	50	100
km	1.6	3.2	4.8	6.4	8.0	16.1	32.2	48.3	64.4	80.5	161

1 gram = 0.035 ounces   1 kilo = 1000 g = 2.2 pounds

g	100	250	500
oz	3.5	8.75	17.5

1 oz = 28.35 g
1 lb = 0.45 kg

kg	0.5	1	2	3	4	5	6	7	8	9	10
lb	1.1	2.2	4.4	6.6	8.8	11.0	13.2	15.4	17.6	19.8	22.0

kg	20	30	40	50	60	70	80	90	100
lb	44	66	88	110	132	154	176	198	220

lb	0.5	1	2	3	4	5	6	7	8	9	10	20
kg	0.2	0.5	0.9	1.4	1.8	2.3	2.7	3.2	3.6	4.1	4.5	9.0

1 litre = 1.75 UK pints/2.13 US pints

1 UK pint = 0.57 l   1 UK gallon = 4.55 l
1 US pint = 0.47 l   1 US gallon = 3.79 l

centigrade/Celsius $C = (F - 32) \times 5/9$

C	-5	0	5	10	15	18	20	25	30	36.8	38
F	23	32	41	50	59	64	68	77	86	98.4	100.4

Fahrenheit $F = (C \times 9/5) + 32$

F	23	32	40	50	60	65	70	80	85	98.4	101
C	-5	0	4	10	16	18	21	27	29	36.8	38.3

CONVERSION TABLES

English-German

A

a, an* eine(e) [**ine**(-uh)]
  10 marks a bottle 10 Mark
  pro Flasche
about: about twenty etwa
  zwanzig [**etvah**]
  at about 5 o'clock gegen fünf
  Uhr [**gay**gen]
  a film about Germany ein Film
  über Deutschland [**OO**ber]
above über [**OO**ber]
abroad im Ausland [**ow**ssland]
  to go abroad ins Ausland
  gehen
absolutely (I agree) genau
  [gen**ow**]
accelerator das Gaspedal
  [**gah**ss-pedahl]
accept akzeptieren
  [aktsept**ee**ren]
accident der Unfall [**oo**nfal]
  there's been an accident es
  hat einen Unfall gegeben
  [geg**ay**ben]
accommodation die Unterkunft
  [**oo**nter-koonft]
  see room
accurate genau [gen**ow**]
ache der Schmerz [shmairts]
  my back aches mein Rücken
  tut weh [toot vay]
across: across the road über die
  Straße [**OO**ber]
adapter der Adapter
address die Adresse [adress-uh]
  what's your address? was ist
  Ihre Adresse? [**eer**-uh]

In German addresses, the house
number follows the street name
and the post code precedes the
town, eg:

  Gerd Schuster
  Mühlbachstr. 35
  50462 Köln

address book das Adreßbuch
  [adr**e**ssb**OO**KH]
admission charge der Eintritt
  [**ine**-tritt]
adult der Erwachsene
  [airv**a**ksen-uh]
advance: in advance im voraus
  [f**o**rowss]
aeroplane das Flugzeug
  [fl**OO**ktsoyk]
after nach [na**KH**]
  after you nach Ihnen [**ee**nen]
afternoon der Nachmittag
  [n**a**KHmit-tahk]
  in the afternoon am
  Nachmittag
  this afternoon heute
  Nachmittag [h**oy**t-uh]
aftershave das After-shave
aftersun cream die Après-
  Lotion [apr**ay**-lohts-yohn]
afterwards danach [dana**KH**]
again wieder [**vee**der]
against gegen [**gay**gen]
age das Alter [**al**-ter]
ago: a week ago vor einer
  Woche [for **ine**-er]
  an hour ago vor einer Stunde
agree: I agree ich bin
  einverstanden [**ine**-fair-

shtanden]

AIDS Aids

air die Luft [looft]

by air mit dem Flugzeug
[**floo**ktsoyk]

air-conditioning die
Klimaanlage [kl**ee**ma-
anlahg-uh]

airmail: by airmail per Luftpost
[pair l**oo**ftpost]

airmail envelope der Luftpost-
Briefumschlag [l**oo**ftposst
br**ee**f-oomshlahk]

airport der Flughafen [fl**oo**k-
hahfen]

to the airport, please zum
Flughafen bitte [tsoom]

airport bus der Flughafenbus
[fl**oo**k-hafenbooss]

aisle seat der Sitz am Gang

alarm clock der Wecker
[v**e**cker]

alcohol der Alkohol

alcoholic alkoholisch [alko-
h**oh**lish]

all: all the boys alle Jungen
[**a**l-uh]

all the girls alle Mädchen

all of it alles [**a**l-ess]

all of them alle

that's all, thanks das ist alles,
danke

allergic: I'm allergic to ... ich bin
allergisch gegen ... [ish bin
all**ai**rgish g**ay**gen]

allowed: is it allowed? ist es
erlaubt? [airl**ow**pt]

all right ok**ay**

I'm all right ich bin okay

are you all right? bist du/sind
Sie okay?

almond die Mandel

almost fast [fasst]

alone allein [al-**ine**]

alphabet das Alphabet [alfa-
b**ay**t]

a	ah	j	yot	s	ess
b	bay	k	kah	t	tay
c	tsay	l	el	u	oo
d	day	m	em	v	fow
e	ay	n	en	w	vay
f	eff	o	oh	x	eeks
g	gay	p	pay	y	**oo**psilon
h	hah	q	koo	z	tset
i	ee	r	air	ß	ess-tset

Alps die Alpen

already schon [shohn]

also auch [owKH]

although obwohl [opv**oh**l]

altogether insgesamt

aluminium foil die Alufolie
[**ah**loo-f**oh**l-yuh]

always immer

am*: I am ich bin [ish]

a.m.: at seven a.m. um
sieben Uhr morgens [oom –
oor]

amazing (surprising) erstaunlich
[airsht**own**lish]
(very good) fant**a**stisch

ambulance der
Krankenwagen [kr**a**nken-
vahgen]

call an ambulance! rufen Sie
einen Krankenwagen [r**oo**fen
zee **ine**-en]

In the event of an emergency, dial 110. This puts you through to the police, who will summon an ambulance for you.

America Amerika [am**ai**reeka]
American (adj) amerikanisch [amairik**ah**nish]
  I'm American (man/woman) ich bin Amerik**a**ner/ Amerik**a**nerin
among unter [**oo**nter]
amount die Menge [m**e**ng-uh]
  (money) der Betrag [betr**ah**k]
amp: a 13 amp fuse eine dreizehn-Ampere-Sicherung [amp**air** z**i**sheroong]]
and und [oont]
angry wütend [v**OO**tent]
animal das Tier [teer]
ankle der Knöchel [kn**ur**shel]
anniversary (wedding) der Hochzeitstag [h**o**KH-tsites-tahk]
annoy: this man's annoying me dieser Mann belästigt mich [bel**e**stisht mish]
annoying ärgerlich [**ai**rgerlish]
another ein anderer [ine **a**nderer]
  can we have another room? können wir ein anderes Zimmer haben?
  another beer, please noch ein Bier, bitte [noKH ine]
antibiotics die Antibiotika [anti-bee-**oh**teeka]
antifreeze das Frostschutz-

mittel [fr**o**st-shoots-mittel]
antihistamine das **A**ntihistamin
antique: is it an antique? ist es antik? [ant**ee**k]
antique shop das Antiquitätengeschäft [antikvit**ay**ten-gesheft]
antiseptic das Antis**e**ptikum
any: have you got any bread/ tomatoes? haben Sie Brot/ Tomaten? [h**ah**ben zee]
  sorry, I don't have any tut mir leid, ich habe keine [t**oo**t meer lite, ish h**ah**buh k**i**ne-uh]
anybody jemand [y**ay**mant]
  does anybody speak English? spricht jemand **E**nglisch?
  there wasn't anybody there es war keiner da [k**y**ner]
anything etwas [**e**tvass]

•••••• DIALOGUES ••••••

anything else? sonst noch etwas?
nothing else, thanks sonst nichts, danke [nishts, d**a**nk-uh]

would you like anything to drink? möchten Sie etwas trinken? [m**ur**shten]
I don't want anything, thanks ich möchte nichts, danke [nishts]

apart from abgesehen von [**a**p-gezay-en fon]
apartment die Wohnung [v**oh**noong]
apartment block der Wohnblock [v**oh**nblock]
appendicitis die Blinddarm-entzündung [bl**i**nt-darm-ent-

ts**oo**ndoong]

aperitif der Aperitif [apairee-t**ee**f]

apology die Entschuldigung [ent-sh**oo**ldigoong]

appetizer die Vorspeise [for-shpize-uh]

apple der **A**pfel

appointment der Termin [tairm**ee**n]

•••••• DIALOGUE ••••••

good afternoon, how can I help you? guten Tag, kann ich Ihnen behilflich sein? [g**oo**ten tahk, kan ish **ee**nen behilflish zine]

I'd like to make an appointment ich möchte einen Termin vereinbaren [fair-**ine**-bahren]

what time would you like? welche Zeit wäre Ihnen recht? [velsh-uh tsite v**ai**r-uh **ee**nen resht]

three o'clock drei Uhr [oor]

I'm afraid that's not possible, is four o'clock all right? tut mir leid, das ist nicht möglich, ist vier Uhr in Ordnung? [m**ur**glish]

yes, that will be fine ja, das ist mir recht [meer]

the name was …? Ihr Name war …? [eer n**ah**m-uh vahr]

apricot die Aprikose [aprik**oh**z-uh]

April der April [a-pr**i**ll]

are*: we are wir sind [veer zint]

you are du bist/Sie sind [doo …/zee]

they are sie sind [zee]

area die Gegend [g**ay**gent]

area code die Vorwahl [f**o**rvahl]

arm der Arm

arrange: will you arrange it for us? können Sie das für uns regeln? [r**ay**geln]

arrival die Ankunft [**a**nkoonft]

arrive ankommen

when do we arrive? wann kommen wir an? [van kommen veer an]

has my fax arrived yet? ist mein Fax schon angekommen?

we arrived today wir sind heute angekommen

art die Kunst [koonst]

art gallery die Kunstgalerie [k**oo**nstgal-leree]

artist der Künstler [k**oo**nstler]

as: as big as so groß wie [zoh grohss vee]

as soon as possible so bald wie möglich [m**ur**glish]

ashtray der Aschenbecher [**a**shen-besher]

ask fragen [fr**ah**gen]

I didn't ask for this das habe ich nicht bestellt [dass h**ah**b-uh ish nisht besht**e**llt]

could you ask him to …? könnten Sie ihn bitten …? [k**ur**nten zee een b**i**tten]

asleep: she's asleep sie schläft [shl**ay**ft]

aspirin das Kopfschmerzmittel [k**o**pf-shmairts-mittel]

asthma das Asthma [**a**st-mah]

astonishing erstaunlich [airsht**ow**nlish]

at: at the hotel im Hotel
at the station am B**a**hnhof
at six o'clock um 6 Uhr [oom]
at Günter's bei Günter [by]
athletics Leichtathletik [l**y**sht-at-laytik]
attractive attraktiv [atrakt**ee**f]
aubergine die Aubergine [ohbairJ**ee**n-uh]
August der August [owg**oo**st]
Australia Australien [owstr**ah**lee-en]
Australian (adj) australisch [owstr**ah**lish]
I'm Australian (man/woman) ich bin Australier [owstr**ah**lee-er]/ Australierin
Austria Österreich [**ur**ster-rysh]
Austrian (man/woman) der Österreicher [**ur**ster-rysher]/ die Österreicherin
(adj) österreichisch [**ur**ster-rysh-ish]
the Austrians die Österreicher
Austrian Alps die österreichischen **A**lpen
Austrian Tirol Tirol [tee-r**oh**l]
automatic (car) der Automatikwagen [owto-m**ah**tik-vahgen]
automatic teller (US) der Geldautomat [g**e**lt-owtomaht]
autumn der Herbst [hairpst]
in the autumn im Herbst
avenue die Allee [all**ay**]
average (not good) mittelmäßig [m**i**ttel-maysish]
(ordinary) durchschnittlich

[d**oo**rsh-shnitt-lish]
on average im D**u**rchschnitt
awake: is he awake? ist er wach? [vaKH]
away: go away! gehen Sie weg! [g**a**y-en zee vek]
is it far away? ist es weit? [vite]
awful furchtbar [f**oo**rsht-bar]
axle die Achse [**a**x-uh]

B

baby das Baby
baby food die Babynahrung [-nahroong]
baby's bottle das Fläschchen [fl**e**sh-shen]
baby-sitter der B**a**bysitter
back (of body) der Rücken [r**oo**cken]
(back part) die Rückseite [r**oo**ck-zite-uh]
at the back hinten
can I have my money back? kann ich mein Geld zurückbekommen? [tsoor**oo**ck-bekommen]
to come back zur**ü**ckkommen
to go back zur**ü**ckgehen [-g**a**y-en]
backache die Rücken-schmerzen [r**oo**cken-shmairtsen]
bacon der Speck [shpeck]
bad schlecht [shlesht]
a bad headache schlimme Kopfschmerzen [shl**i**mm-uh]
badly schlecht [shlesht]

bag die Tasche [t**a**sh-uh]
  (handbag) die Handtasche [h**a**nt-tash-uh]
  (suitcase) die Reisetasche [r**y**zuh-tash-uh]
baggage das Gepäck [gep**e**ck]
baggage check (US) die Gepäckaufbewahrung [gep**e**ck-owfbevahroong]
baggage claim die Gepäckrückgabe [gep**e**ck-r**oo**ck-gahb-uh]
bakery die Bäckerei [becker-**ī**]
balcony der Balkon [bal-k**oh**n]
  a room with a balcony ein Zimmer mit Balkon [ine ts**i**mmer]
bald kahl
ball (large) der Ball [bal]
  (small) die Kugel [k**oo**gel]
ballet das Ballett [bal-**e**tt]
ballpoint pen der Kugelschreiber [k**oo**gel-shryber]
Baltic Sea die Ostsee [**o**st-zay]
banana die Banane [ban**ah**n-uh]
band (musical) die Band [bent]
bandage der Verband [fairb**a**nt]
bank (money) die Bank

Most banks are open from 9 a.m. to 4 p.m. or 4.30 p.m. Some close for an hour at lunchtime. On Thursdays, city centre branches will often be open until 6 p.m.; if you are changing money, make your transaction at one desk and then collect →

your money from another desk; the bank clerk is likely to say: 'Sie bekommen ihr Geld an der Kasse' [zee bek**o**mmen eer gelt an dair k**a**ssuh]. The German unit of currency is the mark (**die Mark, die D-Mark, DM**) which consists of 100 **Pfennige (Pf)**. Denominations are 1, 2, 5, 10, 50 Pf, 1, 2, 5 DM (coins) and 10, 20, 50, 100, 200, 500, 1000 DM (notes).

bank account das Bankkonto [b**a**nk-konto]
bar die Kneipe [k-n**ī**pe-uh]

In bars, it is not customary to pay for your drink at the same time as you order; a record of your orders will be kept (often on a beer mat) and you pay on leaving; you can expect table service in all bars and pubs. In cities some bars are normally open until early in the morning. Closing time is much less of a concept in Germany. The legal limit for driving is an alcohol level of 80 millilitres.

bar of chocolate die Tafel Schokolade [t**ah**fel shoko-l**ah**d-uh]
barber's der Frisör [friz**ur**]
basket der Korb [korp]
  (in shop) der Einkaufskorb

[ine-kowfs-korp]
bath das Bad [baht]
  can I have a bath? kann ich
  ein Bad nehmen? [**nay**men]
bathroom das Bad [baht]
  with a private bathroom mit
  eigenem Bad [**ī**-gen-em]
bath towel das Badehandtuch
  [b**ah**duh-hant-tOOKH]
battery die Batterie [batter**ee**]
Bavaria Bayern [b**y**-ern]
Bavarian Alps die Bayrischen
  Alpen [b**y**-rishen]
be* sein [zine]
beach der Strand [shtrant]
beach mat die Strandmatte
  [shtr**ant**-mat-uh]
beach umbrella der
  Sonnenschirm [z**onnen**-
  sheerm]

In North Germany, you will
find wicker beach chairs which
have a top piece that goes
over your head; they are
called: **Strandkörbe** [strant-
kurbuh].

beans die Bohnen
  runner beans die Stangen-
  bohnen [sht**angen**-]
  broad beans dicke B**oh**nen
  [d**ick**-uh]
beard der Bart
beautiful schön [shurn]
because weil [vile]
  because of ... wegen ...
  [v**ay**gen]
bed das Bett

I'm going to bed ich gehe zu
Bett [ish g**ay**-uh-tsOO]
bed and breakfast
  Übernachtung mit
  Frühstück [ꝏbern**a**KHtoong
  mit fr**ꝏ**shtꝏck]
bedroom das Schlafzimmer
  [shl**ah**f-tsimmer]
beef das Rindfleisch [r**int**-flysh]
beer das Bier [beer]
  two beers, please zwei Bier,
  bitte [b**itt**-uh]

Some useful beer vocabulary:

Alsterwasser [**a**lster-vasser]
shandy
Alt a darker beer, vaguely like
bitter
Export lager
Faßbier [f**a**ssbeer] draught
beer
ein großes Bier [ine gr**oh**ssess
beer] a large beer
eine Halbe [**ine**-uh h**a**lb-uh]
half a litre
ein Helles [ine h**e**lless] a lager
ein kleines Bier [ine kl**ine**-ess
beer] a small beer
eine Maß [mahss] a litre (in
South Germany)
Pils strong lager
Starkbier [sht**a**rkbeer] strong
beer
Radler [r**ah**tler] shandy
Weißbier [v**ice**-beer] pale
wheat-type beer
Weizenbier [v**y**tsen-beer] pale
wheat-type beer

beer mug der Bierkrug
[b**ee**rkr**oo**k]

before vorher [f**o**rhair]

before that davor [daf**o**r]

before me vor mir

begin: when does it begin?
wann fängt es an? [van fengt
ess an]

beginner (man/woman) der
Anfänger [**a**nfeng-er]/die
Anfängerin

beginning: at the beginning am
Anfang

behind hinten

behind me hinter mir

beige beige [bayJ]

Belgian (adj) belgisch [b**e**lgish]

Belgium Belgien [b**e**l-gee-en]

believe glauben [gl**ow**ben]

below unten [**oo**nten]

below ... unter ... [**oo**nter]

belt der Gürtel [g**oo**rtel]

bend (in road) die Kurve [k**oo**rv-
uh]

Berlin Wall die (Berliner)
Mauer [(bairl**ee**ner) m**ow**-er]

berth (on ship) die Kabine
[kab**ee**n-uh]

beside: beside the ... neben
dem/der ... [n**ay**ben daym/
dair]

best beste [b**e**st-uh]

better besser

are you feeling better? geht es
dir/Ihnen besser? [gayt ess
deer/**ee**nen]

between zwischen [tsv**i**shen]

beyond jenseits (+gen) [y**ay**n-
zites]

bicycle das Fahrrad [f**ah**r-raht]

big groß [grohss]

too big zu groß [ts**oo**]

it's not big enough es ist nicht
groß genug [nisht – gen**oo**k]

bike das Rad [raht]

(motorbike) das Motorrad
[mot**oh**r-raht]

bikini der Bikini

bill die Rechnung [r**e**shnoong]

(US: money) der Geldschein
[g**e**lt-shine]

could I have the bill, please?
kann ich bitte bezahlen? [kan
ish b**i**tt-uh bets**ah**len]

bin der Abfalleimer [**a**pfal-ime-
er]

bin liners die Mülltüten [m**oo**ll-
t**oo**ten]

binding (ski) die Bindung
[b**i**ndoong]

bird der Vogel [f**oh**gel]

biro® der Kugelschreiber
[k**oo**gel-shryber]

birthday der Geburtstag
[geb**oo**rts-tahk]

happy birthday! herzlichen
Glückwunsch zum
Geburtstag! [h**ai**rts-lishen
gl**oo**ckvoonsh tsoom]

biscuit das Plätzchen [pl**e**ts-
shen]

bit: a little bit ein bißchen [ine
b**i**ss-shen]

a big bit ein großes Stück
[gr**oh**ss sht**oo**ck]

a bit of ... ein Stück von ...

a bit expensive etwas teuer

bite (by insect) der Stich [shtish]

(by dog) der Biß [biss]

bitter (taste etc) **bitter**

black schwarz [shvarts]

Black Forest der Schwarzwald
[shv**a**rts-valt]

blanket die Decke [d**e**ck-uh]

bless you! Gesundheit!
[gez**oo**nt-hite]

blind blind [blint]

blinds die Jalousie [Jall**oo**zee]

blister die Blase [bl**ah**z-uh]

blocked (road, sink) **verstopft**
[fairsht**o**pft]

block of flats der Wohnblock
[v**oh**nblock]

blond blond [blont]

blood das Blut [bl**oo**t]

high blood pressure h**o**her
Blutdruck [bl**oo**t-droock]

blouse die Bluse [bl**oo**z-uh]

blow-dry (verb) **fönen** [f**u**rnen]

I'd like a cut and blow-dry
schneiden und fönen, bitte
[shn**y**den oont]

blue blau [blow]

blusher das Rouge [r**oo**J]

boarding house die Pension
[pangz-y**oh**n]

boarding pass die Bordkarte
[b**o**rtkart-uh]

boat das Boot [boht]

(for passengers) **das Schiff** [shiff]

body der Körper [k**u**rper]

boil (water, potatoes) **kochen**
[k**o**KHen]

boiled egg ein gekochtes Ei
[gek**o**KHtess ī]

bone der Knochen [k-n**o**KHen]

bonnet (of car) **die Haube**

book das Buch [b**oo**KH]

to book buchen [b**oo**KHen],
bestellen [besht**e**llen]

can I book a seat? kann ich
einen Platz reservieren
lassen? [rezair-v**ee**ren]

•••••• DIALOGUE ••••••

I'd like to book a table for two ich
möchte einen Tisch für zwei
Personen bestellen [ish m**u**rsht-uh
ine-en tish f**oo**r tsvy pairz**oh**nen]
what time would you like it booked
for? für wann ist die
Reservierung? [rezair-v**ee**roong]
half past seven halb acht
that's fine das geht in Ordnung
[gayt in **o**rtnoong]
and your name? Ihr Name, bitte?
[n**ah**m-uh]

bookshop die Buchhandlung
[b**oo**KH-hantloong]

bookstore (US) **die**
Buchhandlung

boot (footwear) **der Stiefel**
[sht**ee**fel]
(of car) **der Kofferraum**
[k**o**ffer-rowm]

border (of country) **die Grenze**
[gr**e**nts-uh]

bored: I'm bored ich habe
langeweile [ish h**a**hb-uh lang-
uh-vile-uh]

boring langweilig [l**a**ngvile-ish]

born: I was born in Manchester
ich bin in Manchester
geboren [geb**oh**ren]
I was born in 1960 ich bin

neunzehnhundertsechzig
geboren

borrow leihen [l**y**-en]
   may I borrow ...? kann ich ...
   leihen?

both beide [b**y**-duh]

bother: sorry to bother you with
   this es tut mir leid, Sie damit
   zu belästigen [ess t**oo**t meer
   lite zee dah**i**t tsoo bel**e**stigen]

bottle die Flasche [fl**a**sh-uh]
   a bottle of dry white wine eine
   Flasche tr**o**ckenen
   Wei**ß**wein

bottle-opener der Flaschenöffner [fl**a**shen-urfner]

bottom (of person) der H**i**ntern
   at the bottom of the hill am
   Fu**ß** des Berges [f**oo**ss]

box die Schachtel [sh**a**KHtel]
   (wooden) die Kiste [k**i**st-uh]

box office die Kasse [k**a**ss-uh]

boy der Junge [y**oo**ng-uh]

boyfriend der Freund [froynt]

bra der BH [bay-h**ah**]

bracelet das Armband
   [**a**rmbant]

brake die Bremse [bremz-uh]

brandy der Weinbrand [v**i**ne-
   brant]

bread das Brot [broht]
   some more bread, please
   noch etwas Brot, bitte
   [**e**tvass]
   white bread das Wei**ß**brot
   [v**i**ce-broht]
   brown bread das Graubrot
   [gr**ow**-broht]
   wholemeal bread das

Vollkornbrot [f**o**llkorn-broht]

break (verb) brechen [br**e**shen]
   I've broken ... mir ist ...
   kaputtgegangen [meer –
   kap**oo**t-gegangen]
   I think I've broken my wrist ich
   gl**au**be, ich h**a**be mir das
   H**a**ndgelenk gebrochen
   [gebr**o**KHen]

breakdown die Panne [p**a**nn-uh]

If you break down on a
motorway, go to one of the
emergency telephones; arrows
on the marker posts along the
hard shoulder will direct you
to the nearest one. The Stra**ß**en-
wacht [shtr**ah**ssenvaKHt] will
give free assistance. (You will
have to pay for any parts.) The
largest German motoring
association is the ADAC [ah-day-
ah-ts**ay**] which has links with
other international motoring
organizations. Note that it
is compulsory to carry a
warning triangle as well as a
first-aid kit.

---

breakdown service die
   Pannenhilfe [p**a**nnen-hilf-uh]

break down (in car) eine Panne
   haben [**i**ne-uh p**a**nn-uh
   h**ah**ben]
   I've broken down ich habe
   eine Panne

breakfast das Frühstück
   [fr**oo**shtック]
   English/full breakfast ein

englisches Frühstück [eng-
lish-ess]
break-in: I've had a break-in bei
mir ist eingebrochen
worden [by meer ist ine-
gebroKHen vorden]
breast die Brust [broost]
breathe atmen [ahtmen]
breeze die Brise [breez-uh]
brewery die Brauerei [brower-i]
bridge (over river) die Brücke
[brOOck-uh]
brief kurz [koorts]
briefcase die Aktentasche
[akten-tash-uh]
bright (light etc) hell
bright red hellrot [hell-roht]
brilliant (idea) glänzend
[glentsent]
(person) großartig [grohss-
artish]
bring bringen
I'll bring it back later ich
bringe es später zurück
[bring-uh ess shpayter
tsOOrOOck]
Britain Großbritannien [grohss-
britannee-en]
British britisch [breetish]
brochure die Broschüre
[broshOOr-uh]
broken kaputt
bronchitis die Bronchitis [bron-
sheetis]
brooch die Brosche [brosh-uh]
broom der Besen [bayzen]
brother der Bruder [brOOder]
brother-in-law der Schwager
[shvahger]

brown braun [brown]
bruise der blaue Fleck
[blow-uh]
brush die Bürste [bOOrst-uh]
(artist's) der Pinsel [pinzel]
Brussels Brüssel [brOOssel]
bucket der Eimer [ime-er]
buffet car der Speisewagen
[shpize-uh-vahgen]
buggy (for child) der
Sportwagen [shport-vahgen]
building das Gebäude
[geboyd-uh]
bulb (light bulb) die Birne
[beern-uh]
bumper die Stoßstange
[shtohss-shtang-uh]
bunk das Bett
bureau de change die
Wechselstube [veksel-
shtOOb-uh]
burglary der Einbruch [ine-
brooKH]
burn die Verbrennung [fair-
brennoong]
(verb) brennen
burnt: this is burnt das ist
angebrannt [an-gebrannt]
burst: a burst pipe ein
geplatztes Rohr
bus der Bus [booss]
what number bus is it to ...?
welcher Bus fährt nach ...?
[velsher booss fairt naKH]
when is the next bus to ...?
wann fährt der nächste Bus
nach ...? [naykst-uh]
what time is the last bus?
wann fährt der letzte Bus?

[le**ts**t-uh]

**could you let me know when
we get there? können Sie mir
Bescheid sagen, wenn wir
da sind?** [**kur**nen zee meer
besh**ite** z**ah**gen]

Get tickets from ticket machines
at the bus stop or, in some
areas, from the driver; in some
parts of Germany tickets
must be purchased in
advance. Multiple tickets –
Mehrfahrten-karten [**m**air-
fahrtenkarten] cut down the
cost of travel considerably.

•••••• DIALOGUE ••••••

**does this bus go to ...? fährt
di**e**ser Bus nach ...?** [fairt]
**no, you need a number ... nein, Sie
müssen mit der ... fahren
where does it leave from? wo fährt
er ab?** [vo]

business das Geschäft [gesh**eft**]
bus station der Busbahnhof
[b**oo**ss-bahnhohf]
bus stop die Bushaltestelle
[b**oo**ss-halt-uh-shtell-uh]
bust der Busen [b**oo**zen]
busy (restaurant etc) **voll** [foll]
(telephone) **besetzt** [bez**e**tst]
**I'm busy tomorrow morgen
bin ich beschäftigt** [besh**ef**-
tisht]
but aber [**ah**ber]
butcher's der Metzger [m**e**tsger]
butter die Butter [b**oo**tter]

button der Knopf [k-nopf]
buy kaufen [k**ow**fen]
**where can I buy ...? wo kann
ich ... bek**o**mmen?** [voh]
**by: by bus/car mit dem Bus/
Auto** [d**aym**]
written by ... geschrie**ben von
by the window am F**e**nster
by the sea am Meer
by Thursday bis Donnerstag
bye auf Wiedersehen** [owf-
veederzayn]

C

cabbage der Kohl
cable car die Drahtseilbahn
[dr**ah**tzile-bahn]
café das Café [kaff**ay**]

Cafés serve coffee, tea and
cakes, alcoholic drinks and
snacks but not full meals.
Some **Konditoreien** (see 'cake
shop') are also cafés, serving
coffee and cakes.

---

cagoule das Windhemd [v**i**nt-
hemt]
cake der Kuchen [k**OO**KHen]
cake shop die Konditorei
[kondeetor-**ī**]
call (verb) **rufen** [r**OO**fen]
(to phone) **anrufen** [**a**nr**OO**fen]
**what's it called? wie heißt
das?** [vee hyst dass]
**he/she is called ... er/sie
heißt ...
please call a doctor bitte**

rufen Sie einen Arzt
**please give me a call at 7.30
am tomorrow morning**
könnten Sie mich morgen
früh um sieben Uhr dreißig
wecken? [k**ur**nten zee mish
m**o**rgen fr**oo** – v**e**cken]
please ask him to call me
s**a**gen Sie ihm b**i**tte, er
möchte mich anrufen
[m**ur**sht-uh]
call back: I'll call back later ich
komme später noch einmal
wieder [ish k**o**mm-uh shp**ay**ter
noKH **i**ne-mahl v**ee**der]
(phone back) ich rufe später
noch einmal an [r**oo**f-uh]
**call round: I'll call round
tomorrow** ich komme
morgen vorbei [k**o**mm-uh –
for-b**y**]
camcorder der C**a**mcorder
camera die K**a**mera
camera shop der Fotoladen
[f**o**to-lahden]
camp (verb) zelten [ts**e**lten]
camping gas das Campinggas
[k**e**mping-gahss]
campsite der Campingplatz
[k**e**mpingplats]

Sites are officially graded on a
scale beginning at 'good' and
working up to 'excellent'. Even
the lowest grade have toilet and
washing facilities and a shop
nearby on the site, while the
grandest are virtually open-air →

hotels with swimming pools,
supermarkets and various other
comforts. Many sites, especially
those in popular holiday areas,
are nearly always full from June
to September, and you should
arrive early in the afternoon for
a good chance of getting in. Most
campsites close down in the
winter.

can (tin) die Dose [d**oh**z-uh]
a can of beer eine Dose Bier
can*: can you ...? kannst du/
können Sie ...? [d**oo**/k**ur**nen
zee]
can I have ...? kann ich ...
haben? [h**ah**ben]
I can't ... ich kann nicht...
[nisht]
Canada K**a**nada
Canadian kan**a**disch
[kan**ah**dish]
I'm Canadian (man/woman) ich
bin Kanadier [kan**ah**dee-er]/
Kanadierin
canal der Kanal [kan**ah**l]
cancel (reservation) rückgängig
machen [r**oo**ck-gengish
m**a**KHen]
candle die Kerze [k**air**ts-uh]
candy (US) die Süßigkeiten
[z**oo**ssish-kyten]
canoe das Kanu [kahn**oo**]
canoeing das Kanufahren
[kahn**oo**-fahren]
can-opener der Dosenöffner
[d**oh**zen-urfner]

cap (hat) eine Mütze [m**oo**ts-uh]
(of bottle) der Deckel
car das Auto [**ow**to]
by car mit dem **Au**to
carafe die Karaffe [kar**aff**-uh]
a carafe of house white, please
eine Karaffe wei**ß**en
Tafelwein, bitte
caravan der Wohnwagen
[v**oh**nvahgen]
caravan site der
Wohnwagenplatz
[v**oh**nvahgen-plats]
carburettor der Vergaser [fair-
g**ah**zer]
card (birthday etc) die Karte
[k**art**-uh]
here's my (business) card hier
ist meine Karte
cardigan die Strickjacke
[sht**rick**-yack-uh]
cardphone das Kartentelefon
careful vorsichtig [f**or**-zishtish]
be careful! seien Sie
vorsichtig! [z**y**-en zee]
caretaker der Hausmeister
[h**ow**ss-myster]
car ferry die Autofähre [**ow**to-
fair-uh]
car hire die Autovermietung
[**ow**to-fairmeetoong]
carnival der Karneval [k**arn**-
uh-val]
car park der Parkplatz
[p**ark**plats]
carpet der Teppich [t**epp**ish]
carriage (of train) der Wagen
[v**ah**gen]
carrier bag die Tragetasche

[tr**ahg**-uh-tash-uh]
carrot die Möhre [m**ur**-uh]
carry tragen [tr**ah**gen]
carry-cot die
Säuglingstragetasche
[z**oy**glings-trahg-uh-tash-uh]
carton (of orange juice etc) die
Packung [p**ack**oong]
carwash (place) die
Autowaschanlage [**ow**to-
vash-anlahg-uh]
case (suitcase) der Koffer
cash das Bargeld [b**ah**rgelt]
(verb) einlösen [**ine**-lurzen]
will you cash this for me?
können Sie das für mich
einlösen? [k**ur**nen]
cash desk die Kasse [k**a**ss-uh]
cash dispenser der
Geldautomat [g**elt**-owtomaht]
cassette die Kassette
[kass**ett**-uh]
cassette recorder der
Kass**ett**enrecorder
castle das Schloß [shloss]
casualty department die
Unfallstation [**oo**nfal-shtats-
yohn]
cat die Katze [k**ats**-uh]
catch fangen
where do we catch the bus
to ...? wo können wir den
Bus nach ... bekommen?
cathedral der Dom [dohm]
Catholic (adj) katholisch
[kat**oh**lish]
cauliflower der Blumenkohl
[bl**oo**menkohl]
cave die Höhle [h**ur**l-uh]

ceiling die Decke [**deck**-uh]

celery der Sellerie [**z**elleree]

cellar (for wine) der Weinkeller [**vine**-keller]

cemetery der Friedhof [**freet**-hohf]

Centigrade* Celsius [ts**e**lzee-oos]

centimetre* der Zentimeter [ts**e**ntimayter]

central zentral [tsentr**ah**l]

central heating die Zentralheizung [tsentr**ah**l-hytsoong]

centre das Zentrum [ts**e**ntroom]
  how do we get to the city centre? wie kommt man zum Stadtzentrum? [tsoom sht**a**tt-sentroom]

cereal die Zerealien [tsairay-**ah**lee-en]

certainly sicher [**z**isher]
  certainly not ganz bestimmt nicht [gants besht**i**mmt nisht]

chair der Stuhl [sht**oo**l]

chairlift der Sessellift [**ze**ssel-lift]

champagne der Champagner [shamp**a**n-yer]

change (noun: money) das Wechselgeld [**v**eksel-gelt]
  to change (money) wechseln [**w**ekseln]
  to change a reservation umbuchen [**oo**mb**oo**kHen]
  can I change this for ...? kann ich das gegen ... umtauschen? [g**ay**gen ... **oo**m-towshen]
  I don't have any change ich habe kein Kleingeld [h**ah**b-uh kine kl**ine**-gelt]
  can you give me change for a 50 mark note? können Sie einen 50-Mark-Schein wechseln? [k**ur**nen zee **ine**-en – shine]

•••••• DIALOGUE ••••••

do we have to change (trains/buses)? müssen wir umsteigen? [m**oo**ssen veer **oo**m-shtygen]

yes, change at Düsseldorf ja, Sie müssen in Düsseldorf umsteigen

no, it's direct nein, das ist eine Direktverbindung

changed: to get changed sich umziehen [zish **oo**m-tsee-en]

chapel die Kapelle [kapell-uh]

charge der Preis [price]

charge (verb) verlangen [fairl**a**ngen]

charge card die Kreditkarte [krayd**ee**t-kart-uh]
  see credit card

cheap billig [b**i**llish]
  do you have anything cheaper? haben Sie etwass billigeres? [h**ah**ben zee **e**tvass b**i**lligeress]

check (verb) überprüfen [**oo**ber-pr**oo**fen]
  could you check the ... please? könnten Sie die ... überprüfen, bitte? [k**ur**nten zee die ...]
  (US) der Scheck [sheck]
  (in restaurant etc) die Rechnung [r**e**shnoong]

check-in der Check-in

check in (at hotel) sich anmelden [zish **a**nmelden]

(at airport) einchecken [**ine**-checken]

where do we have to check in?
wo müssen wir einchecken?

cheek (of face) die Backe [b**a**ck-uh]

cheerio! (bye-bye) tschüs! [ch**oo**ss]

cheers! (toast) Prost! [prohst]
(thanks) danke [d**a**nkuh]

cheese der Käse [k**ay**z-uh]

chemist's die Apotheke [apot**ay**k-uh]

> German pharmacists sell
> prescribed and non-prescribed
> drugs. There are all-night
> pharmacists in bigger towns and
> cities; they work on a rota
> system and you can find the
> address of the one that is open
> on the door of any pharmacist
> as well as in local papers (look
> under **Nachtdienst** – night
> service).

cheque der Scheck [sheck]

do you take cheques? nehmen
Sie Schecks? [n**ay**men zee
shecks]

cheque book das Scheckheft [sh**e**ck-heft]

cheque card die Scheckkarte [sh**e**ck-kart-uh]

cherry die Kirsche [k**ee**rsh-uh]

chess Schach [shaKH]

chest (body) die Brust [broost]

chewing gum der Kaugummi [k**ow**-goommee]

chicken (as food) das Hähnchen [h**ay**nshen]

chickenpox die Windpocken [v**i**ntpocken]

child das Kind [kint]
children die Kinder

child minder die Tagesmutter [t**ah**gess-mootter]

children's pool das
Kinderschwimmbecken
[kinder-shvimmbecken]

children's portion der
Kinderteller [kinder-teller]

chin das Kinn

china (noun) das Porzellan [portsell**ah**n]

Chinese (adj) chinesisch [shin**ay**zish]

chips die Pommes frites [pom
frit]

chocolate die Schokolade [shokol**ah**d-uh]
milk chocolate die
Milchschokolade [milsh-]
plain chocolate die
Bitterschokolade

chocolates die Pralinen [pral**ee**nen]

hot chocolate der Kakao [kak**ow**]

choose wählen [v**ay**len]

Christian name der Vorname [forn**ah**m-uh]

Christmas Weihnachten [v**y**naKHten]

Christmas Eve der
Heiligabend [hylish-**ah**bent]

merry Christmas! frohe
Weihnachten [fr**oh**-uh]

church die Kirche [keersh-uh]

cider der Apfelwein [apfel-vine]

cigar die Zigarre [tsigarr-uh]

cigarette die Zigarette [tsigarett-uh]

cigarette lighter das Feuerzeug [foyer-tsoyk]

cinema das Kino [keeno]

circle der Kreis [krice]
(in theatre) der Balkon [balkohn]

city die Stadt [shtatt]

city centre die Innenstadt [innenshtatt]

clean (adj) sauber [zowber]
can you clean this for me? können Sie dies für mich reinigen? [kurnen zee deess foor mish rynigen]

cleaning solution (for contact lenses) die Reinigungslösung [rynigoongs-lurzoong]

cleansing lotion (cosmetic) die Reinigungscreme [rynigoongs-kraym]

clear klar

clever klug [klook]

cliff die Klippe [klipp-uh]

climbing das Bergsteigen [bairk-shtygen]

cling film die Frischhaltefolie [frish-halt-uh-fohlee-uh]

clinic die Klinik [kleenik]

cloakroom (for coats) die Garderobe [garderohb-uh]

clock die Uhr [oor]

close schließen [shleessen]

what time do you close? wann schließen Sie?

we close at 8 pm on weekdays and 6 pm on Saturdays wir schließen wochentags um zwanzig Uhr und samstags um achtzehn Uhr [voKHen-tahks oom – zams-tahks]

do you close for lunch? haben Sie mittags geschlossen? [geshlossen]

yes, between 1 and 2.30 pm ja, von dreizehn Uhr bis vierzehn Uhr dreißig

closed geschlossen [geshlossen]

cloth (fabric) der Stoff [shtoff]
(for cleaning etc) der Lappen

clothes die Kleider [klyder]

clothes line die Wäscheleine [vesh-uh-line-uh]

clothes peg die Wäscheklammer [vesh-uh-klammer]

cloud die Wolke [volk-uh]

cloudy wolkig [volkish]

clutch (of car) die Kupplung [kooploong]

coach (bus) der Bus [booss]
(on train) der Wagen [vahgen]

coach station der Busbahnhof [boossbahnhohf]

coach trip die Busreise [boossrize-uh]

coast die Küste [koost-uh]
on the coast an der Küste

coat (long coat) der Mantel
(jacket) die Jacke [yack-uh]

coathanger der Kleiderbügel [klyderboogel]

cockroach die Küchenschabe

42

[kOOshen-shahb-uh]
cocoa der Kakao [kakow]
code (for phoning) die Vorwahl
[forvahl]
  what's the (dialling) code for
  Berlin? was ist die Vorwahl
  für Berlin?
coffee der Kaffee [kaffay]
  two coffees, please zwei
  Kaffee bitte

You can generally expect to be
served ground coffee when or-
dering a coffee. It is often served
in a small pot (Kännchen
[kennshen] containing approximately two cups. Note that the
milk served with your coffee
is usually evaporated milk.
Italian coffees like Cappuccino
and Espresso are also quite
popular.

coin die Münze [mOOnts-uh]
Coke® die Cola [kohla]
cold (adj) kalt
  I'm cold mir ist kalt [meer]
  I have a cold ich bin erkältet
  [ish bin airkeltet]
collapse: he's collapsed er ist
  zusammengebrochen [air ist
  tsoozammengebroKHen]
collar der Kragen [krahgen]
collect sammeln
  I've come to collect ... ich
  komme, um ... abzuholen
  [ish komm-uh oom ... ap-tsoo-
  hohlen]
collect call das R-Gespräch

[air-geshpraysh]
college das College
Cologne Köln [kurln]
colour die Farbe [farb-uh]
  do you have this in other
  colours? haben Sie dies noch
  in anderen Farben? [hahben
  zee deess noKH in ander-en
  farben]
colour film der Farbfilm [farp-
  film]
comb (noun) der Kamm
come kommen

•••••• DIALOGUE ••••••
  where do you come from?
  woher kommen Sie? [vohair]
  I come from Edinburgh ich
  komme aus Edinburgh [ish
  komm-uh owss]

come back zurückkommen
  [tsOOrOOck-kommen]
  I'll come back tomorrow ich
  komme morgen zurück
  [komm-uh]
come in hereinkommen [hair-
  ine-kommen]
comfortable (hotel etc)
  komfortabel [komfortahbel]
compact disc die Compact-
  Disc
company (business) die Firma
  [feerma]
compartment (on train) das
  Abteil [aptile]
compass der Kompaß
  [kompass]
complain sich beschweren [zish
  beshvairen]

complaint die Beschwerde
[beshv**ai**rd-uh]
I have a complaint ich möchte
mich beschweren [m**ur**sht-uh
mish beshv**ai**ren]
completely völlig [f**ur**lish]
computer der Computer
['computer']
concert das Konzert [konts**ai**rt]
concussion die Gehirn-
erschütterung [geh**ee**rn-
airsh**oo**tteroong]
conditioner (for hair) der
Festiger
condom das Kondom
[kond**oh**m]
conference die Konferenz
[konf**ai**rents]
confirm bestätigen
[besht**ay**tigen]
congratulations! herzlichen
Glückwunsch! [h**ai**rtslishen
gl**oo**ckvoonsh]
connecting flight der
Anschlußflug [**a**nshlooss-
flook]
connection (in travelling) die
Verbindung [fairb**i**ndoong]
conscious (medically) bei
Bewußtsein [by bev**oo**st-zine]
constipation die Verstopfung
[fair-sht**o**pfoong]
consulate das Konsulat
[konzool**ah**t]
contact: **where can I contact
him?** wo kann ich ihn
erreichen? [vo – een
air-r**y**shen]
contact lenses die

Kontaktlinsen [kont**a**kt-linzen]
contraceptive das
Verhütungsmittel
[fairh**oo**toongs-mittel]
convenient (time, location)
günstig [g**oo**nstish]
that's not convenient das ist
nicht sehr günstig [nisht zair]
cook kochen [k**o**KHen]
not cooked (underdone) nicht
gar [nisht gahr]
cooker der Herd [hairt]
cookie (US) das Plätzchen
[pl**e**ts-shen]
cooking utensils die
Küchengeräte [k**oo**shen-
gerayt-uh]
cool kühl [k**oo**l]
cork der Korken
corkscrew der Korkenzieher
[k**o**rken-tsee-er]
corner: **on the corner** an der
Ecke [**e**ck-uh]
in the corner in der Ecke
cornflakes die Corn-flakes
correct (right) richtig [r**i**shtish]
corridor der Gang
cosmetics die Kosmetika
[kosm**a**ytika]
cost (verb) k**o**sten
how much does it cost? was
kostet das? [vass k**o**stet dass]
cot (for baby) das Kinderbett
cotton die Baumwolle
[b**o**wmvoll-uh]
cotton wool die Watte [v**a**t-uh]
couch (sofa) die Couch
couchette der Liegewagen
[l**ee**g-uh-v**a**hgen]

cough (noun) der Husten [h**oo**sten]

cough medicine das Hustenmittel [h**oo**sten-mittel]

could: could you ...? könnten Sie...? [**kur**nten zee]

could I have ...? könnte ich ... haben? [**kur**nt-uh ish ... h**ah**ben]

I couldn't ... ich konnte nicht... [ish k**o**nnt-uh nisht]

country das Land [lant]

countryside die Landschaft [l**a**nt-shafft]

couple (man and woman) das Paar [pahr]

a couple of ... ein paar... [ine pahr]

courier der Reiseleiter [**rize**-uh-lyter]

course (of meal) der Gang

of course natürlich [nat**oo**rlich]

of course not natürlich nicht [nisht]

cousin (male) der Vetter [**fe**tter] (female) die Kusine [k**oo**z**een**-uh]

cow die Kuh [k**oo**]

crab die Krebs [kr**ay**ps]

cracker (biscuit) der Kräcker [kr**e**cker]

craft shop der Handwerksladen [h**a**ntvairks-lahden]

crash (noun) der Zusammenstoß [ts**oo**-z**a**mmen-shtohss]

I've had a crash ich hatte einen Unfall [ish h**a**tt-uh **ine**-

en **oo**nfal]

crazy verrückt [fair-r**oo**ckt]

cream (on milk, in cake) die Sahne [z**ah**n-uh] (lotion) die Creme [kraym] (colour) cremefarben [kr**ay**m-farben]

creche (for babies) die Kinderkrippe [k**i**nderkripp-uh]

credit card die Kreditkarte [kred**ee**t-kart-uh]

Although credit cards and charge cards are accepted in a number of larger shops they are not as popular yet as in Great Britain and the US. Do not expect to be able to pay by credit card in supermarkets or at service stations.

•••••• DIALOGUE ••••••

can I pay by credit card? kann ich mit Kreditkarte bezahlen? [bets**ah**len]

which card do you want to use? mit welcher Karte möchten Sie bezahlen? [v**e**lsher]

what's the number? was ist die Nummer? [n**oo**mmer]

and the expiry date? und das Ablaufdatum? [**a**plowf-dahtoom]

crisps die Chips [chips]

crockery das Geschirr [gesh**ee**r]

crossing (by sea) die Überfahrt [**oo**berfahrt]

crossroads die Kreuzung [kr**oy**tsoong]

crowd die Menge [meng-uh]
crowded (streets, bars) voll [foll]
crown (on tooth) die Krone
[krohn-uh]
cruise (by ship) die Kreuzfahrt
[kroyts-fahrt]
crutches die Krücken [kroock-
en]
cry weinen [vynen]
cucumber die Gurke [goork-uh]
cup die Tasse [tass-uh]
 a cup of ... please eine
 Tasse ..., bitte [ine-uh]
cupboard der Schrank [shrank]
curly (hair) kraus [krowss]
current (electrical, in water) der
 Strom [shtrohm]
 (in sea) die Strömung
 [shtrurmoong]
curtains die Vorhänge
[forheng-uh]
cushion das Kissen
custom der Brauch [browKH]
Customs der Zoll [tsoll]
cut der Schnitt [shnitt]
cut (verb) schneiden [shnyden]
 I've cut myself ich habe mich
 geschnitten [ish hahb-uh mish
 geshnitten]
cutlery das Besteck [beshteck]
cycling das Radfahren
[rahtfahren]
cyclist (man/woman) der
 Radfahrer [rahtfahrer]/die
 Radfahrerin
Czech (adj) tschechisch
[cheshish]
 (language) Tschechisch
Czech Republic die

Tschechische Republik
[cheshish-uh repoo-bleek]

D

dad der Vater [fahter]
daily täglich [tayglish]
damage (verb) beschädigen
[beshaydigen]
 I'm sorry, I've damaged this
 tut mir leid, ich habe es
 beschädigt [toot meer lite]
damaged beschädigt
[beshaydisht]
damn! verdammt! [fairdamt]
damp feucht [foysht]
dance (noun) der Tanz [tants]
dance (verb) tanzen [tantsen]
 would you like to dance?
 möchtest du/möchten Sie
 tanzen? [murshtest doo/
 murshten zee]
dangerous gefährlich
[gefairlish]
Danish dänisch [daynish]
Danube die Donau [dohnow]
dark dunkel [doonkel]
 it's getting dark es wird
 dunkel [veert]
date*: what's the date today?
 welches Datum ist heute?
 [velshess dahtoom ist hoyt-uh]
 let's make a date for next
 Monday wir sollten einen
 Termin für nächsten Montag
 vereinbaren [ine-en tairmeen
 foor – fair-ine-bahren]
dates (fruit) die Datteln fpl
daughter die Tochter [toKHter]

daughter-in-law die
Schwiegertochter [shv**ee**ger-
toKHter]

dawn das Morgengrauen
[m**o**rgen-growen]

at dawn bei Tagesanbruch
[by t**ah**gess-anbrooKH]

day der Tag [tahk]

the day after am Tag danach
[dan**a**KH]

the day after tomorrow
übermorgen [**OO**bermorgen]

the day before am Tag zuvor
[tsOO**fo**r]

the day before yesterday
vorgestern [f**o**rgestern]

every day jeden Tag [y**ay**den]

all day den ganzen Tag [dayn
g**a**ntsen]

in two days' time in zwei
Tagen [t**ah**gen]

have a nice day schönen Tag
noch [sh**ur**nen – noKH]

day trip der Tagesausflug
[t**ah**gess-owssflook]

dead tot [toht]

deaf taub [towp]

deal (business) das Geschäft
[gesh**e**ft]

it's a deal abgemacht [ap-
gem**a**KHt]

death der Tod [toht]

decaffeinated coffee
koffeinfreier Kaffee [koffay-
een-fry-er k**a**ffay]

December der Dezember
[dayts**e**mber]

decide entscheiden [ent-
sh**y**den]

we haven't decided yet wir
haben uns noch nicht
entschieden [veer h**ah**ben
oonss noKH nisht ent-sh**ee**den]

decision die Entscheidung [ent-
sh**y**doong]

deck (on ship) das Deck

deckchair der Liegestuhl [leeg-
uh-sht**OO**l]

deduct abziehen [**a**p-tsee-en]

deep tief [teef]

definitely bestimmt [besht**i**mmt]

definitely not ganz bestimmt
nicht [gants]

degree (qualification) der
Abschluß [**a**pshlooss]

delay die Verzögerung [fair-
ts**ur**geroong]

deliberately absichtlich
[**a**pzishtlish]

delicatessen der Feinkostladen
[f**ine**-kost-lahden]

delicious köstlich [k**ur**stlish]

deliver liefern [l**ee**fern]

delivery (of mail) die Zustellung
[ts**OO**-shtelloong]

Denmark Dänemark [d**ay**n-uh-
mark]

dental floss die Zahnseide
[ts**ah**nzide-uh]

dentist der Zahnarzt [ts**ah**n-
artst]

see **doctor**

•••••• D I A L O G U E ••••••

it's this one here es ist dieser hier
[d**ee**zer heer]

this one? dieser?

no that one nein, dieser [nine]

here? hier? [heer]
yes ja [yah]

dentures das Gebiß [geb**i**ss]
deodorant das Deodor**a**nt
department die Abteilung [ap-t**y**loong]
department store das Kaufhaus [**kow**fhowss]
departure die Abreise [**a**p-rize-uh]
departure lounge die Abflughalle [**a**pfl**oo**k-hal-uh]
depend: it depends es kommt darauf an [ess kommt dar**ow**f an]
it depends on ... es hängt von ... ab [hengt fon ... ap]
deposit (as security) die Kaution [kowts-y**oh**n]
(as part payment) die Anzahlung [**a**ntsahloong]
description die Beschreibung [beshr**y**boong]
dessert der Nachtisch [n**a**KHtish]
destination das Reiseziel [r**i**ze-uh-tseel]
develop entwickeln [entv**i**ckeln]

•••••• DIALOGUE ••••••

could you develop these films?
können Sie diese Filme entwickeln? [k**u**rnen zee d**ee**z-uh film-uh]
when will they be ready? wann sind sie fertig? [f**ai**rtish]
tomorrow afternoon morgen nachmittag

how much is the four-hour service?
was kostet der Vier-Stunden-Service? [sht**oo**nden]

diabetic (man/woman) der Diabetiker [dee-ab**ay**tiker]/die Diabetikerin
diabetic foods diabetische Kost [dee-ab**ay**tish-uh]
dial (verb) wählen [**vay**len]
dialling code die Vorwahl [**for**vahl]

For direct international calls from Germany, dial the country code (given below), the area code (minus the first 0), and finally the subscriber number:

UK: 0044   Australia: 0061
Ireland: 00353
New Zealand: 0064
US & Canada: 001

If you're calling from within the former GDR, and not from a city, the major snag is that codes change according to the place from where you're dialling. To find the dialling code you're obliged to use the direct phone service facilities to be found in main post offices and railway stations, or at least go there to find out the code you require. Once you have this code, it's easy enough to call abroad from any booth.
see also **phone**

diamond der Diamant [dee-amant]

diaper (US) die Windel [vindel]

diarrhoea der Durchfall [doorshfal]

diary (business etc) der Terminkalender [tairmeen-kalender]
(for personal experiences) das Tagebuch [tahg-uh-booKH]

dictionary das Wörterbuch [vurterbooKH]

didn't*
see not

die sterben [shtairben]

diesel der Diesel

diet die Diät [dee-ayt]
I'm on a diet ich mache eine Diät [ish maKH-uh ine-uh]
I have to follow a special diet ich muß nach einer Diät leben [mooss naKH ine-er – layben]

difference der Unterschied [oontersheet]
what's the difference? was ist der Unterschied?

different verschieden [fair-sheeden]
this one is different dieses ist anders
a different table ein anderer Tisch

difficult schwer [shvair]

difficulty die Schwierigkeit [shveerish-kite]

dinghy (rubber) das Schlauchboot [shlowKHboht]
(sailing) das Dingi [ding-gee]

dining room das Speisezimmer [shpize-uh-tsimmer]

dinner (evening meal) das Abendessen [ahbentessen]
to have dinner zu Abend essen [tsoo]

direct (adj) direkt [deerekt]
is there a direct train? gibt es eine direkte Zugverbindung? [tsook-fairbindoong]

direction die Richtung [rishtoong]
which direction is it? in welcher Richtung ist es? [velsher]
is it in this direction? ist es in dieser Richtung? [deezer]

directory enquiries die Auskunft [owsskoonft]

The number for directory enquiries is 119.

dirt der Schmutz [shmoots]

dirty schmutzig [shmootsish]

disabled behindert
is there access for the disabled? gibt es Zugang für Behinderte? [geept ess tsoogang foor behindert-uh]

disappear verschwinden [fairshvinden]
it's disappeared es ist verschwunden [fairshvoonden]

disappointed enttäuscht [ent-toysht]

disappointing enttäuschend

[ent-**toy**shent]

disaster die Katastrophe
[katast**roh**f-uh]

disco die Diskothek [diskot**ayk**]

discount der Rabatt [rabb**at**]
  is there a discount? gibt es
  einen Rabatt? [geept ess
  ine-en]

disease die Krankheit [**krank**-
  hite]

disgusting widerlich
  [**vee**derlish]

dish (meal) das Gericht [ge**ri**sht]
  (bowl) der **Te**ller

dishcloth das Spültuch
  [shp**oo**lt**oo**KH]

disinfectant das
  Desinfektionsmittel
  [dezinfekts-**yoh**ns-mittel]

disk (for computer) die Diskette
  [disk**ett**-uh]

disposable diapers (US) die
  Papierwindeln [pap**eer**-
  vindeln]

disposable nappies die
  Papierwindeln

distance die Entfernung [ent-
  fairnoong]
  in the distance weit weg [vite
  vek]

distilled water destilliertes
  Wasser [destill**eer**tess **va**sser]

district das Gebiet [ge**bee**t]

disturb stören [sht**ur**-ren]

diversion (detour) die Umleitung
  [**oo**m-lytoong]

diving board das Sprungbrett
  [shpr**oo**ngbrett]

divorced geschieden

[ges**hee**den]

dizzy: I feel dizzy mir ist
  schwindlig [meer ist shv**i**ntlish]

do tun [t**oo**n]
  what shall we do? was sollen
  wir tun? [vass z**o**llen veer
  t**oo**n]
  how do you do it? wie
  machen Sie das? [vee ma**KH**en
  zee]
  will you do it for me? können
  Sie das für mich tun?
  [k**ur**nen]

•••••• DIALOGUES ••••••

how do you do? guten Tag
[g**oo**ten t**áh**k]

nice to meet you freut mich [froyt
mish]

what do you do? (work) was
machst du/machen Sie
beruflich? [vass ma**KH**st d**oo**/
ma**KH**en zee ber**oo**flish]

I'm a teacher, and you? ich bin
Lehrer, und Sie?

I'm a student ich bin Stud**e**nt

what are you doing this evening?
was machst du/machen Sie
heute abend? [ma**KH**st d**oo**/ma**KH**en
zee h**oy**t-uh **ah**bent]

**we're going out for a drink, do you
want to join us?** wir gehen einen
trinken, möchtest du/möchten
Sie mitkommen? [m**ur**shtest d**oo**/
m**ur**shten zee]

do you want cream? möchtest du/
möchten Sie Sahne?

I do, but she doesn't ich ja, aber
sie nicht [yah]

doctor der Arzt [artst]
we need a doctor wir
brauchen einen Arzt [veer
br**ow**KHen **ine**-en]
please call a doctor bitte
rufen Sie einen Arzt [b**i**tt-uh
r**oo**fen zee]

> British and other EU nationals
> are entitled to free medical care
> in Germany on production of a
> form E111, available from main
> post offices. Without this form,
> you'll have to pay in full for all
> medical treatment, which is
> expensive. Whether or not you
> get an E111, it's sensible to take
> out some form of travel insur-
> ance. For dental treatment,
> however, you should expect to
> be asked to pay part of the costs.

•••••• DIALOGUE ••••••

where does it hurt? wo tut es
weh? [vo t**oo**t ess vay]
right here genau hier [gen**ow** heer]
does that hurt now? tut es jetzt
weh? [yetst]
yes ja
take this to the pharmacist gehen
Sie hiermit zur Apotheke [g**ay**-en
zee h**ee**rmit ts**oo**r apot**ay**k-uh]

document das Dokument
[dok**oo**m**e**nt]
dog der Hund [hoont]
doll die Puppe [p**oo**p-uh]
domestic flight der Inlandflug
[**i**nlant-fl**oo**k]

don't*
see **not**
don't do that! tu das/tun Sie
das nicht! [t**oo** dass/t**oo**n zee
dass nisht]
door die Tür [t**oo**r]
doorman der Portier [porty**ay**]
double d**o**ppelt
double bed das D**o**ppelbett
double room das
Doppelzimmer [d**o**ppel-
tsimmer]
doughnut der Berliner
[bairl**ee**ner]
down: **down here** hier unten
[heer **oo**nten]
put it down over there setzen
Sie es hier ab [z**e**tsen zee ess
heer ap]
it's down there on the right es
ist hier unten rechts
it's further down the road es
ist weiter die Straße entlang
[v**y**ter dee shtr**ah**ss-uh entl**a**ng]
downhill skiing der
Abfahrtslauf [**a**pfahrts-lowf]
downmarket (restaurant etc)
weniger anspruchsvoll
[v**a**yniger **a**nshprooKHsfoll]
downstairs unten [**oo**nten]
dozen das Dutzend [d**oo**tsent]
half a dozen sechs Stück
[zeks sht**oo**ck]
drain (in sink, street) der Abfluß
[**a**p-flooss]
draught beer das Faßbier
[**fa**ssbeer]
draughty: **it's draughty** es zieht
[ess tseet]

drawer die Schublade
[sh**oo**plahd-uh]

drawing die Zeichnung
[ts**y**shnoong]

dreadful furchtbar [f**oo**rshtbar]

dream der Traum [trowm]

dress das Kleid [klite]

dressed: to get dressed sich
anziehen [zish **a**ntsee-en]

dressing (for cut) der Verband
[fairb**a**nt]

   salad dressing die Salatsoße
[zal**ah**tzohss-uh]

dressing gown der Bademantel
[b**ah**d-uh-mantel]

drink (alcoholic) der Drink
(non-alcoholic) das Getränk
[getr**e**nk]

   drink (verb) trinken

   a cold drink ein k**a**ltes
Getränk

   can I get you a drink? kann
ich Ihnen etwas zu trinken
besorgen? [**e**tvass ts**oo** –
bez**o**rgen]

   what would you like to drink?
was möchtest du/möchten
Sie zu trinken? [m**u**rshtest
d**OO**/m**u**rshten zee]

   no thanks, I don't drink nein
danke, ich trinke nicht
[tr**i**nk-uh nisht]

   I'll just have a drink of water
ich m**ö**chte nur **e**twas
W**a**sser

drinking water das Trinkwasser
[tr**i**nkvasser]

   is this drinking water? ist das
Trinkwasser?

drive (verb) f**a**hren

   we drove here wir sind mit
dem Auto gekommen [veer
zint mit daym **ow**to gek**o**mmen]

   I'll drive you home ich fahre
Sie nach Hause [ish f**a**hr-uh
zee naKH h**ow**z-uh]

driver (man/woman) der F**a**hrer/
die F**a**hrerin

driving licence der
Führerschein [f**OO**rer-shine]

drop: just a drop please (of drink)
nur einen Tropfen [noor **ine**-
en]

drug (medical) das Medikam**e**nt

   drugs (narcotics) die Drogen
fpl [dr**oh**gen]

drunk (adj) betrunken
[betr**oo**nken]

drunken driving Trunkenheit
am Steuer [tr**oo**nken-hite am
sht**oy**er]

dry (adj) trocken

If you'd like a really dry wine,
ask for it 'herb' [hairp]

---

dry-cleaner die chemische
Reinigung [sh**ay**mish-uh
r**y**nigoong]

duck die Ente [**e**nt-uh]

due: he was due to arrive
yesterday er sollte gestern
ankommen [air z**o**llt-uh]

   when is the train due? wann
kommt der Zug an? wann
kommt der Zug an?

dull (pain) dumpf [doompf]
(weather) trüb [tr**OO**p]

dummy (baby's) der Schnuller

[shn**oo**ller]

during während [v**ai**rent]

dust der Staub [shtowp]

dusty staubig [sht**ow**bish]

dustbin die Mülltonne
[m**oo**lltonn-uh]

Dutch (adj) holländisch
[h**o**llendish]
(language) Holländisch

duty-free (goods) zollfreie
Waren [ts**o**llfry-uh v**ah**ren]

duty-free shop der Duty-free-
Shop

duvet das Federbett [f**ay**derbet]

E

each (every) jeder [y**ay**der]
how much are they each? was
kosten sie pro Stück? [vass
k**o**sten zee pro sht**oo**k]

ear das Ohr

earache Ohrenschmerzen
[**oh**ren-shmairtsen]

early früh [fr**oo**]
early in the morning früh am
Morgen
I called by earlier ich war
schon einmal hier [sh**oh**n
ine-mahl heer]

earring der Ohrring

east der Osten
in the east im Osten

Easter Ostern [**oh**stern]

easy leicht [lysht]

eat essen
we've already eaten, thanks
danke, wir haben schon
gegessen [h**ah**ben shohn]

eau de toilette das Eau de
toilette

EC die EG [ay-g**ay**]

economy class die Touristen-
klasse [t**oo**risten-klass-uh]

egg das Ei [ī]

Eire Irland [**ee**rlant]

either: either … or … entweder…
oder… [**e**ntvayder … **oh**der]
either, I don't mind egal
welcher [ayg**ah**l velsher]

elastic der Gummi [g**oo**mmee]

elastic band das Gummiband
[g**oo**mmeebant]

elbow der Ellbogen

electric elektrisch [ayl**e**ktrish]

electric fire das elektrische
Heizgerät [ayl**e**ktrish-uh h**i**tes-
gerayt]

electrician der Elektriker
[ayl**e**ktriker]

electricity der Strom [shtrohm]
see voltage

elevator (US) der Aufzug
[**ow**f-ts**oo**k]

else: something else etwas
anderes [**e**tvass **a**nderess]
somewhere else woanders
[vo-**a**nders]

•••••• DIALOGUE ••••••

would you like anything else?
möchten Sie noch etwas?
[m**u**rshten]
no, nothing else, thanks danke,
das ist alles [d**a**nk-uh dass ist
al-ess]

embassy die Botschaft [b**oh**t-
shafft]

emergency der Notfall
[n**oh**t-fal]
this is an emergency! dies ist
ein Notfall! [deess ist ine]
emergency exit der Notausgang
[n**oh**t-owssgang]
empty leer [lair]
end das Ende [**e**nd-uh]
at the end of the street am
Ende der Straße
end (verb) enden
when does it end? wann ist es
zu Ende? [vann ist ess tsoo
end-uh]
engaged (toilet, telephone) besetzt
[bez**e**tst]
(to be married) verlobt
[fairl**oh**pt]
engine der Motor [m**oh**tohr]
England England [**e**ng-lant]
English englisch [**e**ng-lish]
I'm English (man/woman) ich bin
Engländer [**e**ng-lender]/
Engländerin
do you speak English?
sprichst du/sprechen Sie
Englisch? [shprisht d**OO**/
shpr**e**shen zee]
enjoy: **to enjoy oneself** sich
amüsieren [zish am**OO**z**ee**ren]

•••••• DIALOGUE ••••••

how did you like the film? wie hat
dir/Ihnen der Film gefallen? [vee
hat deer/**ee**nen dair]
I enjoyed it very much – did you?
er hat mir sehr gut gefallen –
dir/Ihnen auch? [meer zair g**OO**t –
deer/**ee**nen owKH]

enjoyable unterhaltsam [oonter-
h**a**lt-zahm]
(meal) angenehm
[**a**n-genaym]
enlargement (of photo) die
Vergröß erung
[fairgr**ur**sseroong]
enormous enorm [ayn**o**rm]
enough genug [gen**OO**k]
there's not enough ... es ist
nicht genug ... da [ess ist
nisht]
it's not big enough es ist nicht
groß genug
that's enough das genügt
[dass gen**OO**kt]
entrance der Eingang
[**ine**-gang]
envelope der Umschlag
[**oo**mshlahk]
epileptic (man/woman) der
Epileptiker/die
Epileptikerin
equipment (for climbing etc) die
Ausrüstung [**ow**ss-
r**OO**stoong]
error der Fehler [f**ay**ler]
especially besonders
[bez**o**nders]
essential wesentlich
[v**ay**zentlish]
it is essential that ... es ist
unbedingt notwendig,
daß... [**oo**nbedingt
n**oh**tvendish]
Estonia Estland [**e**stlant]
EU die EU [ay-**OO**]
Eurocheque der Euroscheck
[**oy**ro-sheck]

Eurocheque card die Euroscheckkarte [**o**yro-sheck-kart-uh]

Europe Europa [oyro**h**pa]

European europäisch [oyrohp**ay**ish]

even sogar [zog**ah**r], selbst [zelpst]

even if ... sogar wenn..., selbst wenn ... [ven]

evening der Abend [**ah**bent]

this evening heute abend [h**oy**t-uh]

in the evening am Abend

evening meal das Abendessen [**ah**bent-essen]

eventually schließlich [shl**ee**sslish]

ever jemals [**yay**mahls]

•••••• DIALOGUE ••••••

have you ever been to Heidelberg? waren Sie schon einmal in Heidelberg? [v**ah**ren zee shohn **ine**-mahl]

yes, I was there two years ago ja, ich war vor zwei Jahren da [for – y**ah**ren]

every jeder [**yay**der]

every day jeden Tag [**yay**den tahk]

everyone jeder [**yay**der]

everything alles [**al**-ess]

everywhere überall [**oo**ber-al]

exactly! genau! [gen**ow**]

exam die Prüfung [pr**oo**foong]

example das Beispiel [b**y**shpeel]

for example zum Beispiel [tsoom]

excellent hervorragend [hairf**or**-rahgent]

excellent ausgezeichnet [owss-getsy**sh**net]

except außer [**ow**sser]

excess baggage das Übergewicht [**oo**bergevisht]

exchange rate der Wechselkurs [v**e**ckselkoorss]

exciting (day, holiday) aufregend [**ow**f-raygent]

(film) spannend [shp**a**nnent]

excuse me (to get past) entschuldigen Sie! [ent-sh**oo**ldigen zee]

(to get attention) Entschuldigung! [ent-sh**oo**ldigoong]

(to say sorry) Verzeihung [fair-ts**y**-oong]

exhaust (pipe) der Auspuff [**ow**sspooff]

exhausted erschöpft [airsh**ur**pft]

exhibition die Ausstellung [**ow**ss-shtelloong]

exit der Ausgang [**ow**ssgang]

where's the nearest exit? wo ist der nächste Ausgang? [dair n**ay**kst-uh]

expect erwarten [airv**a**rten]

expensive teuer [t**oy**er]

experienced erfahren [airf**ah**ren]

explain erklären [airkl**ai**ren]

can you explain that? könnten Sie mir das erklären? [k**ur**nten zee meer]

express (mail) per Expreß [pair
ekspress]
(train) der Schnellzug
[shnelltsook]
extension (telephone) der
Anschluß [anshlooss]
extension 21, please
Anschluß einundzwanzig
bitte [bitt-uh]
extension lead die
Verlängerungsschnur
[fairlengeroongs-shnoor]
extra: can we have an extra
one? können wir noch eins
haben? [kurnen veer noKH ine-
ss hahben]
do you charge extra for that?
kostet das extra?
extraordinary außergewöhnlich
[owsser-gevurnlish]
extremely äußerst [oysserst]
eye das Auge [owg-uh]
will you keep an eye on my
suitcase for me? könnten Sie
auf meinen Koffer
aufpassen? [kurnten zee –
owfpassen]
eyebrow pencil der
Augenbrauenstift
[owgenbrowen-shtift]
eye drops die Augentropfen
[owgen-tropfen]
eyeglasses (US) die Brille
[brill-uh]
eyeliner der Eyeliner
eye make-up remover der
Augen-Make-up-
Entferner [owgen-'make-up'-
entfairner]

eye shadow der Lidschatten
[leet-shatten]

F

face das Gesicht [gezisht]
factory die Fabrik [fabreek]
Fahrenheit* Fahrenheit
faint (verb) ohnmächtig werden
[ohnmeshtish vairden]
she's fainted sie ist
ohnmächtig geworden [zee
ist ... gevorden]
I feel faint mir ist ganz
schwach [meer ist gants
shvaKH]
fair (funfair) der Jahrmarkt
[yahrmarkt]
(trade) die Messe [mess-uh]
fair (adj) fair
fairly ziemlich [tseemlish]
fake die Fälschung [felshoong]
fall (verb) fallen [fal-en]
she's had a fall sie ist
hingefallen [zee ist hin-
gefal-en]
(US: autumn) der Herbst
[hairpst]
false falsch [falsh]
family die Familie [fameelee-uh]
famous berühmt [beroomt]
fan (electrical) der Ventilator
[ventilah-tor]
(hand held) der Fächer [fesher]
(sports) der Fan [fen]
fan belt der Keilriemen [kile-
reemen]
fantastic fantastisch
far weit [vite]

•••••• DIALOGUE ••••••

is it far from here? ist es weit von hier? [fon heer]

no, not very far nein, nicht sehr weit [nisht zair]

well how far? wie weit denn? [vee]

it's about 10 kilometres es sind etwa zehn Kilometer [etvah]

fare der Fahrpreis [**fahr**price]

farm der Bauernhof [**bo**wernhohf]

fashionable modisch [**moh**dish]

fast schnell

fat (person) dick
(on meat) das Fett

father der Vater [**fah**ter]

father-in-law der Schwiegervater [shv**ee**ger-fahter]

faucet (US) der Wasserhahn [**va**sserhahn]

fault der Fehler [**fay**ler]

sorry, it was my fault tut mir leid, es war mein Fehler [mine]

it's not my fault es ist nicht meine Schuld [nisht m**ine**-uh shoolt]

faulty defekt [day**fe**kt]

favourite Lieblings- [l**ee**plings]

fax das Fax [faks]

fax (verb) (person) per Fax benachrichtigen [pair faks ben**a**KH-rishtigen]
(document) **fa**xen

February der Februar [**fay**broo-ahr]

feel fühlen [f**oo**len]

I feel hot mir ist heiß [meer ist hice]

I feel unwell mir ist nicht gut [nisht g**oo**t]

I feel like going for a walk mir ist nach einem Spaziergang [naKH]

how are you feeling? wie fühlen Sie sich? [vee f**oo**len zee zish]

I'm feeling better es geht mir besser [ess gayt meer]

felt-tip (pen) der Filzstift [filts-shtift]

fence der Zaun [tsown]

fender (US) die Stoßstange [sht**oh**ss-shtang-uh]

ferry die Fähre [f**air**-uh]

festival das Festival [**fe**stivahl]

fetch holen [h**oh**len]

I'll fetch him ich hole ihn [h**oh**l-uh]

will you come and fetch me later? können Sie mich später abholen? [k**ur**nen zee mish sh**pay**ter **a**phohlen]

feverish: she's still feverish sie hat noch immer Fieber [zee hat noKH immer f**ee**ber]

few: a few ein paar [ine pahr]

a few days ein paar Tage

fiancé: my fiancé mein Verlobter [mine fairl**oh**pter]

fiancée: my fiancée meine Verlobte [m**ine**-uh fairl**oh**pt-uh]

field das Feld [felt]

fight der Kampf

fill füllen [f**oo**llen]

fill in ausfüllen [**ow**ssfoollen]

do I have to fill this in? muß
ich das ausfüllen? [mooss]
fill up voll machen [foll ma**KH**en]
fill it up, please volltanken
bitte [**f**olltanken bitt-uh]
filling (in sandwich) der Belag
[bel**ah**k]
(in cake, tooth) die Füllung
[f**oo**lloong]
film der Film

•••••• DIALOGUE ••••••

do you have this kind of film?
haben Sie diesen Film? [h**ah**ben
zee d**ee**zen]
yes, how many exposures? ja, wie
viele Aufnahmen? [vee v**eel**-uh
owfnahmen]
36 sechsunddreißig [seksoont-
dr**y**ssish]

film processing die
Filmentwicklung [film-
entvickloong]
filter coffee der Filterkaffee
[f**i**lter-kaffay]
filter papers das Filterpapier
[f**i**lter-papeer]
filthy dreckig [dr**e**ckish]
find finden
I can't find it ich kann es
nicht finden [ish kann ess
nisht]
I've found it ich habe es
gefunden [gef**oo**nden]
find out herausfinden
[her**ow**ss-finden]
could you find out for me?
könnten Sie das für mich
herausfinden? [k**ur**nten zee

dass foor mish]
fine (weather) schön [shurn]
(punishment) die Geldstrafe
[g**e**lt-shtrahf-uh]

•••••• DIALOGUES ••••••

how are you? wie geht's? [vee
gayts]
I'm fine thanks danke, gut [g**oo**t]

is that OK? ist das ok**a**y?
that's fine thanks in Ordnung,
danke [**o**rtnoong]

finger der Finger [f**i**ng-er]
finish (verb) beenden
[buh-**e**nden]
I haven't finished yet ich bin
noch nicht fertig [ish bin no**KH**
nisht f**ai**rtish]
when does it finish? wann ist
es zu Ende? [van ist ess tsoo
end-uh]
fire das Feuer [f**oy**-er]
can we light a fire here?
können wir hier ein Feuer
machen? [k**ur**nen veer heer –
ma**KH**en]
it's on fire es brennt
fire alarm der Feueralarm [f**oy**-
er-alarm]
fire brigade die Feuerwehr
[f**oy**-er-vair]

In the event of a fire, phone 112.

fire escape die Feuertreppe
[f**oy**-er-trepp-uh], die
Feuerleiter [f**oy**-er-lyter]
fire extinguisher der

Feuerlöscher [**foy**-er-lursher]

first erster [**air**ster]

I was first ich war der/die
erste [dair/dee **air**st-uh]

at first zuerst [tsoo-**air**st]

the first time das erste Mal

first on the left die erste
Straße links

first aid die Erste Hilfe [**air**st-uh
hilf-uh]

first aid kit die Erste-Hilfe-
Ausrüstung [**air**st-uh hilf-uh
owssroostoong]

first class erster Klasse [**air**ster
kl**a**ss-uh]

first floor der erste Stock [**air**st-
uh shtock]
(US) das Erdgeschoß [**air**t-
geshoss]

first name der Vorname
[**for**nahm-uh]

fish der Fisch [fish]

fishmonger's der Fischhändler
[**fish**-hentler]

fit (attack) der Anfall [**a**n-fal]

it doesn't fit me es paßt mir
nicht [ess passt meer nisht]

fitting room der Anproberaum
[**a**nprohb-uh-rowm]

fix (arrange, sort out) regeln
[**ray**geln]

can you fix this? (repair)
können Sie das reparieren?
[kurnen zee dass repar**ee**ren]

fizzy sprudelnd [shpr**oo**delnt]

flag die Fahne [**fah**n-uh]

flannel der Waschlappen
[**va**shlappen]

flash (for camera) der Blitz

flat (apartment) die Wohnung
[**voh**noong]
(adj) flach [flaKH]

I've got a flat tyre ich habe
einen Platten [ish h**ah**b-uh
ine-en]

flavour der Geschmack
[geshm**a**ck]

flea der Floh

flight der Flug [flook]

flight number die Flugnummer
[fl**oo**k-noommer]

flippers die Schwimmflossen
[shv**i**mflossen]

flood die Flut [floot]

floor (of room) der Fußboden
[**foo**ssbohden]
(storey) das Stockwerk
[sht**o**ckvairk]

on the floor auf dem Boden
[owf daym b**oh**den]

on the third floor im dritten
Stock

florist der Blumenhändler
[bl**oo**men-hentler]

flour das Mehl [mayl]

flower die Blume [bl**oo**m-uh]

flu die Grippe [gr**i**pp-uh]

fluent: he speaks fluent German
er spricht fließend Deutsch
[air shprisht fl**ee**ssent doytch]

fly (insect) die Fliege [fl**ee**g-uh]

fly (verb) fliegen [fl**ee**gen]

fly in einfliegen [**ine**-fleegen]

fly out abfliegen [**a**pfleegen]

fog der Nebel [**nay**bel]

foggy: it's foggy es ist neblig
[**nay**blish]

folk dancing der Volkstanz

[follks-tants]

folk music die Volksmusik [follks-moozeek]

follow folgen
  follow me folgen Sie mir [zee meer]

food das Essen

food poisoning die Lebensmittelvergiftung [laybensmittel-fairgiftoong]

food shop/store das Lebensmittelgeschäft [laybensmittel-gesheft]

foot* der Fuß [fooss]
  on foot zu Fuß [tsoo]

football der Fußball [foossbal]

football match das Fußballspiel [foossbal-shpeel]

for für [foor]
  do you have something for ...? (headaches/diarrhoea etc) haben Sie etwas gegen ...? [hahben zee etvass gaygen]

•••••• DIALOGUES ••••••

who's the bratwurst? für wen ist die Bratwurst? [vayn]
that's for me das ist für mich [mish]
and this one? und das hier?
that's for her das ist für sie [zee]

where do I get the bus for Stuttgart? wo fährt der Bus nach Stuttgart ab? [vo fairt – naKH]
the bus for Stuttgart leaves from Schillerstraße der Bus nach Stuttgart fährt von der Schillerstraße

how long have you been here for?
wie lange sind Sie schon hier?
[vee lang-uh zint zee shohn heer]
I've been here for two days, how about you? ich bin seit zwei Tagen hier, und Sie? [zite]
I've been here for a week ich bin seit einer Woche hier

forehead die Stirn [shteern]

foreign ausländisch [owsslendish]

foreigner (man/woman) der Ausländer [owsslender]/die Ausländerin

forest der Wald [vallt]

forget vergessen [fairgessen]
  I forget, I've forgotten ich habe es vergessen [ish hahb-uh ess]

fork (for eating) die Gabel [gahbel]
  (in road) die Abzweigung [ap-tsvygoong]

form (document) das Formular [formoolahr]

formal (dress) formell

fortnight zwei Wochen [tsvy voKHen]

fortress die Festung [festoong]

fortunately glücklicherweise [gloock-lisher-vize-uh]

forward: could you forward my mail? könnten Sie meine Post nachsenden? [kurnten zee mine-uh posst naKH-zenden]

forwarding address die Nachsendeadresse [naKHzend-uh-adress-uh]

foundation cream die Grundierungscreme

[groond**ee**roongs-kraym]

fountain der Brunnen
[br**oo**nnen]

foyer das Foyer [foy-y**ay**]

fracture der Bruch [brooKH]

France Frankreich [fr**a**nk-rysh]

free frei [fry]
(no charge) kostenlos
[k**o**stenlohss], gratis [gr**ah**tiss]
is it free (of charge)? ist es
gratis?

freeway (US) die Autobahn
[**ow**tobahn]

freezer die Gefriertruhe
[gefr**ee**tr**oo**-uh]

French (adj) französisch
[frants**ur**zish]
(language) Französisch

French fries die Pommes frites
[pom frit]

frequent häufig [h**oy**fish]
how frequent is the bus to
Kiel? wie oft fährt der Bus
nach Kiel? [vee oft fairt]

fresh frisch [frish]

fresh orange juice der
natürliche Orangensaft
[nat**oo**rlish-uh or**o**nJenzaft]

Friday Freitag [fr**y**tahk]

fridge der Kühlschrank
[k**oo**lshrank]

fried gebraten [gebr**ah**ten]

fried egg das Spiegelei
[shp**ee**gel-ī]

friend (man/woman) der Freund
[fr**oy**nt]/die Freundin
[fr**oy**ndin]

friendly freundlich [fr**oy**ntlish]

from von [fon]

when does the next train from
Bremen arrive? wann kommt
der nächste Zug aus Bremen
an? [der n**ay**kst-uh ts**oo**k owss]

from Monday to Friday von
Montag bis Freitag

from next Thursday ab
nächsten Donnerstag

where are you from? woher
kommst du/kommen Sie? [voh**air**
kommst d**oo**/k**o**mmen zee]
I'm from Slough ich bin aus
Slough [ish bin owss]

front die Vorderseite
[f**o**rderzite-uh]
in front vorn [forn]
in front of the hotel vor dem
Hotel [for]
at the front vorn [forn]

frost der Frost

frozen gefroren

frozen food die Tiefkühlkost
[t**ee**fk**oo**lkost]

fruit das Obst [ohpst]

fruit juice der Fruchtsaft
[fr**oo**KHtzaft]

fry braten [br**ah**ten]

frying pan die Bratpfanne
[br**ah**t-pfan-uh]

full voll [foll]
it's full of ... es ist **v**oller...
I'm full ich bin satt [ish bin
zatt]

full board die Vollpension
[f**o**llpangz-yohn]

fun: it was fun es hat Spaß
gemacht [ess hat shpahss

gem**a**KHt]

funfair das Volksfest [f**o**llks-fest]

funicular railway die Seilbahn [z**i**le-bahn]

funny (strange) seltsam [z**e**ltzahm]

(amusing) komisch [k**oh**mish]

furniture die Möbel [m**u**rbel]

further weiter [v**y**ter]

it's further down the road es ist weiter die Straße entlang

•••••• DIALOGUE ••••••

how much further is it to the castle? wie weit ist es noch bis zum Schloß? [vee vite ist ess noKH bis tsoom]

about 3 kilometres etwa drei Kilometer [**e**tvah]

fuse (noun) die Sicherung [z**i**sheroong]

the lights have fused die Sicherung ist durchgebrannt [d**oo**rsh-gebrannt]

fuse box der Sicherungskasten [z**i**sheroongs-kasten]

fuse wire der Schmelzdraht [shm**e**lts-draht]

future die Zukunft [ts**oo**koonft]

in future in Zukunft

G

gallon* die Gallone [gal**oh**n-uh]

game das Spiel [shpeel]

(meat) das Wild [vilt]

garage (for fuel) die Tankstelle [t**a**nk-shtell-uh]

(for repairs) die Werkstatt [v**ai**rkshtatt]

(for parking) die Garage [gar**ah**J-uh]

garden der Garten

garlic der Knoblauch [k-n**oh**blowKH]

gas das Gas [gahss]

(US: gasoline) das Benzin [bents**ee**n]

gas cylinder (camping gas) die Gasflasche [g**ah**ss-flash-uh]

gasoline (US) das Benzin [bents**ee**n] see **petrol**

gas permeable lenses luftdurchlässige Kontaktlinsen [l**oo**ft-doorsh-lessig-ug kont**a**kt-linzen]

gas station (US) die Tankstelle [t**a**nk-shtell-uh]

gate das Tor [tohr]

(at airport) der Flugsteig [fl**oo**k-shtike]

gay schwul [shv**oo**l]

gay bar die Schwulenkneipe [shv**oo**len-k-nipe-uh]

gear (in car etc) der Gang

gearbox das Getriebe [getr**ee**b-uh]

gear lever der Schaltknüppel [sh**a**ltkn**oo**ppel]

general allgemein [al-gem**ine**]

Geneva Genf

gents (toilet) die Herrentoilette [h**ai**ren-twalett-uh]

genuine echt [esht]

German (man/woman) der/die Deutsche [d**oy**tch-uh]

(adj) deutsch [doytch]

(language) Deutsch

the Germans die Deutschen

German measles die Röteln [**rur**teln]

Germany Deutschland [d**oy**tchlant]

get (obtain) bekommen

(fetch) holen [h**oh**len]

(become) werden [v**ai**rden]

will you get me another one, please? bringen Sie mir bitte noch eins [noKH ine-ss]

do you know where I can get them? wissen Sie, wo ich sie bek**o**mmen kann?

how do I get to ...? wie komme ich nach...? [vee k**o**mm-uh ish naKH]

to get old alt werden [v**ai**rden]

•••••• DIALOGUE ••••••

can I get you a drink? möchtest du/möchten Sie etwas trinken? [m**ur**shtest d**OO**/m**ur**shten zee **e**tvass]

no, I'll get this one, what would you like? nein, das ich meine Runde, was möchten Sie? [m**i**ne-uh r**oo**nd-uh]

a glass of red wine ein Glas Rotwein

get back (return) zurückkommen [tsoor**oo**ck-kommen]

get in (arrive) ankommen [**a**n-kommen]

get off aussteigen [**ow**ss-shtygen]

where do I get off? wo muß ich aussteigen? [vo mooss ish

get on (to train etc) einsteigen [**ine**-shtygen]

get out (of car etc) aussteigen [**ow**ss-shtygen]

get up (in the morning) aufstehen [**ow**f-shtay-en]

gift das Geschenk [gesh**e**nk]

gift shop der Geschenkladen [gesh**e**nk-lahden]

gin der Gin

a gin and tonic, please einen Gin Tonic, bitte [**ine**-en]

girl das Mädchen [m**ay**dshen]

girlfriend die Freundin [fr**oy**ndin]

give geben [g**ay**ben]

I gave it to him ich habe es ihm gegeben [ish h**ah**b-uh ess eem geg**ay**ben]

will you give this to ...? bitte geben Sie dies ...

give back zurückgeben [tsoor**oo**ck-gayben]

glad froh

glass das Glas [glahss]

a glass of wine ein Glas Wein

glasses (spectacles) die Brille [br**ill**-uh]

gloves die Handschuhe [h**a**ntsh**oo**-uh]

glue der Klebstoff [kl**ay**p-shtoff]

go gehen [g**ay**-en]

(by car, train etc) f**ah**ren

we'd like to go to the Black Forest wir möchten zum Schwarzwald fahren [veer m**ur**shten tsoom]

where are you going? wohin gehen/fahren Sie? [voh**i**n]

where does this bus go?
wohin fährt dieser Bus?
[fairt]
let's go gehen wir
she's gone (left) sie ist
gegangen
where has he gone? wohin ist
er gegangen?
I went there last week ich war
letzte Woche da
hamburger to go Hamburger
zum Mitnehmen [tsoom]
go away weggehen [vek-gay-en]
go away! gehen Sie weg!
go back (return) zurückgehen
[tsoorOOck-gay-en]
go down (the stairs etc)
hinuntergehen [hinoonter-
gay-en]
go in hineingehen [hin-ine-
gay-en]
go out (in the evening) ausgehen
[owss-gay-en]
do you want to go out tonight?
möchten Sie heute abend
ausgehen? [murshten zee
hoyt-uh ahbent]
go through gehen durch [gay-
en doorsh]
go up (the stairs etc)
hinaufgehen [hinowf-gay-en]
goat die Ziege [tseeg-uh]
God Gott
goggles (ski) die Skibrille
[sheebrill-uh]
gold das Gold [gollt]
golf Golf
golf course der Golfplatz [golf-
plats]

good gut [goot]
good! gut!
it's no good es hat keinen
Zweck [ess hat kine-en tsveck]
goodbye auf Wiedersehen [owf-
veederzayn]
good evening guten Abend
[gooten ahbent]
Good Friday der Karfreitag
[kar-frytahk]
good morning guten Morgen
[gooten morgen]
good night gute Nacht [goot-uh
naKHt]
goose die Gans [ganss]
got: we've got to ... wir
müssen ... [veer moossen]
I've got to ... ich muß ...
[mooss]
have you got any ...? haben
Sie ...? [hahben zee]
government die Regierung
[regeeroong]
gradually allmählich
[al-maylish]
grammar die Grammatik
gram(me) das Gramm
granddaughter die Enkelin
[enk-uh-lin]
grandfather der Großvater
[grohssfahter]
grandmother die Großmutter
[grohssmootter]
grandson der Enkel
grapefruit die Grapefruit
grapefruit juice der
Grapefruitsaft [-zaft]
grapes die Trauben [trowben]
grass das Gras [grahss]

grateful dankbar

gravy die Soße [zohss-uh]

great (excellent) großartig [grohss-artish]

that's great! das ist toll! [tol]

a great success ein großer Erfolg [grohss-er]

Great Britain Großbritannien [grohss-britannee-en]

Greece Griechenland [greeshenlant]

greedy gefräßig [gefrayssish]

Greek griechisch [greeshish]

green grün [groon]

green card (car insurance) die grüne Karte [groon-uh kart-uh]

greengrocer's der Gemüse-händler [gemooz-uh-hentler]

grey grau [grow]

grill (on cooker) der Grill

grilled gegrillt

grocer's der Lebensmittelhändler [laybensmittel-hentler]

ground der Boden [bohden]

on the ground auf dem Boden

ground floor das Erdgeschoß [airt-geshoss]

group die Gruppe [groop-uh]

guarantee die Garantie [garantee]

is it guaranteed? ist darauf Garantie? [darowf]

guest der Gast

guesthouse die Pension [pangz-yohn]

To escape the formality of a hotel, look for one of the plentiful **Pensionen** which may be rooms above a bar or a restaurant or simply space in a private house; in urban areas these cost about the same as a hotel but in the countryside are usually less expensive. An increasingly prevalent budget option (especially in busy holiday areas) is bed and breakfast accommodation in a private house (look for signs saying **Fremdenzimmer** or **Zimmer frei**). These are seldom other than a really good deal. However, very few German cities have private rooms on offer other than to relieve congestion when there's a trade fair on. Also in the more rural areas, and particularly plentiful along the main touring routes, are country inns or guesthouses (**Gasthäuser**). These are often in an atmospheric old building and the cost includes breakfast. Farmhouse holidays are increasingly popular and in many ways are the best bargains of all. Full lists of these are available from local tourist offices and the only major snag is that this option is really only feasible if you have your own transport.

guide (person) der Reiseleiter
[ry-zuh-lyter]
guidebook der Reiseführer [ry-
zuh-foorer]
guided tour die Rundfahrt
[roontfahrt]
(on foot) der Rundgang
[roontgang]
guitar die Gitarre [gitarr-uh]
gum (in mouth) das Zahnfleisch
[tsahn-flysh]
gun das Gewehr [gevair]
gym das Fitneßstudio
[fitness-sht00dee-oh]

H

hair das Haar [hahr]
hairbrush die Haarbürste
[hahrboorst-uh]
haircut der Haarschnitt
[hahrshnit]
hairdresser der Frisör [frizur]

Hairdressers are usually closed
on Mondays.

hairdryer der Fön® [furn]
hair gel das Haargel [hahr-gayl]
hairgrip die Haarklemme
[hahrklem-uh]
hair spray das Haarspray
[hahr-shpray]
half* halb [halp]
half an hour eine halbe
Stunde [ine-uh halb-uh
shtoond-uh]
half a litre ein halber Liter
[halber leeter]

about half that etwa die
Hälfte [etvah dee helft-uh]
half board die Halbpension
[halp-pangz-yohn]
half-bottle die halbe Flasche
[halb-uh flash-uh]
half fare der halbe Fahrpreis
[halb-uh fahr-price]
half price: at half price zum
halben Preis [tsoom halben
price]
hall (in house) die Diele [deel-
uh]
ham der Schinken [shinken]

German ham will normally be
thinly sliced and slightly
smoked. If you want ham as
you'd normally get it at home,
you should ask for 'gekochter
Schinken'.

hamburger der Hamburger
[hemburger]
hammer der Hammer
hand die Hand [hant]
handbag die Handtasche [hant-
tash-uh]
handbrake die Handbremse
[hantbremz-uh]
handkerchief das Taschentuch
[tashen-t00KH]
handle (on door) die Klinke
[klink-uh]
(on suitcase etc) der Griff
hand luggage das Handgepäck
[hant-gepeck]
hang-gliding das Drachen-
fliegen [draKHen-fleegen]

hangover der Kater [kahter]
I've got a hangover ich habe
einen Kater [ish hahb-uh
ine-en]
happen geschehen [geshay-en]
what's happening? was ist
los? [lohss]
what has happened? was ist
passiert? [passeert]
happy glücklich [glOOcklish]
I'm not happy about this ich
bin damit nicht zufrieden
[ish bin dahmit nisht
tsOOfreeden]
harbour der Hafen [hahfen]
hard hart
(difficult) schwer [shvair]
hard-boiled egg ein
hartgekochtes Ei
[hartgekoKHtess ī]
hard lenses harte
Kontaktlinsen [hart-uh
kontakt-linzen]
hardly kaum [kowm]
hardly ever fast nie [fasst nee]
hardware shop die
Eisenwarenhandlung
[īzenvahren-hantloong]
hat der Hut [hoot]
hate (verb) hassen
have* haben [hahben]
can I have a ...? kann ich ein
... haben? [kan ish]
can we have some ...? können
wir etwas ... haben? [kurnen
veer etvass]
do you have ...? hast du/
haben Sie...? [dOO/... zee]
what'll you have? (drink) was

möchtest du/möchten Sie?
[vass murshtest dOO/murshten
zee]
I have to leave now ich muß
jetzt gehen [mooss yetst
gay-en]
do I have to ...? muß ich ...?
hayfever der Heuschnupfen
[hoy-shnoopfen]
hazelnuts die Haselnüsse
[hahzel-nOOss-uh]
he* er [air]
head der Kopf
headache die Kopfschmerzen
[kopf-shmairtsen]
headlights die Scheinwerfer
[shine-vairfer]
headphones die Kopfhörer
[kopf-hur-rer]
health food shop der Bioladen
[bee-oh-lahden]
healthy gesund [gezoont]
hear hören [hur-ren]

•••••• DIALOGUE ••••••

can you hear me? können Sie
mich hören? [kurnen zee mish]
I can't hear you ich kann Sie nicht
hören [ish kan zee nisht]

hearing aid das Hörgerät [hur-
gerayt]
heart das Herz [hairts]
heart attack der Herzinfarkt
[hairts-infarkt]
heat die Hitze [hits-uh]
heater (in room) der Ofen
[ohfen]
(in car) die Heizung [hytsoong]
heating die Heizung [hytsoong]

heavy schwer [shvair]

heel (of foot) die Ferse [**fai**rz-uh]

(of shoe) der Absatz [**a**pzats]

could you heel these? können Sie mir hier die Absätze erneuern? [**ku**rnen zee meer heer dee **a**psets-uh airn**oy**ern]

heelbar die Absatzbar [**a**pzatsbar]

height (of mountain) die Höhe [h**ur**-uh]

(of person) die Größe [gr**ur**ss-uh]

helicopter der Hubschrauber [h**oo**p-shrowber]

hello hallo

Shaking hands when meeting people (whether they are friends, business partners or strangers) is routine in Germany. It may sometimes be regarded as impolite or stand-offish not to shake hands.

helmet (for motorcycle) der Helm

help die Hilfe [h**i**lf-uh]

(verb) **h**elfen

help! Hilfe!

can you help me? können Sie mir helfen? [**ku**rnen zee meer helfen?]

thank you very much for your help vielen Dank für Ihre Hilfe [**fee**len dank f**oo**r **ee**r-uh]

helpful hilfreich [h**i**lf-rysh]

hepatitis die Hepatitis [hepat**ee**tiss]

her*: I haven't seen her ich habe sie nicht gesehen [zee]

give it to her geben Sie es ihr [eer]

with her mit ihr

for her für sie

that's her das ist sie

that's her towel das ist ihr Handtuch

herbal tea der Kräutertee [kr**oy**ter-tay]

herbs die Kräuter [kr**oy**ter]

here hier [heer]

here is/are ... hier ist/sind [zint]

here you are (offering) bitte [b**i**tt-uh]

hers*: that's hers das gehört ihr [dass geh**ur**t eer]

hey! he! [hay]

hi! h**a**llo

hide verstecken [fairsht**e**cken]

high hoch [hohKH]

highchair der Hochstuhl [h**oh**KH-sht**oo**l]

highway (US) die Autobahn [**ow**tobahn]

hill der Berg [bairk]

him*: I haven't seen him ich habe ihn nicht gesehen [een]

give it to him geben Sie es ihm [eem]

with him mit ihm

for him für ihn

that's him das ist er [air]

hip die Hüfte [h**oo**ft-uh]

hire: for hire zu vermieten [ts**oo** fairm**ee**ten]

(verb) m**ie**ten [m**ee**ten]

where can I hire a bike? wo kann ich ein Fahrrad

mieten? [vo kan ish ine **fahr**-raht]

see also rent

his*: it's his car es ist sein Auto [zine]

that's his das ist seins [zine-ss]

hit (verb) schlagen [shl**ah**gen]

hitch-hike trampen [tr**e**mpen]

hobby das Hobby

hold (verb) h**a**lten

hole das Loch [loKH]

holiday der Urlaub [**OO**rlowp]

on holiday im Urlaub

Holland Holland [h**o**l-lant]

home das Zuhause [ts**oo**h**ow**z-uh]

at home (in my house etc) zu Hause

(in my country) bei uns [by oonss]

we go home tomorrow wir fahren morgen nach Hause [veer **fah**ren m**o**rgen naKH]

honest ehrlich [**air**lish]

honey der Honig [h**oh**nish]

honeymoon die Flitterwochen [fl**i**ttervoKHen]

hood (US: of car) die Haube [h**ow**b-uh]

hope h**o**ffen

I hope so hoffentlich [h**o**ffentlish]

I hope not hoffentlich nicht [nisht]

hopefully hoffentlich [h**o**ffentlish]

horn (of car) die Hupe [h**oo**p-uh]

horrible schrecklich

horse das Pferd [pfairt]

horse riding Reiten [r**y**ten]

hospital das Krankenhaus [kranken-howss]

hospitality die Gastfreund-schaft [g**a**st-froynt-shafft]

thank you for your hospitality vielen Dank für Ihre Gastfreundschaft [**fee**len dank foor **eer**-uh]

hot heiß [hice]

(spicy) scharf [sharf]

I'm hot mir ist heiß [meer]

it's hot today es ist heiß heute [h**oy**t-uh]

hotel das Hotel

see room

An immensely complicated grading system applies to German hotels, with no fewer than 80 classifications according to price and services provided. Despite this, they're all more or less the same: clean, comfortable and functional with conveniences like TV, phone and en suite bathroom usually taken for granted in the medium range establishments upwards. You should always call into the nearest tourist office to check any special deals which they may have with local establishments; this can result in you spending less than the figures quoted on the official hotel lists which every tourist →

office provides. Many tourist offices charge around DM3 for finding you a room, but others perform the service gratis. You should take care not to turn up in a large town or city when there's a trade fair or **Messe** taking place.

hotel room: in my hotel room in meinem Hotelzimmer [**mine**-em hot**el**-tsimmer]

hot spring die Thermalquelle [tairm**ah**l-kvell-uh]

hour die Stunde [sht**oo**nd-uh]

house das Haus [howss]

house wine der Tafelwein [**tah**fel-vine]

hovercraft das Luftkissenboot [**loo**ft-kissenboht]

how wie [vee]

  how many? wie viele? [**feel**-uh]

  how do you do? guten Tag! [**goo**ten tahk]

•••••• DIALOGUES ••••••

how are you? wie geht es dir/Ihnen? [gayt ess deer/**ee**nen]

fine, thanks, and you? danke, gut, und dir/Ihnen? [dank-uh g**oo**t oont]

how much is it? was kostet das?

75 marks fünfundsiebzigMark

I'll take it ich nehme es [ish n**aym**-uh ess]

humid feucht [foysht]

humour der Humor [hoom**oh**r]

Hungarian ungarisch

[**oo**ngahrish]

Hungary Ungarn [**oo**ngarn]

hungry hungrig [h**oo**ngrish]

  I'm hungry ich habe Hunger [ish h**ah**buh h**oo**ng-er]

  are you hungry? hast du/haben Sie Hunger? [doo/h**ah**ben zee]

hurry (verb) sich beeilen [zish buh-**ī**len]

  I'm in a hurry ich habe es eilig [ish h**ah**b-uh ess **ī**lish]

  there's no hurry es eilt nicht [**ī**lt nisht]

  hurry up! beeilen Sie sich!

hurt (verb) weh tun [vay t**oo**n]

  it really hurts es tut echt weh [t**oo**t esht vay]

husband der Mann

hydrofoil das Tragflächenboot [tr**ah**kfleshenboht]

hypermarket der Verbrauchermarkt [fair-br**ow**KHer-markt]

I

I ich [ish]

ice das Eis [ice]

  with ice mit Eis

  no ice, thanks kein Eis, danke [kine ice, d**a**nk-uh]

ice cream das Eis [ice]

ice-cream cone die Tüte Eiskrem [t**oo**t-uh **ice**-kraym]

ice lolly das Eis am Stiel [ice am shteel]

ice rink die Schlittschuhbahn [shl**i**tt-shoo-bahn]

ice skates die Schlittschuhe
[shlitt-shoo-uh]
idea die Idee [eeday]
idiot der Idiot [eedee-oht]
if wenn [ven]
ignition die Zündung
[tsoondoong]
ill krank
I feel ill ich fühle mich krank
[ish fool-uh mish]
illness die Krankheit [krankhite]
imitation (leather etc)
nachgemacht [naKH-gemaKHt]
immediately sofort [zofort]
important wichtig [vishtish]
it's very important es ist sehr
wichtig [ist zair]
it's not important es ist nicht
wichtig [nisht]
impossible unmöglich [oon-
murglish]
impressive beeindruckend [be-
ine-droockent]
improve verbessern [fair-
bessern]
I want to improve my German
ich möchte mein Deutsch
aufbessern [ish mursht-uh
mine doytch owf-bessern]
in: it's in the centre es ist im
Zentrum
in my car in meinem Auto
in Munich in München
in two days from now in zwei
Tagen [tahgen]
in May im Mai
in English auf Englisch [owf
eng-lish]
in German auf Deutsch

[doytch]
is he in? ist er da?
in five minutes in fünf
Minuten [minooten]
inch* der Zoll [tsoll]
include enthalten [ent-halten]
does that include meals? ist
das einschließlich der
Mahlzeiten? [ine-shleeslish
dair mahl-tsyten]
is that included? ist das im
Preis enthalten? [price]
inconvenient ungünstig
[oongoonstish]
incredible (very good, amazing)
unglaublich [oon-glowplish]
Indian indisch [indish]
indicator (on car) der Blinker
indigestion die
Magenverstimmung
[mahgen-fair-shtimmoong]
indoor pool das Hallenbad
[hallenbaht]
indoors drinnen
inexpensive billig [billish]
infection die Infektion [infekts-
yohn]
infectious ansteckend
[anshteckent]
inflammation die Entzündung
[ent-tsoondoong]
informal (clothes, occasion, meeting)
zwanglos [tsvang-lohss]
information die Information
[informats-yohn]
do you have any information
about ...? haben Sie
Informationen über ...?
[hahben zee informats-yohnen

ꝏber]

information desk der
Informationsschalter
[informats-y**oh**ns-shalter]

injection die Spritze [shpr**i**ts-uh]

injured verletzt [fairl**e**tst]
she's been injured sie ist
verletzt [zee]

in-laws die Schwiegereltern
[shv**ee**ger-eltern]

inner tube der Schlauch
[shl**ow**KH]

innocent unschuldig [**oo**n-
shooldish]

insect das Insekt [inz**e**kt]

insect bite der Insektenstich
[inz**e**kten-shtish]
do you have anything for
insect bites? haben Sie etwas
für Insektenstiche? [h**ah**ben
zee **e**tvass f**oo**r]

insect repellent das
Insektenbekämpfungsmittel
[inz**e**kten-bek**e**mpfoongs-mittel]

inside **i**nnen
inside the hotel im Hotel
let's sit inside setzen wir uns
nach dr**i**nnen [z**e**tsen veer
oonss naKH]

insist I insist ich bestehe
darauf [ish besht**ay**-uh
dar**ow**f]

insomnia die Schlaflosigkeit
[shl**ah**f-lohzish-kite]

instant coffee der Pulverkaffee
[p**oo**lver-kaffay]

instead statt dessen [sht**a**tt]
instead of ... anstelle von ...
[ansht**e**ll-uh fon]

give me that one instead
geben Sie mir statt dessen
das [g**ay**ben zee meer shtatt
d**e**ssen dass]

insulin das Insulin [inz**oo**l**ee**n]

insurance die Versicherung
[fairz**i**sheroong]

intelligent intelligent
[intellig**e**nt]

interested: I'm interested in ...
ich interessiere mich für...
[ish interess**ee**r-uh mish f**oo**r]

interesting interess**a**nt
that's very interesting das ist
sehr interessant [zair]

international international
[internats-yon**ah**l]

interpret dolmetschen
[d**o**lmetchen]

interpreter (man/woman) der
Dolmetscher [d**o**lmetcher]/die
Dolmetscherin

intersection (US) die Kreuzung
[kr**oy**tsoong]

interval (at theatre) die Pause
[p**ow**z-uh]

into in
I'm not into ... ich stehe nicht
auf ... [ish sht**ay**-uh nisht owf]

introduce vorstellen [f**o**r-
shtellen]
may I introduce ...? darf ich
Ihnen ... vorstellen? [ish
eenen]

invitation die Einladung [**i**ne-
lahdoong]

invite einladen [**i**ne-lahden]

Ireland Irland [**ee**rlant]

Irish irisch [**ee**rish]

I'm Irish (man/woman) ich bin
Ire/Irin [ish bin **eer**-uh/**ee**rin]
iron (for ironing) das Bügeleisen
[b**oo**gel-īzen]
 can you iron these for me?
 könnten Sie diese Sachen
 für mich bügeln? [**kur**nten
 zee d**ee**z-uh za**kH**en f**oo**r mish
 b**oo**geln]
is* ist
island die Insel [**i**nzel]
it* es; er; sie [ess, air, zee]
 it is ... es ist ...
 is it ...? ist es...?
 where is it? wo ist es? [vo]
 it's him er ist es
 it was ... es war... [var]
Italian (adj) italienisch [ital-
 yaynish]
 (language) Italienisch
Italy Italien [it**ah**lee-en]
itch: it itches es juckt [ess
 yoockt]

J

jack (for car) der Wagenheber
 [**vah**gen-hayber]
jacket die Jackett [Jack**ett**]
jar das Glas [glahss]
jam die Marmelade [marm-uh-
 l**ah**d-uh]
jammed: it's jammed es klemmt
January der Januar [y**a**nooar]
jaw der Kiefer [k**ee**fer]
jazz der Jazz
jealous eifersüchtig
 [**ī**ferzooshtish]
jeans die Jeans

jellyfish die Qualle [kv**a**ll-uh]
jersey der Pullover [pooll**oh**ver]
jetty der Steg [shtayk]
Jewish jüdisch [y**oo**dish]
jeweller's das Juweliergeschäft
 [yoov-uh-l**eer**-gesheft]
jewellery der Schmuck
 [shmoock]
job die Arbeit [**a**rbite]
jogging das Joggen
 I'm going jogging ich gehe
 joggen [ish g**ay**-uh]
joke der Witz [vits]
journey die Reise [**rize**-uh]
 have a good journey! gute
 Reise! [g**oo**t-uh]
jug die Kanne [k**a**nn-uh]
 a jug of water ein Krug mit
 Wasser [kr**oo**k mit v**a**sser]
juice der Saft [zaft]
July der Juli [y**oo**lee]
jump (verb) springen
 [shpr**i**ngen]
jumper der Pullover
 [pooll**oh**ver]
jump leads das Starthilfekabel
 [sht**a**rt-hilf-uh-kahbel]
junction die Kreuzung
 [kr**oy**tsoong]
June der Juni [y**oo**nee]
just (only) nur [n**oo**r]
 just two nur zwei
 just for me nur für mich [f**oo**r
 mish]
 just here genau hier [gen**ow**
 heer]
 not just now nicht jetzt [nisht
 yetst]
 we've just arrived wir sind

gerade angekommen [veer
zint gerahd-uh an-gekommen]

K

keep behalten
  keep the change der Rest ist
  für Sie [dair rest ist foor zee]
  can I keep it? kann ich es
  behalten?
  please keep it bitte behalten
  Sie es
ketchup der Ketchup
kettle der Wasserkessel
  [vasser-kessel]
key der Schlüssel [shloossel]
  the key for room 201, please
  den Schlüssel für Zimmer
  zweihunderteins, bitte [dayn
  – foor tsimmer]
key ring der Schlüsselring
  [shloossel-ring]
kidneys die Nieren [neeren]
kill töten [turten]
kilo* das Kilo [keelo]
kilometre* der Kilometer [keelo-
  mayter]
  how many kilometres is it
  to ...? wieviel Kilometer sind
  es nach ...? [veefeel]
kind (generous) nett
  that's very kind das ist sehr
  nett [zair]

•••••• DIALOGUE ••••••

which kind do you want? welche
möchtest du/möchten Sie?
[velsh-uh murshtest doo/murshten
zee]

I want this/that kind ich möchte
diese hier/die da [ish mursht-uh
deez-uh heer/dee da]

king der König [kurnish]
kiosk der Kiosk
kiss der Kuß [kooss]
  (verb) küssen [koossen]
kitchen die Küche [koosh-uh]
kitchenette die Kochnische
  [koKHneesh-uh]
Kleenex® die Papiertücher
  [papeer-toosher]
knee das Knie [k-nee]
knickers das Höschen [hurss-
  shen]
knife das Messer
knitwear die Strickwaren
  [shtrick-vahren]
knock (verb) klopfen
knock down anfahren
  he's been knocked down er ist
  angefahren worden [air ist
  an-gefahren vorden]
knock over (object) umstoßen
  [oom-shtohssen]
  (pedestrian) anfahren
know (somebody, a place) kennen
  (something) wissen [vissen]
  I don't know ich weiß nicht
  [ish vice nisht]
  I didn't know that das wußte
  ich nicht [voost-uh]
  do you know where I can
  find ...? wissen Sie, wo ich ...
  finden kann?

ENGLISH ◆ GERMAN | Kn

L

label das Etikett
ladies' (toilets) die
  Damentoilette [**dah**men-
  twalett-uh]
ladies' wear die
  Damenkleidung [**dah**men-
  klydoong]
lady die Dame [**dah**m-uh]
lager das helle Bier [**h**ell-uh
  beer]
  see **beer**
lake der See [zay]
Lake Constance der Bodensee
  [**boh**denzay]
Lake Lucerne der
  Vierwaldstätter See [**fee**rvalt-
  shtetter zay]
lamb das Lamm
lamp die Lampe [**l**amp-uh]
lane (on motorway) die Spur
  [shp**oor**]
  (small road) die Gasse [**g**ass-uh]
language die Sprache
  [shpr**ah**KH-uh]
language course der
  Sprachkurs [shpr**ah**KH-koors]
large groß [grohss]
last letzter [**l**etster]
  last week letzte Woche [letst-
  uh v**o**KH-uh]
  last Friday letzten Fr**ei**tag
  [**l**etsten]
  last night gestern abend
  [**g**estern **ah**bent]
  what time is the last train to
  Hamburg? wann fährt der
  letzte Zug nach Hamburg?

[vann fairt]
late spät [shpayt]
  sorry I'm late tut mir leid, daß
  ich zu spät komme [t**oo**t meer
  lite dass ish ts**oo** shpayt
  k**o**mm-uh]
  the train was late der Zug
  hatte Verspätung [dair ts**oo**k
  h**a**tt-uh fairshp**ay**toong]
  we must go, we'll be late wir
  müssen gehen, sonst
  kommen wir zu spät [veer
  m**oo**ssen g**ay**-en zonst k**o**mmen
  veer ts**oo**]
  it's getting late es wird spät
  [ess veert]
later später [shp**ay**ter]
  I'll come back later ich
  komme später wieder [ish
  k**o**mm-uh – v**ee**der]
  see you later bis später
  later on nachher [naKH-h**ai**r]
latest spätester [shp**ay**tester]
  by Wednesday at the latest
  spätestens bis Mittwoch
  [shp**ay**testens biss]
Latvia Lettland [**l**ettlant]
laugh (verb) lachen [l**a**KHen]
launderette der Waschsalon
  [**v**ash-zall**o**ng]
laundromat (US) der
  Waschsalon
laundry (clothes) die Wäsche
  [**v**esh-uh]
  (place) die Wäscherei
  [vesher**ī**]
lavatory die Toilette [twal**e**tt-uh]
law das Gesetz [gez**e**ts]
lawn der Rasen [**rah**zen]

lawyer der Rechtsanwalt [**re**shts-anvallt]

laxative das Abführmittel [**a**pfoor-mittel]

lazy faul [fowl]

lead (electrical) das Kabel [**kah**bel]

lead (verb) führen [**foo**ren]

where does this road lead to? wohin führt diese Straße? [**vo**hin foort d**ee**z-uh sht**rah**ss-uh]

leaf das Blatt

leaflet der Handzettel [**ha**nt-tsettel]

leak die undichte Stelle [**oo**ndisht-uh sht**e**ll-uh] (verb) lecken

the roof leaks das Dach ist undicht

learn lernen [**lair**nen]

least: not in the least nicht im mindesten [nisht im **mi**ndesten]

at least mindestens

leather das Leder [**lay**der]

leave verlassen [fair**la**ssen]

I am leaving tomorrow ich reise morgen ab [ish **ri**ze-uh **mo**rgen ap]

he left yesterday er ist gestern abgereist [**a**p-geryst]

may I leave this here? kann ich das hierlassen? [**hee**rlassen]

I left my coat in the bar ich habe meinen Mantel in der Bar gelassen [**hah**b-uh m**i**ne-en]

when does the bus for

Saarbrücken leave? wann fährt der Bus nach Saarbrücken? [vann fairt dair booss naKH]

leek der Lauch [lowKH]

left links

on the left links

to the left nach links [naKH]

turn left biegen Sie links ab [**bee**gen zee – ap]

there's none left es ist alle [**a**luh]

left-handed linkshändig [l**i**nks-hendish]

left luggage (office) die Gepäckaufbewahrung [gep**e**ck-owfbevahroong]

leg das Bein [bine]

lemon die Zitrone [tsitr**oh**n-uh]

lemonade die Limonade [limon**ah**d-uh]

lemon tea der Zitronentee [tsitr**oh**nentay]

lend leihen [**ly**-en]

will you lend me your ... ? könnten Sie mir Ihr ... leihen? [k**ur**nten zee meer eer]

lens (of camera) das Objektiv [ob-yekt**ee**f]

lesbian die Lesbierin [l**e**sbee-erin]

less weniger [**va**yniger]

less than weniger als

less expensive nicht so teuer [nisht zoh]

lesson die Stunde [sht**oo**nd-uh]

let (allow) lassen

will you let me know? können Sie mir Bescheid sagen?

[kurnen zee meer beshite
zahgen]

I'll let you know ich werde
Ihnen Bescheid sagen [ish
vaird-uh eenen]

let's go for something to eat
gehen wir etwas essen [gay-
en veer etvass]

let off absetzen [apzetsen]

will you let me off at ...?
können Sie mich in ...
absetzen? [kurnen zee mish]

letter der Brief [breef]

do you have any letters for
me? ist ein Brief für mich
angekommen? [ine breef foor
mish an-gekommen]

letterbox der Briefkasten
[breefkasten]

Letterboxes in Germany are
yellow. Collection times are
indicated at the front. A red dot
denotes Sunday collection.

lettuce der Kopfsalat
[kopfzalaht]

lever der Hebel [haybel]

library die Bücherei [boosheri]

licence die Genehmigung
[genaymigoong]

(driving) der Führerschein
[foorer-shine]

lid der Deckel

lie (tell untruth) lügen [loogen]

lie down sich hinlegen [zish
hinlaygen]

life das Leben [layben]

lifebelt der Rettungsgürtel

[rettoongs-goortel]

lifeguard (on beach) der
Rettungsschwimmer
[rettoongs-shvimmer]

life jacket die Schwimmweste
[shvimm-vest-uh]

lift (in building) der Aufzug [owf-
tsook]

could you give me a lift?
könnten Sie mich
mitnehmen? [kurnten zee
mish mitnaymen]

would you like a lift? kann ich
Sie mitnehmen?

lift pass (for ski lift) der Liftpaß
[liftpas]

a daily/weekly lift pass ein
Liftpaß für einen Tag/eine
Woche [foor ine-en tahk/ine-
uh voKH-uh]

light das Licht [lisht]

(not heavy) leicht [lysht]

do you have a light? (for
cigarette) haben Sie Feuer?
[hahben zee foyer]

light green hellgrün
[hellgroon]

light bulb die Glühbirne
[gloobeern-uh]

I need a new light bulb ich
brauche eine neue Birne
[noy-uh]

lighter (cigarette) das Feuerzeug
[foyer-tsoyk]

lightning der Blitz [blits]

like mögen [murgen]

I like it es gefällt mir [ess
gefelt meer]

I don't like it es gefällt mir

ENGLISH ❖ GERMAN | Le

nicht [nisht]

I like going for walks ich gehe gern spazieren [ish **gay**-uh gairn]

I like you ich mag dich [ish mahk dish]

do you like ...? magst du/ mögen Sie...? [**mah**kst doo/ **mur**gen zee]

I'd like a beer ich möchte gern ein Bier [**mur**sht-uh gairn]

I'd like to go swimming ich würde gern schwimmen gehen [**voo**rd-uh]

would you like a drink? möchtest du/möchten Sie etwas trinken?

would you like to go for a walk? möchtest du/möchten Sie einen Spaziergang machen?

what's it like? wie ist es? [vee]

I want one like this ich möchte so eins [zoh ine-ss]

lime die Limone [lim**ohn**-uh]

lime cordial der Limonensaft [lim**ohn**enzaft]

line (on paper) die Linie [**lee**nee-uh]

(telephone) die Leitung [**ly**toong]

could you give me an outside line? könnten Sie mir ein Amt geben? [**kur**nten zee meer ine amt **gay**ben]

lips die Lippen

lip salve der Lippen-Fettstift [**fett**-shtift]

lipstick der Lippenstift [**lippen**-shtift]

liqueur der Likör [lik**ur**]

listen zuhören [ts**oo**-hur-ren]

Lithuania Litauen [**lit**owen]

litre* der Liter [**lee**ter]

a litre of white wine ein Liter Weißwein

little klein [kline]

just a little, thanks danke, nur ein bißchen [**d**ank-uh noor ine biss-shen]

a little milk etwas Milch [**e**tvass]

a little bit more ein bißchen mehr [mair]

live leben [**lay**ben]

we live together wir wohnen zusammen [veer **voh**nen tsoo**za**mmen]

•••••• DIALOGUE ••••••

where do you live? wo wohnen Sie? [vo **voh**nen zee]

I live in London ich **woh**ne in London

lively lebhaft [**lay**p-haft]

liver die Leber [**lay**ber]

loaf das Brot [broht]

lobby (in hotel) das Foyer [foy-**yay**]

lobster der Hummer [**ho**mmer]

local örtlich [**urt**lish]

can you recommend a local restaurant? können Sie ein Restaurant am Ort empfehlen? [**ku**rnen zee ine resto**rong** am ort emp**fay**len]

lock das Schloß [shloss]
(verb) abschließen [ap-shleessen]
it's locked es ist abgeschlossen [ap-geshlossen]
lock in einschließen [ine-shleessen]
lock out ausschließen [owss-shleessen]
I've locked myself out ich habe mich ausgesperrt [ish hahb-uh mish owss-geshpairt]
locker (for luggage etc) das Schließfach [shleessfaKH]
lollipop der Lutscher [lootcher]
London London [lon-don]
long lang
how long will it/does it take? wie lange dauert es? [vee lang-uh dowert ess]
a long time eine lange Zeit [ine-uh lang-uh tsite]
one day/two days longer ein Tag/zwei Tage länger [leng-er]
long distance call das Ferngespräch [fairn-gespraysh]
look: I'm just looking, thanks danke, ich sehe mich nur um [dank-uh, ish zay-uh mish noor oom]
you don't look well du siehst nicht gut aus [doo zeest nisht goot owss]
look out! passen Sie auf! [passen zee owf]
can I have a look? kann ich mal sehen? [kann ish mahl

zay-en]
look after sich kümmern um [zish koommern oom]
look at ansehen [anzay-en]
look for suchen [zooKHen]
I'm looking for ... ich suche... [ish zooKH-uh]
look forward to sich freuen auf [zish froyen owf]
I'm looking forward to it ich freue mich darauf [ish froy-uh mish darowf]
loose (handle etc) lose [lohz-uh]
lorry der Lastwagen [lasst-vahgen]
lose verlieren [fairleeren]
I've lost my way ich habe mich verlaufen [ish hahb-uh mish fairlowfen]
I'm lost, I want to get to ... ich weiß nicht, wo ich bin, ich möchte nach ... [vice nisht vo ish bin ish mursht-uh naKH]
I've lost my handbag ich habe meine Handtasche verloren [fairlohren]
lost property (office) das Fundbüro [foont-booroh]
lot: a lot, lots viel [feel]
not a lot nicht sehr viel [nisht zair]
a lot of people viele Leute [feel-uh]
a lot bigger viel größer
I like it a lot mag es sehr [ish mahk ess zair]
lotion die Lotion [lohts-yohn]
loud laut [lowt]
lounge (in house) das

Wohnzimmer [**voh**n-
tsimmer]
(in hotel) die Lounge
(in airport) der Warteraum
[**vart**-uh-rowm]
love die Liebe [**leeb**-uh]
(verb) lieben [**lee**ben]
I love Germany ich liebe
Deutschland
lovely herrlich [**hair**lish]
low (prices, bridge) niedrig
[**need**rish]
luck das Glück [gl**oo**ck]
good luck! viel Glück [feel]
luggage das Gepäck [ge**peck**]
luggage trolley der Kofferkuli
[**koffer**-k**oo**li]
lump (on body) die Beule
[**boyl**-uh]
lunch das Mittagessen
[**mitt**ahkessen]
lungs die Lungen [**loong**-en]
Luxembourg Luxemburg
[**look**semboork]
luxurious luxuriös [looksooree-
urss]
luxury der Luxus [**look**sooss]

M

machine die Maschine
[mash**een**-uh]
mad (insane) verrückt [fair-
r**oo**ckt]
(angry) böse [b**ur**z-uh]
made: what is it made of?
woraus ist es? [**voh**rowss]
(food) was ist da drin?
[vass]

magazine die Zeitschrift [ts**ite**-
shrift]
maid (in hotel) das
Zimmermädchen [ts**immer**-
maydshen]
maiden name der
Mädchenname [**may**dshen-
nahm-uh]
mail die Post
is there any mail for me? ist
Post für mich da? [f**oo**r
mish]
mailbox der Briefkasten
[**breef**kasten]
see letterbox
main Haupt- [howpt]
main course das Hauptgericht
[**howp**t-gerisht]
main post office die Hauptpost
[**howp**t-posst]
main road die Hauptstraße
[**howp**t-shtrahss-uh]
mains switch der
Hauptschalter [**howp**t-
shalter]
make (brand name) die Marke
[**mark**-uh]
(verb) machen [ma**KH**en]
I make it 200 marks nach
meiner Rechnung sind
das zweihundert Mark
[na**KH** m**ine**-er **r**eshnoong zint
dass]
make-up das Make-up
man der Mann
manager der Geschäftsführer
[ge**sheft**s-f**oo**rer]
can I see the manager? kann
ich den Geschäftsführer

sprechen? [dayn – shpreshen]

manageress die
Geschäftsführerin [geshefts-
ffoorerin]

manual (car) ein Auto mit
Handschaltung [owto mit
hant-shaltoong]

many viele [feel-uh]

not many nicht viele [nisht]

map (of city) der Stadtplan
[shtat-plahn]

(road map) die Straßenkarte
[shtrahssen-kart-uh]

(geographical) die Landkarte
[lantkart-uh]

March der März [mairts]

margarine die Margarine
[margareen-uh]

market der Markt

marmalade die
Orangenmarmelade
[oronJen-marmelahd-uh]

married: I'm married ich bin
verheiratet [ish bin
fairhyrahtet]

are you married? sind Sie
verheiratet? [zint zee]

mascara die Wimperntusche
[vimpern-toosh-uh]

match (football etc) das Spiel
[shpeel]

matches die Streichhölzer
[shtrysh-hurltser]

material (fabric) der Stoff [shtoff]

matter: it doesn't matter das
macht nichts [maKHt nishts]

what's the matter? was ist los?
[vass ist lohss]

mattress die Matratze

[matrats-uh]

May der Mai [my]

may: may I have another one?
kann ich noch eins haben?
[ish noKH ine-ss hahben]

may I come in? darf ich
hereinkommen? [hairine-
kommen]

may I see it? kann ich es
sehen? [zay-en]

maybe vielleicht [feelysht]

mayonnaise die Mayonnaise
[my-oh-nayz-uh]

me* mich [mish]

that's for me das ist für mich

send it to me schicken Sie es
mir [meer]

me too ich auch [ish owKH]

meal die Mahlzeit [mahltsite]

•••••• DIALOGUE ••••••

did you enjoy your meal? hat es
Ihnen geschmeckt? [eenen
geshmeckt]

it was excellent, thank you es war
ausgezeichnet, danke [var owss-
getsyshnet, dank-uh]

mean (verb) bedeuten
[bedoyten]

what do you mean? was
meinen Sie damit? [vass
mine-en zee]

•••••• DIALOGUE ••••••

what does this word mean? was
bedeutet dieses Wort? [vass
bedoytet deezess vort]

it means ... in English auf Englisch
bedeutet es ... [owf eng-lish]

measles die Masern [m**a**hzern]

meat das Fleisch [flysh]

mechanic der Mechaniker
[mesh**ah**niker]

medicine die Medizin
[medits**ee**n]

medium (size) m**i**ttlerer

medium-dry (wine) halbtrocken
[h**a**lp-trocken]

medium-rare (steak) medium
[m**ay**dee-oom]

medium-sized mittelgroß
[m**i**ttelgrohss]

meet treffen
nice to meet you freut mich
[froyt mish]
where shall I meet you? wo
treffen wir uns? [vo – veer
oonss]

meeting die Besprechung
[besh**pre**shoong]

meeting place der Treffpunkt
[treff-poonkt]

melon die Melone [mel**oh**n-uh]

men die Männer [m**e**nner]

mend reparieren [repar**ee**ren]
could you mend this for me?
können Sie das reparieren?
[k**u**rnen zee]

menswear die Herrenkleidung
[h**ai**ren-klydoong]

mention erwähnen [airv**ay**nen]
don't mention it gern
geschehen [gairn gesh**ay**-en]

menu die Speisekarte [shp**i**ze-
uh-kart-uh]
may I see the menu, please?
kann ich bitte die
Speisekarte h**a**ben? [b**i**tt-uh]

see **Menu Reader** on page 213

message die Nachricht
[n**a**KHrisht]
are there any messages for
me? ist eine Nachricht für
mich hinterl**a**ssen **w**orden?
[**ine**-uh – f**oo**r mish]
I want to leave a message for
... ich möchte eine Nachricht
für ... hinterlassen [ish
m**ur**sht-uh]

metal das Metall

metre* der Meter [m**ay**ter]

microwave (oven) der
Mikrowellenherd
[m**ee**krovellen-hairt]

midday der Mittag
at midday mittags [m**i**ttahgs]

middle: in the middle in der
Mitte [dair m**i**tt-uh]
in the middle of the night
mitten in der Nacht
the middle one der m**i**ttlere
[m**i**ttler-uh]

midnight die Mitternacht
[m**i**tter-naKHt]
at midnight um Mitternacht
[oom]

might: I might vielleicht
[feel**y**sht]
I might not vielleicht nicht
[nisht]
I might want to stay another
day vielleicht bleibe ich
noch einen Tag länger
[bl**i**be-uh ish noKH **ine**-en tahk
l**e**ng-er]

migraine die Migräne
[migr**ay**n-uh]

mild (taste, weather) mild [milt]

mile* die Meile [**mile**-uh]

milk die Milch [milsh]

milkshake der Milchshake

millimetre* der Millimeter [**m**illimayter]

minced meat das Hackfleisch [h**a**ckflysh]

mind: never mind macht nichts [maKHt nishts]

I've changed my mind ich habe es mir anders überlegt [ish h**ah**b-uh ess meer **a**nders ooberl**ay**kt]

•••••• DIALOGUE ••••••

do you mind if I open the window? macht es Ihnen etwas aus, wenn ich das Fenster öffne? [maKHt ess **ee**nen **e**tvass˚owss venn ish]

no, I don't mind nein, das ist mir gleich [meer gl**y**sh]

mine*: it's mine es gehört mir [geh**u**rt meer]

mineral water das Mineralwasser [miner**ah**lvasser]

mint (sweet) das Pfefferminz [pfefferm**i**nts]

minute die Minute [min**oo**t-uh]

in a minute gleich [glysh]

just a minute Moment mal [mohm**e**nt mahl]

mirror der Spiegel [shp**ee**gel]

Miss Frau [frow]

Miss! (waitress etc) Fräulein [fr**oy**line]

miss (bus, train) verpassen [fairp**a**ssen]

(regret absence of) vermissen [fairm**i**ssen]

I missed the bus ich habe den Bus verpaßt [ish h**ah**b-uh dayn booss fairp**a**sst]

missing: to be missing fehlen [f**ay**len]

there's a suitcase missing ein Koffer fehlt

mist der Nebel [n**ay**bel]

mistake der Fehler [f**ay**ler]

I think there's a mistake ich glaube, da ist ein Fehler [ish gl**ow**b-uh]

sorry, I've made a mistake tut mir leid, ich habe einen Fehler gemacht [t**oo**t meer lite ish h**ah**b-uh **ine**-en]

misunderstanding das Mißverständnis [m**i**ss-fairshtentniss]

mix-up: sorry, there's been a mix-up tut mir leid, etwas ist schiefgelaufen [t**oo**t meer lite, **e**tvass ist sh**ee**f-gelowfen]

modern modern [mod**ai**rn]

modern art gallery die Galerie für moderne Kunst [gal-er**ee** foor mod**ai**rn-uh koonst]

moisturizer die Feuchtigkeitscreme [f**oy**shtishkites-kraym]

moment: I'll be back in a moment ich bin gleich wieder da [glysh v**ee**der]

Monday der Montag [m**oh**ntahk]

money das Geld [gelt]

month der Monat [m**oh**naht]

monument das Denkmal

[denkmahl]
moon der Mond [mohnt]
moped das Moped [mohpet]
more* mehr [mair]
  can I have some more water,
  please? kann ich bitte noch
  etwas Wasser haben? [ish
  bitt-uh noKH etvass]
  more expensive/interesting
  teurer/interessanter [toyrer]
  more than 50 über fünfzig
  [oober]
  more than that mehr als das
  a lot more viel mehr [feel]

•••••• D I A L O G U E ••••••

  would you like some more?
  möchten Sie noch etwas?
  [murshten zee noKH etvass]
  no, no more for me, thanks nein
  danke, das ist genug [nine dank-
  uh dass ist genook]
  how about you? und Sie? [oont
  zee]
  I don't want any more, thanks ich
  möchte nichts mehr, danke
  [nishts]

morning der Morgen
  this morning heute morgen
  [hoyt-uh]
  in the morning am Morgen
most: I like this one most of all
  dies gefällt mir am besten
  [deess gefellt meer]
  most of the time die meiste
  Zeit [dee myst-uh tsite]
  most tourists die meisten
  Touristen [mysten]
mostly meistens [mystens]

mother die Mutter [mootter]
motorbike das Motorrad
  [motohr-raht]
motorboat das Motorboot
  [motohr-boht]
motorway die Autobahn
  [owtobahn]
mountain der Berg [bairk]
  in the mountains in den
  Bergen [dayn bairgen]
mountaineering das
  Bergsteigen [bairk-shtygen]
mouse die Maus [mowss]
moustache der Schnurrbart
  [shnoorr-bart]
mouth der Mund [moont]
mouth ulcer die Mundfäule
  [moont-foyl-uh]
move bewegen [bevaygen]
  (move house) umziehen [oom-
  tsee-en]
  he's moved to another room er
  ist in ein anderes Zimmer
  gezogen [air ist in ine anderess
  tsimmer getsohgen]
  could you move your car?
  könnten Sie Ihr Auto
  wegfahren? [kurnten zee eer
  owto veckfahren]
  could you move up a little?
  könnten Sie etwas
  aufrücken? [etvass owf-
  rOOcken]
  where has it moved to? (shop,
  gallery) wo ist es jetzt? [vo]
movie der Film
movie theater (US) das Kino
  [keeno]
Mr Herr [hair]

Mrs Frau [frow]

Ms Frau [frow]

much viel [feel]

much better/worse viel besser/schlechter [shleshter]

much hotter viel heißer

not much nicht viel [nisht]

not very much nicht sehr viel [zair]

I don't want very much ich möchte nicht so viel

mud der Dreck

mug (for drinking) die Tasse [tass-uh]

I've been mugged ich bin überfallen worden [ish bin ooberfallen vorden]

mum die Mutter [mootter]

mumps der Mumps [moomps]

Munich München [moonshen]

museum das Museum [moozayoom]

mushrooms die Pilze [pilts-uh]

music die Musik [moozeek]

musician der Musiker [mooziker]

Muslim moslemisch [moslaymish]

mussels die Muscheln [moosheln]

must*: I must ich muß... [ish mooss]

I mustn't drink alcohol ich darf keinen Alkohol trinken [kine-en]

mustard der Senf [zenf]

my*: my room mein Zimmer [mine]

my family meine Familie

[mine-uh]

my parents meine Eltern

myself: I'll do it myself ich mache es selbst [ish maKH-uh ess zelpst]

by myself allein [alline]

N

nail (finger, metal) der Nagel [nahgel]

nail varnish der Nagellack [nahgel-lack]

name der Name [nahmuh]

The familiar **du** and first names are used in informal relationships, for example, between friends and relatives, or when talking to children. In formal situations, or when talking to older people you don't know, **Sie** is used, combined with the address **Herr** or **Frau** (Mr or Mrs/Ms) + surname. In less formal situations, Germans immediately adopt first name terms.

---

my name's John ich heiße John [ish hice-uh]

what's your name? wie heißen Sie? [vee hice-en zee]

what is the name of this street? wie heißt diese Straße? [vee hysst]

napkin die Serviette [zairvee-ett-uh]

nappy die Windel [vindel]

narrow eng

nasty (person) gemein [gem**ine**]
(weather, accident) furchtbar
[**foo**rshtbar]

national national [nats-yohn**ah**l]

nationality die
Staatsangehörigkeit [sht**ah**ts-
an-gehurishkite]

natural natürlich [nat**oo**rlish]

nausea die Übelkeit [**OO**belkite]

navy (blue) marineblau
[mar**ee**n-uh-blow]

near nah
is it near the city centre? ist es
nahe dem Stadtzentrum?
[n**ah**-uh daym]
do you go near the Branden-
burg gate? fahren Sie in die
Nähe des Brandenburger
T**o**res? [f**ah**ren zee in dee
n**ay**-uh]
where is the nearest ...? wo ist
der nächste ...? [vo ist dair
n**ay**kst-uh]

nearby in der Nähe [dair n**ay**-
uh]

nearly fast [fasst]

necessary notwendig
[n**oh**tvendish]

neck der Hals [halss]

necklace die Halskette
[h**a**lskett-uh]

necktie (US) die Krawatte
[krav**a**tt-uh]

need: I need ... ich brauche ...
[ish br**ow**KH-uh]
do I need to pay? muß ich
bezahlen? [mooss]

needle die Nadel [n**ah**del]

negative (film) das Negativ

neither: neither (one) of them
keiner (von ihnen) [k**i**ne-er
fon **ee**nen]
neither ... nor ... weder ...
noch ... [v**ay**der ... noKH]

nephew der Neffe [n**eff**-uh]

net (in sport) das Netz

Netherlands die Niederlande
[n**ee**derland-uh]

network map der
Nahverkehrsplan
[n**ah**fairkairs-plahn]

never nie [nee]

•••••• D I A L O G U E ••••••

have you ever been to Mainz?
waren Sie schon einmal in
Mainz? [v**ah**ren zee shohn **ine**-
mahl]
no, never, I've never been there
nein, ich war noch nie da [noKH]

new neu [noy]

news (radio, TV etc) die
Nachrichten [n**a**KHrishten]

newsagent's der
Zeitungshändler [ts**y**toongs-
hentler]

newspaper die Zeitung
[ts**y**toong]

newspaper kiosk der
Zeitungskiosk [ts**y**toongs-
kee-osk]

New Year Neujahr [n**oy**-yahr]
Happy New Year! frohes
neues Jahr [fr**oh**-ess
n**oy**ess yar]

Many Germans celebrate New Year's Eve at a **Silvester-party**; midnight firework displays are traditional events.

New Year's Eve Silvester [zilv**e**ster]

New Zealand Neuseeland [noyz**ay**lant]

New Zealander: I'm a New Zealander (man/woman) ich bin Neuseeländer [noyz**ay**lender]/ Neeseeländerin

next nächster [n**ay**kster]
the next turning/street on the left die nächste **A**bzweigung/ Straße links [n**ay**kst-uh]
at the next stop an der nächsten **H**altestelle [n**ay**ksten]
next **week** nächste **W**oche
next to neben [n**ay**ben]

nice (food) gut [g**oo**t]
(looks, view etc) hübsch [h**oo**psh]
(person) nett

niece die Nichte [n**i**sht-uh]

night die Nacht [naKHt]
at night nachts
good night gute Nacht [g**oo**t-uh]

• • • • • • DIALOGUE • • • • • •

do you have a single room for one night? haben Sie ein Einzelzimmer für eine Nacht? [h**ah**ben zee ine **ine**-tsel-tsimmer f**oo**r **ine**-uh]
yes ja [yah]
how much is it per night? was

kostet es pro Nacht?
it's 150 marks for one night eine Übernachtung kostet hundertfünfzig Mark [oober-n**a**KHtoong]
thank you, I'll take it danke, ich nehme es [n**ay**m-uh]

nightclub der Nachtklub [n**a**KHtkloob]

nightdress das Nachthemd [n**a**KHt-hemt]

night porter der Nachtportier [n**a**KHt-port-yay]

no nein [nine]
I've no change ich habe kein Kle**i**ngeld [kine]
there's no ... left es ist kein ... übrig [**oo**brish]
no way! auf keinen Fall [owf k**i**ne-en fal]
oh no! (upset) nein!

nobody keiner [k**i**ne-er]
there's nobody there es ist keiner da

noise der Lärm [lairm]

noisy: it's too noisy es ist zu laut [ts**oo** lowt]

non-alcoholic alkoholfrei [alkoh**oh**lfry]

none keiner [k**i**ne-er]

nonsmoking compartment das Nichtraucherabteil [n**i**shtrowKHer-aptile]

noon der Mittag [m**i**ttahk]

no-one keiner [k**i**ne-er]

nor: nor do I ich auch nicht [owKH nisht]

normal normal [norm**ah**l]

north der Norden
in the north im Norden
north of Leipzig nördlich von
Leipzig [n**ur**tlish fon]
northeast der Nordosten [nort-
osten]
northern nördlich [n**ur**tlish]
North Sea die Nordsee [n**or**tzay]
northwest der Nordwesten
[nortv**e**sten]
Northern Ireland Nordirland
[nort-**ee**rlant]
Norway Norwegen [n**o**rvaygen]
Norwegian (adj) norwegisch
[n**o**rvaygish]
nose die Nase [n**ah**z-uh]
nosebleed Nasenbluten
[n**ah**zen-bl**oo**ten]
not* nicht [nisht]
no, I'm not hungry nein, ich
h**a**be keinen H**u**nger
[k**i**ne-en]
I don't want any, thank you ich
möchte keine, danke
[m**ur**sht-uh k**i**ne-uh d**a**nk-uh]
it's not necessary es ist nicht
nötig
I didn't know that das wußte
ich nicht [v**oo**st-uh]
not that one – this one nicht
den – diesen [dayn – d**ee**zen]
note (banknote) der Geldschein
[g**e**lt-shine]
notebook das Notizbuch
[nohte**e**ts-b**oo**KH]
notepaper (for letters) das
Briefpapier [br**ee**f-papeer]
nothing nichts [nishts]
nothing for me, thanks nichts

für mich, danke
nothing else sonst nichts
[zonst]
novel der Roman [rom**ah**n]
November der November
now jetzt [yetst]
number die Nummer
[n**oo**mmer]
I've got the wrong number ich
habe mich verwählt [h**a**hb-uh
mish fairv**ay**lt]
what is your phone number?
was ist Ihre Telefon-
nummer? [**ee**r-uh telef**oh**n-
noommer]
number plate das
Nummernschild [n**oo**mmern-
shilt]
Nuremburg Nürnberg [n**oo**rn-
bairk]
nurse (female) die
Krankenschwester [kr**a**nken-
shvester]
(male) der Krankenpfleger
[kr**a**nken-pflayger]
nursery slope der
Anfängerhügel [**a**nfenger-
h**oo**gel]
nut (for bolt) die
Schraubenmutter
[shr**ow**benmootter]
nuts die Nüsse [n**oo**ss-uh]

O

occupied (toilet) besetzt
[bez**e**tst]
o'clock*: it's nine o'clock es ist
neun Uhr [**oo**r]

October der Oktober

odd (strange) merkwürdig
[ma**i**rk-v**oo**rdish]

of* von (+dat) [fon]

the name of the hotel der
Name des Hotels

off (lights) aus [owss]

it's just off Goethestraße es ist
ganz in der Nähe der
Goethestraße [gants in dair
n**ay**-uh]

we're off tomorrow wir reisen
morgen ab [veer r**y**zen]

offensive anstößig [an-
sht**u**rssish]

office das Büro [b**oo**r**oh**]

often oft

not often nicht oft [nisht]

how often are the buses? wie
oft f**a**hren die Busse? [vee]

oil (for car, for salad) das Öl [url]

ointment die Salbe [z**a**lb-uh]

OK ok**ay**

are you OK? sind Sie okay?

is that OK with you? ist das in
Ordnung? [**o**rtnoong]

is it OK if I ...? kann ich ... ?

that's OK thanks (it doesn't
matter) d**a**nke, das ist in
Ordnung

I'm OK (nothing for me, I've got
enough) nein, d**a**nke [nine]
(I feel OK) mir geht's gut [meer
gayts g**oo**t]

is this train OK for ...? fährt
d**ie**ser Zug nach ...?

I said I'm sorry, OK ich habe
doch gesagt, es tut mir leid
[h**a**hb-uh do**KH** gez**a**hkt]

old alt

•••••• DIALOGUE ••••••

how old are you? wie alt bist du/
sind Sie? [vee alt bist d**oo**/zint zee]

I'm twenty-five ich bin
fünfundzwanzig

and you? und du/Sie? [oont]

old-fashioned altmodisch
[**a**ltmohdish]

old town (old part of town) die
Altstadt [**a**lt-shtatt]

in the old town in der
Altstadt

olive oil das Olivenöl [ol**ee**ven-
url]

olives die Oliven [ol**ee**ven]

omelette das Omelette [oml**ett**]

on* auf [owf]

on the street/beach auf der
Straße/am Strand

is it on this road? ist es auf
dieser Straße?

on the plane im Flugzeug

on Saturday am Samstag

on television im Fernsehen

I haven't got it on me ich habe
es nicht bei mir [h**a**hb-uh ess
nisht by meer]

this one's on me (drink) diese
Runde ist auf meine
Rechnung [d**ee**z-uh r**oo**nd-uh
ist owf m**i**ne-uh r**e**shnoong]

the light wasn't on das Licht
war nicht an

what's on tonight? was gibt es
h**eu**te **a**bend? [vass geept ess]

once (one time) einmal [**i**ne-
mahl]

at once (immediately) sofort
[zof**o**rt]

one* ein(e) [**ine**(-uh)]
(as figure) eins [ine-ss]
the white one der wei**ß**e
[dair]

one-way ticket die einfache
Fahrkarte [**ine**-faKH-uh f**ah**r-
kartuh]

onion die Zwiebel [tsv**ee**bel]

only nur [n**OO**r]
only one nur einer
it's only 6 o'clock es ist erst
sechs Uhr [airst]
I've only just got here ich bin
gerade erst **a**ngekommen
[ger**ah**d-uh airst]

on/off switch der Ein/Aus-
Schalter [ine-**ow**ss-shalter]

open (adj) **o**ffen

open (verb) **ö**ffnen [**u**rfnen]
when do you open? wann
machen Sie auf? [van m**a**KHen
zee owf]
I can't get it open ich
bekomme es nicht auf
[bek**o**mm-uh]
in the open air im Freien
[fr**y**-en]

opening times die
Öffnungszeiten [**u**rfnoongs-
tsyten]

open ticket die unbeschränkte
Fahrkarte [**oo**nbeshrenkt-uh
f**ah**rkart-uh]

opera die Oper [**oh**per]

operation (medical) die
Operation [operats-y**oh**n]

operator (telephone) die

Vermittlung [fairm**i**ttloong]

opposite: the opposite direction
die entgegengesetzte
Richtung [entg**ay**gen-gezetst-
uh r**i**shtoong]
the bar opposite die Kn**ei**pe
gegenüber [gaygen-**oo**ber]
opposite my hotel gegenüber
m**ei**nem Hotel

optician der Augenarzt
[**ow**genartst]

or oder [**oh**der]

orange (fruit) die Apfelsine
[apfelz**ee**n-uh], die Orange
[or**o**nJ-uh]
(colour) orange

orange juice der Orangensaft
[or**o**nJen-zaft]

orchestra das Orchester
[ork**e**ster]

order: can we order now?
können wir jetzt bestellen?
[k**u**rnen veer yetst besht**e**llen]
I've already ordered, thanks
d**a**nke, ich habe schon
bestellt [h**ah**b-uh shohn
besht**e**llt]
I didn't order this das habe ich
nicht bestellt
out of order au**ß**er Betrieb
[**ow**sser betr**ee**p]

ordinary normal [norm**ah**l]

other andere [**a**nder-uh]
the other one der andere
the other day (recently) neulich
[n**oy**lish]
I'm waiting for the others ich
w**a**rte auf die anderen [dee
anderen]
do you have any others?

haben Sie noch andere?
[h**ah**ben zee noKH]

otherwise sonst [zonst]

our* unser [**oo**nzer]

ours* unserer [**oo**nzerer]

out: he's out (not at home) er ist
nicht da [air ist nisht]

three kilometres out of town
drei Kilom**e**ter au**ß**erhalb
der Stadt [**ow**sserhalp dair
shtatt]

outdoors drau**ß**en [dr**ow**ssen]

outside ... au**ß**erhalb ... (+gen)
[**ow**sser-halp]

can we sit outside? können
wir drau**ß**en sitzen?
[dr**ow**ssen]

oven der Backofen [b**a**ck-ohfen]

over: over here hier [heer]

over there dort drüben
[dr**oo**ben]

over 500 über fünfhundert
[**oo**ber]

it's over (finished) es ist vorbei
[for-b**y**]

**overcharge: you've overcharged
me** Sie haben mir zuviel
berechnet [zee h**ah**ben meer
ts00f**ee**l ber**e**shnet]

overcoat der Mantel

overnight (travel) über Nacht
[**oo**ber naKHt]

overtake überholen
[00berh**oh**len]

owe: how much do I owe you?
was bin ich Ihnen schuldig?
[vass bin ish **ee**nen sh**oo**ldish]

own: my own ... mein
eigener ... [mine **i**gener]

are you on your own? sind Sie
allein hier? [zint zee all**ine**
heer]

I'm on my own ich bin allein
hier

owner (man/woman) der Besitzer
[bez**i**tser]/die Besitzerin

P

pack (verb) p**a**cken

pack: a pack of ... (food, drink etc)
eine P**a**ckung ... [**ine**-uh
p**a**ckoong]

package das Pak**e**t [pak**ay**t]

package holiday die
Pauschalreise
[powsh**ah**lrize-uh]

packed lunch das Lunchpaket
[-pak**ay**t]

packet: a packet of cigarettes
eine Sch**a**chtel Zigar**e**tten
[sh**a**KHtel tsigar**e**tten]

padlock das Vorhängeschloß
[**f**orheng-uh-shloss]

page (of book) die Seite [z**i**te-uh]

could you page Mr ...? können
Sie Herrn ... ausrufen
lassen? [k**u**rnen zee hairn ...
owssroofen]

pain der Schmerz [shmairts]

I have a pain here ich habe
hier Schmerzen [ish h**ah**b-uh
heer]

painful schmerzhaft [shm**ai**rts-
haft]

painkillers das Schmerzmittel
[shm**ai**rts-mittel]

paint die Farbe [f**a**rb-uh]

painting (picture) das Gemälde
[gemeld-uh]

pair: a pair of ... ein Paar ... [ine
pahr]

Pakistani (adj) pakistanisch
[pakist**ah**nish]

palace der Palast

pale blaß [blass]

pale blue zartblau [ts**a**rtblow]

pan die Pfanne [pf**a**nn-uh]

panties das Höschen [h**u**rs-
shen]

pants (underwear: men's) die
Unterhose [**oo**nterhohz-uh]
(women's) das Höschen [h**u**rs-
shen]
(US) die Hose [h**oh**z-uh]

pantyhose die Strumpfhose
[shtr**oo**mpf-hohz-uh]

paper das Papier [pap**ee**r]
(newspaper) die Zeitung
[ts**y**toong]
a piece of paper ein Stück
Papier [ine sht**oo**ck]

paper handkerchiefs die
Papiertaschentücher
[pap**ee**r-tashent**oo**sher]

parcel das Paket [pak**ay**t]

pardon?, (US) pardon me? (didn't
understand) wie bitte? [vee
b**i**tt-uh]

parents: my parents meine
Eltern [m**i**ne-uh **e**ltern]

parents-in-law die
Schwiegereltern [shv**ee**ger-
eltern]

park der Park
(verb) p**a**rken
can I park here? kann man

hier parken? [heer]

parking lot (US) der Parkplatz
[p**a**rkplats]

part ein Teil [tile]

partner (boyfriend, girlfriend) der
Partner/die P**a**rtnerin

party (group) die Gruppe
[gr**oo**pp-uh]
(celebration) die Fete [f**ay**t-uh]

pass (in mountains) der Paß [pas]

passenger der Passagier
[passaJeer]

passport der Paß [pas]

past*: in the past in der
Vergangenheit [dair
fairg**a**ngen-hite]
just past the information office
kurz hinter dem
Auskunftsbüro [koorts]

path der Weg [vayk]

pattern das Muster [m**oo**ster]

pavement der Bürgersteig
[b**OO**rgershtike]
on the pavement auf dem
Bürgersteig

pay (verb) zahlen [ts**a**hlen]
can I pay, please? kann ich
zahlen, bitte? [b**i**tt-uh]
it's already paid for es ist
schon bezahlt [shohn
bets**ah**lt]

•••••• DIALOGUE ••••••

who's paying? wer bezahlt? [vair
bets**ah**lt]

I'll pay ich bezahle

no, you paid last time, I'll pay
nein, du hast letztes Mal bezahlt, ich
bezahle [l**e**tstess mahl]

pay phone der
  Münzfernsprecher [moonts-
  fairnshpresher]
peaceful friedlich [freetlish]
peach der Pfirsich [pfeerzish]
peanuts die Erdnüsse
  [airtnooss-uh]
pear die Birne [beern-uh]
peas die Erbsen [airpsen]
peculiar eigenartig [igen-artish]
pedestrian crossing der
  Fußgängerüberweg
  [foossgeng-er-oobervayk]

Most German pedestrians will
stop at a red light on a
pedestrian crossing whether
there are cars about or not, even
at night! Police are often quick
to hand out on-the-spot fines for
jaywalkers.

pedestrian precinct die
  Fußgängerzone [foossgeng-
  er-tsohn-uh]
peg (for washing) die
  Wäscheklammer [vesh-uh-
  klammer]
  (for tent) der Hering [hairing]
pen der Stift [shtift]
pencil der Bleistift [bly-shtift]
penfriend (boy/girl) der
  Brieffreund [breef-froynt]/die
  Brieffreundin
penicillin das Penizillin
  [penitsilleen]
penknife das Taschenmesser
  [tashen-messer]
pensioner (man/woman) der

Rentner/die Rentnerin
people die Leute [loyt-uh]
  the other people in the hotel
  die anderen Leute im Hotel
  too many people zu viele
  Leute [tsoo feel-uh]
pepper (spice) der Pfeffer
  (vegetable) die Paprikaschote
  [paprika-shoht-uh]
peppermint (sweet) das
  Pfefferminz [pfeffermints]
per: per night pro Nacht [naKHt]
  how much per day? was
  kostet es pro Tag? [tahk]
per cent Prozent [protsent]
perfect perfekt [pairfekt]
perfume das Parfüm [parfoom]
perhaps vielleicht [feelysht]
  perhaps not vielleicht nicht
period (of time) die Zeit [tsite]
  (menstruation) die Periode
  [pairee-ohd-uh]
perm die Dauerwelle
  [dowervell-uh]
permit die Genehmigung
  [genay-migoong]
person die Person [pairzohn]
personal stereo der Walkman®
petrol das Benzin [bentseen]

Types of petrol are Normal
[normahl] (2/3 star, always
unleaded), Super verbleit
[zooper fair-blite] (4 star,
leaded) and Super unverbleit
[oonfair-blite] (4 star, unleaded). Cash payment is the
norm.

petrol can der Reservekanister
[rez**air**v-uh-kanister]
petrol station die Tankstelle
[t**a**nk-shtell-uh]
pharmacy die Apotheke
[apot**ay**k-uh]
see **chemist**
phone das Telefon [telef**oh**n]
(verb) anrufen [**a**n-r**oo**fen]

Phone boxes are yellow
and are either operated by
coins (**Münzfernsprecher**
[m**oo**nts-fairn-shpresher]) or
cards (**Kartentelefon** [k**a**rten-
telef**oh**n]). Phonecards
(**Telefonkarten**) can be
purchased from post offices and
some shops. A phonecard is
worth buying, especially if you're
intending to call home.
However, an easier option is
to use the direct phone
service facilities of the main
post office (**Hauptpost**): a
phone booth will be allocated to
you from the counter marked
Fremd-gespräche, which is also
where you pay once you've
finished.
see **speak** and **dialling code**

phone book das Telefonbuch
[telef**oh**n-b**OO**KH]
phonecard die Telefonkarte
[-**ka**rtuh]
phone number die
Telefonnummer [-n**oo**mmer]
photo das Foto

excuse me, could you take a
photo of us? entschuldigen
Sie, könnten Sie ein Foto
von uns machen? [k**u**rnten
zee ine]
phrase book der Sprachführer
[shpr**ah**KH-f**OO**rer]
piano das Klavier [klav**ee**r]
pickpocket der Taschendieb
[t**a**shen-deep]
pick up: will you be there to pick
me up? werden Sie da sein,
um mich abzuholen? [oom
mish **a**pts**OO**-hohlen]
picnic das Picknick
picture das Bild [bilt]
pie (meat) die Pastete
[past**ay**t-uh]
(fruit) der Kuchen [k**OO**KHen]
piece das Stück [sht**OO**ck]
a piece of ... ein Stück ... [ine]
pill die Pille [p**i**ll-uh]
I'm on the pill ich nehme die
Pille [ish n**ay**m-uh dee]
pillow das Kopfkissen
pillow case der
Kopfkissenbezug [kopfkissen-
bets**OO**k]
pin die Nadel [n**ah**del]
pineapple die Ananas [**a**nanas]
pineapple juice der Ananassaft
[**a**nanas-zaft]
pink rosa [r**oh**za]
pipe (for smoking) die Pfeife
[pf**i**fe-uh]
(for water) das Rohr
pipe cleaner der
Pfeifenreiniger [pf**y**fen-
ryniger]

pity: it's a pity das ist schade [shah**d**-uh]

pizza die Pizza [p**ee**tsa]

place der Platz [plats]

is this place taken? ist dieser Platz besetzt? [d**ee**zer – bez**e**tst]

at your place bei dir/Ihnen [by deer/**ee**nen]

at his place bei ihm [eem]

plain (not patterned) uni [**oo**nee]

plane das Flugzeug [fl**oo**ktsoyk]

by plane mit dem Flugzeug [daym]

plant die Pflanze [pfl**a**nts-uh]

plaster (for cut) das Heftpflaster

plaster cast der Gipsverband [g**i**ps-fairbant]

plastic das Plastik

(credit cards) die Kreditkarten [kred**ee**t-karten]

plastic bag die Plastiktüte [pl**a**stik-t**oo**t-uh]

plate der Teller

platform der Bahnsteig [b**ah**nshtike]

which platform is it, please? welches Gleis, bitte? [v**e**lless glice b**i**tt-uh]

play (verb) spielen [shp**ee**len]

(noun: in theatre) das Stück [sht**oo**ck]

playground der Spielplatz [shp**ee**l-plats]

pleasant angenehm [**a**n-genaym]

please bitte [b**i**tt-uh]

yes please ja bitte [yah]

could you please ...? könnten Sie bitte ...? [k**ur**nten zee]

please don't bitte nicht [nisht]

pleased to meet you! freut mich! [froyt mish]

pleasure die Freude [fr**oy**d-uh]

my pleasure ganz meinerseits [gants m**i**ne-er-zites]

plenty: plenty of ... viel ... [feel]

we've plenty of time wir haben viel Zeit

that's plenty, thanks das reicht, danke [rysht]

pliers die Zange [ts**a**ng-uh]

plug (electrical) der Stecker [sht**e**cker]

(for car) die Zündkerze [ts**oo**ntkairts-uh]

(in sink) der Stöpsel [sht**ur**psel]

plumber der Klempner

p.m.* (in the afternoon) nachmittags [n**a**KHmittahks]

(in the evening) abends [ahbents]

poached egg das pochierte Ei [posh**ee**rt-uh **ī**]

pocket die Tasche [t**a**sh-uh]

point: two point five zwei Komma fünf

there's no point es hat keinen Sinn [k**i**ne-en zin]

points (in car) die Kontakte [kont**a**kt-uh]

poisonous giftig [g**i**ftish]

Poland Polen

Polish polnisch

police die Polizei [polits**ī**]

call the police! rufen Sie die Polizei! [r**oo**fen zee dee]

The German police are not renowned for their friendliness, but they usually treat foreigners with courtesy. It's important to remember that you are expected to carry your ID (your passport, or at least a student card or driving licence) at all times. Traffic offences or any other misdemeanours will result in a rigorous checking of documentation, and on-the-spot fines are best paid without argument. Throughout Germany the number to ring for the police is 110.

policeman der Polizist
[polits**i**st]
police station die Polizeiwache
[polits**i**-vaKH-uh]
policewoman die Polizistin
[polits**i**stin]
polish die Creme [kr**ay**m]
polite höflich [h**ur**flish]
polluted verschmutzt
[fairshm**oo**tst]
pony der Pony [p**o**nnee]
pool (for swimming) das
Schwimmbecken [shv**i**mm-
becken]
poor (not rich) **arm**
(quality) **schlecht** [shlesht]
pop music die Popmusik [p**o**p-
m**oo**zeek]
pop singer (male/female) der
Popsänger [p**o**pzenger]/die
Popsängerin

population die Bevölkerung
[bef**ur**lkeroong]
pork das Schweinefleisch
[shv**i**ne-uh-flysh]
port (for boats) der Hafen
[h**ah**fen]
(drink) der Portwein [p**o**rtvine]
porter (in hotel) der Portier
[port-y**ay**]
portrait das Porträt [portr**ay**]
posh (restaurant, people) vornehm
[f**o**rnaym]
possible möglich [m**ur**glish]
is it possible to ...? ist es
möglich, zu ...?
as ... as possible so ... wie
möglich [zo ... vee]
post (mail) die Post [posst]
to post (verb) **absenden**
could you post this for me?
könnten Sie das für mich
aufgeben? [k**ur**nten zee dass
f**oo**r mish **o**wf-gayben]
postbox der Briefkasten
[br**ee**fkasten]
postcard die Postkarte
[p**o**sstkart-uh]
poster das Plakat [plak**ah**t]
post office die Post

The German postal service is generally fast and reliable. There is no distinction between first and second class post; most deliveries within Germany reach their destination on the next day. Post offices are normally open from 9 a.m. till →

6 p.m. Monday to Friday but
closed on Saturday afternoons.
Some may close for one or two
hours at lunchtime.

poste restante postlagernd
[**p**osst-lahgernt]
pots and pans das
Kochgeschirr [ko**KH**gesheer]
potato die Kart**o**ffel
potato chips (US) die Chips
[chips]
potato salad der Kartoffelsalat
[kart**o**ffel-zal**ah**t]
pottery (objects) die
Töpferwaren [t**ur**pfer-vahren]
pound* (money, weight) das
Pfund [pfoont]
power cut der Stromausfall
[shtr**oh**m-owssfal]
power point die Steckdose
[sht**e**ck-dohz-uh]
practise: I want to practise my
German ich will mein
Deutsch üben [ish vill mine
doytch **oo**ben]
prawns die Kr**a**bben
prefer: I prefer ... ich mag
lieber ... [ish mahk l**ee**ber]
pregnant schwanger
[shv**a**ng-er]
prescription (for chemist) das
Rezept [rayts**e**pt]
present (gift) das Geschenk
[gesh**e**nk]
president der Präsident
[prezeed**e**nt]
pretty hübsch [h**oo**psh]

it's pretty expensive es ist
ganz schön teuer [gants shurn
t**oy**er]
price der Preis [price]
priest der Geistliche
[g**y**stlish-uh]
prime minister der
Premierminister [premy**ay**-
minister]
printed matter die Drucksache
[dr**oo**ck-zaKH-uh]
priority (in driving) die Vorfahrt
[**f**orfahrt]

Where there are no priority
signs, traffic coming from the
right has priority. Priority signs
are either a yellow lozenge
(priority road) or a red-rimmed
triangle with an arrow
(indicating priority for the next
cross-roads).

prison das Gefängnis [gef**e**ng-
niss]
private privat [priv**ah**t]
private bathroom das eigene
Bad [**ī**gen-uh baht]
private room das Einzelzimmer
[**ine**-tseltsimmer]
probably wahrscheinlich
[vahrsh**ine**-lish]
problem das Problem
[probl**ay**m]
no problem! kein Problem
[kine]
program(me) das Programm
promise: I promise ich
verspreche es [fairshrp**e**sh-uh]

pronounce: how is this
pronounced? wie spricht man
das aus? [vee shprisht man dass
owss]
properly (repaired, locked etc)
richtig [**r**ishtish]
protection factor der
Lichtschutzfaktor [**l**isht-
shoots-faktor]
Protestant evangelisch
[ayvang**ay**lish]
public convenience die
öffentliche Toilette
[**ur**fentlish-uh twal**e**tt-uh]
public holiday der gesetzliche
Feiertag [gez**e**tslish-uh **f**ire-
tahk]
pudding (dessert) der Nachtisch
[**n**aKHtish]
pull ziehen [ts**ee**-en]
pullover der Pullover
[pool**oh**vher]
puncture die Reifenpanne
[**r**yfen-pann-uh]
purple violett [vee-oh-l**e**tt]
purse (for money) das
Portemonnaie [port-mon**ay**]
(US) die Handtasche [h**a**nt-
tash-uh]
push schieben [sh**ee**ben]
pushchair der Sportwagen
[shp**o**rt-vahgen]
put tun [t**oo**n]
where can I put …? wo kann
ich … hinstellen? [h**i**n-
shtellen]
could you put us up for the
night? könnten Sie uns heute
nacht unterbringen? [oonss

h**oy**t-uh naKHt **oo**nterbringen]
pyjamas der Schlafanzug
[shl**a**hf-antsook]

Q

quality die Qualität [kvalit**ay**t]
quarantine die Quarantäne
[kvarant**ay**n-uh]
quarter das Viertel [**f**eertel]
quayside: on the quayside am
Kai [ky]
question die Frage [fr**a**hg-uh]
queue die Schlange [shl**a**ng-uh]
quick schnell [shnell]
that was quick das war
schnell [vahr]
what's the quickest way there?
wie komme ich am
schnellsten dorthin? [vee
komm-uh ish am shn**e**llsten
dort-hin]
fancy a quick drink? wollen
wir schnell einen trinken
gehen? [v**o**llen veer – **ine**-en
trinken g**ay**-en]
quickly schnell [shnell]
quiet (place, hotel) ruhig [r**oo**ish]
quiet! Ruhe! [r**oo**-uh]
quite (fairly) ziemlich
[ts**ee**mlish]
(very) ganz [gants]
that's quite right ganz recht
[resht]
quite a lot eine ganze Menge
[**ine**-uh gants-uh m**e**ng-uh]

R

rabbit das Kaninchen
[kaneenshen]

race (for runners, cars) das
Rennen

racket (squash, tennis etc) der
Schläger [shlayger]

radiator (in room) der
Heizkörper [hites-kurper]
(of car) der Kühler [kooler]

radio das Radio [rahdee-oh]
on the radio im Radio

rail: by rail per Bahn [pair]

railway die Eisenbahn
[īzenbahn]

rain der Regen [raygen]
in the rain im Regen
it's raining es regnet [raygnet]

raincoat der Regenmantel
[raygenmantel]

rape die Vergewaltigung
[fairgeval-tigoong]

rare (steak) englisch [eng-lish]

rash (on skin) der Ausschlag
[owss-shlahk]

raspberry die Himbeere
[himbair-uh]

rat die Ratte [ratt-uh]

rate (for changing money) der
Wechselkurs [veksel-koorss]

rather: it's rather good es ist
ganz gut [gants goot]
I'd rather ... ich würde
lieber ... [ish voord-uh leeber]

razor (electric) der
Rasierapparat [razeer-
apparaht]

razor blades die Rasierklingen

[razeer-klingen]

read lesen [layzen]

ready fertig [fairtish]
are you ready? bist du/sind
Sie fertig?
I'm not ready yet ich bin noch
nicht fertig [noKH nisht]

•••••• DIALOGUE ••••••

when will it be ready? wann ist es
fertig? [vann]
it should be ready in a couple of
days es müßte in ein paar Tagen
fertig sein [moosst-uh]

real echt [esht]

really wirklich [veerklish]
that's really great das ist echt
toll [esht tol]

rearview mirror der
Rückspiegel [rook-shpeegel]

reasonable (prices etc)
vernünftig [fairnoonftish]

receipt die Quittung [kvittoong]

recently kürzlich [koortslish]

reception (in hotel, for guests) der
Empfang
at reception am Empfang

reception desk die Rezeption
[retsepts-yohn]

receptionist die
Empfangsperson [empfangs-
pairzohn]

recognize erkennen [airkennen]

recommend: could you
recommend ...? könnten Sie ...
empfehlen? [kurnten zee ...
empfaylen]

record (music) die Schallplatte
[shallplat-uh]

Ra

red rot [roht]

red wine der Rotwein [**roht**vine]

refund (verb) erstatten [air-
sht**atten**]

can I have a refund? kann ich
das Geld zurückbekommen?
[kan ish dass gelt tsoor**OO**ck-
bekommen]

region das Gebiet [geb**eet**]

registered: by registered mail
per Einschreiben [pair **ine**-
shryben]

registration number die
Autonummer [**ow**to-
noommer]

relative der/die Verwandte
[fairv**an**t-uh]

religion die Religion [relig-y**oh**n]

remember: I don't remember ich
kann mich nicht erinnern
[ish kan mish nisht air-**innern**]

I remember ich erinnere mich
[air-**i**nner-uh]

do you remember? erinnern
Sie sich? [zee zish]

rent die Miete [m**eet**-uh]
(verb) mieten [m**eet**en]

for rent zu vermieten [ts**oo**
fairm**eet**en]

•••••• DIALOGUE ••••••

I'd like to rent a car ich möchte
ein Auto mieten [ish m**ur**sht-uh ine
owto]

for how long? für wie lange? [f**oo**r
vee l**a**ng-uh]

two days zwei Tage [t**ah**g-uh]

this is our range das ist unser
Angebot [**oo**nzer **an**-geboht]

I'll take the ... ich nehme den ...
[n**ay**m-uh dayn]

is that with unlimited mileage? ist
das ohne Kilometerbeschränkung? [**oh**n-uh keelo-m**ay**ter-
beshrenkoong]

it is ja [yah]

can I see your licence please? kann
ich bitte Ihren Führerschein
sehen? [**ee**ren f**oo**rer-shine]

and your passport und Ihren Paß
[pas]

is insurance included? ist
Versicherung inbegriffen?

yes, but you pay the first 200
marks ja, aber die ersten
zweihundert Mark müssen Sie
selbst bezahlen [zelpst bets**ah**len]

can you leave a deposit of ...?
könnten Sie eine Anzahlung von
hundert Mark leisten? [**ine**-uh
an-tsahloong – **ly**sten]

rented car das Mietauto [m**eet**-
owto]

repair (verb) reparieren
[repar**ee**ren]

can you repair it? können Sie
es reparieren? [k**ur**nen zee]

repeat wiederholen
[veederh**oh**len]

could you repeat that? können
Sie das noch einmal
wiederholen? [k**ur**nen zee
dass noKH **ine**-mahl]

reservation die Reservierung
[rezairv**ee**roong]

I'd like to make a reservation
ich möchte eine

Reservierung vornehmen
[mu**r**sht-uh **ine**-uh – for-
naymen]

•••••• DIALOGUE ••••••

I have a reservation ich habe eine
Reservierung [ish ha**h**b-uh]
yes sir, what name please? auf
welchen Namen, bitte? [owf
ve**l**shen n**ah**men]

reserve reservieren
[rezairve**e**ren]

•••••• DIALOGUE ••••••

can I reserve a table for tonight?
kann ich für heute abend einen
Tisch reservieren? [kan ish foor
ho**y**t-uh **ah**bent **ine**-en tish]
yes madam, for how many people?
ja, für wieviele Personen? [foor
vee ve**e**l-uh pairz**oh**nen]
for two für zwei [tsvy]
and for what time? und für welche
Zeit? [ve**l**sh-uh tsite]
for eight o'clock für acht Uhr [oor]
and could I have your name
please? und kann ich bitte Ihren
Namen haben? [**ee**ren n**ah**men]
see **alphabet**

rest: I need a rest ich brauche
Erholung [ish br**ow**KH-uh
airh**oh**loong]
  the rest of the group der Rest
  der Gru**pp**e
restaurant das Restaurant
  [restor**o**ng]

Italian, Greek, Turkish and
Chinese restaurants are very
popular with Germans, while
for traditional German food
you're best advised to try a
Gasthaus [ga**st**-howss] (inn) or
even a **Brauhaus** [br**ow**-
howss]. Look out for the set-
price menu (**Tageskarte**
[t**ah**gess-kart-uh]) which
usually offers 3-course meals at
very reasonable prices.

---

rest room (US) die Toilette
  [twal**e**tt-uh]
retired: I'm retired ich bin im
  Ruhestand [ish bin im r**oo**-uh-
  shtant]
return (ticket) die Rückfahrkarte [r**oo**ck-fahrkart-uh]

•••••• DIALOGUE ••••••

a return to Heilbronn eine
Rückfahrkarte nach Heilbr**o**nn
coming back when? wann soll die
Rückfahrt sein? [r**oo**ck-fahrt]

reverse charge call das
  R-Gespräch [**ai**r-geshpraysh]
reverse gear der
  Rückwärtsgang
  [r**oo**ckvairtsgang]
revolting ekelhaft [**ay**kelhaft]
Rhine der Rhein [rine]
rib die Rippe [r**i**pp-uh]
rice der Reis [rice]
rich (person) reich [rysh]
  (food) schwer [shvair]
ridiculous lächerlich [l**e**sherlish]

right (correct) richtig [rishtish]
(not left) rechts [reshts]
you were right Sie hatten
recht [resht]
that's right das stimmt
[shtimmt]
this can't be right das kann
nicht stimmen [nisht
shtimmen]
right! okay!
is this the right road for ...? ist
dies die Straße nach ...?
[deess]
on the right rechts
turn right biegen Sie rechts
ab [beegen zee – ap]
right-hand drive die
Rechtssteuerung [reshts-
shtoyeroong]
ring (on finger) der Ring
I'll ring you ich rufe Sie an
[ish roof-uh zee]
ring back zurückrufen
[tsooroock-roofen]
ripe (fruit) reif [rife]
rip-off: it's a rip-off das ist
Wucher [vooKHer]
rip-off prices Wucherpreise
[vooKHer-prize-uh]
risky riskant
river der Fluß [flooss]
road die Straße [shtrahss-uh]
is this the road for ...? ist dies
die Straße nach ...? [deess
dee – naKH]
down the road die Straße
entlang
road accident der Verkehrsunfall [fairkairss-oonfal]

road map die Straßenkarte
[shtrahssen-kart-uh]
roadsign das Verkehrszeichen
[fairkairs-tsyshen]
rob: I've been robbed ich bin
bestohlen worden [ish bin
beshtohlen vorden]
rock der Felsen [felzen]
(music) der Rock
on the rocks (with ice) mit Eis
[ice]
roll (bread) das Brötchen
[brurtchen]
roof das Dach [daKH]
roof rack der
Dachgepäckträger [daKH-
gepeck-trayger]
room das Zimmer [tsimmer]
in my room in meinem
Zimmer [mine-em]

•••••• DIALOGUE ••••••

do you have any rooms? haben
Sie Zimmer frei? [fry]
for how many people? für wie
viele Personen? [foor vee veel-uh
pairzohnen]
for one/for two für eine Person/
für zwei Personen
yes, we have rooms free ja, wir
haben Zimmer frei
for how many nights will it be? für
wie lange? [foor vee lang-uh]
just for one night nur für eine
Nacht [ine-uh naKHt]
how much is it? was kostet es?
... with bathroom and ... without
bathroom ... mit Bad und ... ohne
Bad [ohn-uh baht]

can I see a room with bathroom kann ich ein Zimmer mit Bad sehen? [**zay**-en]

ok, I'll take it gut, ich nehme es [**naym**-uh]

room service der Zimmerservice [**tsimmer'service'**]

rope das Seil [zile]

rosé (wine) der Roséwein [rohz**ay**-vine]

roughly (approximately) ungefähr [oongef**air**]

round: it's my round das ist meine Runde [m**ine**-uh r**oo**nd-uh]

roundabout (for traffic) der Kreisverkehr [kr**ice**-fairkair]

round trip ticket die Rückfahrkarte [r**oo**ck-fahrkart-uh]

see **return**

route die Strecke [shtr**eck**-uh]

what's the best route? welches ist der beste Weg? [v**el**shess ist dair b**e**st-uh vayk]

rubber (material) das Gummi [g**oo**mmee]

(eraser) der Radiergummi [rad**eer**-goommee]

rubber band das Gummiband [g**oo**mmee-bant]

rubbish (waste) der Abfall [**ap**-fal]

(poor quality goods) der Mist

rubbish! (nonsense) Quatsch! [kvatch]

rucksack der Rucksack [r**oo**ckzack]

rude unhöflich [**oo**n-hurflish]

ruins die Ruinen [roo-**ee**nen]

rum der Rum [roomm]

rum and coke ein Rum mit Cola [k**oh**la]

run (person) rennen, laufen [l**ow**fen]

how often do the buses run? wie oft fahren die Busse? [vee oft f**ah**ren dee b**oo**ss-uh]

I've run out of money ich habe kein Geld mehr [ish h**ah**b-uh kine gelt mair]

rush hour die Rush-hour

S

sad traurig [tr**ow**rish]

saddle der Sattel [z**a**ttel]

safe (not in danger) sicher [z**i**sher]

(not dangerous) ungefährlich [**oo**n-gefairlish]

safety pin die Sicherheitsnadel [z**i**sher-hites-nahdel]

sail das Segel [z**ay**gel]

sailboard das Windsurfbrett [v**i**nt-surfbrett]

sailboarding das Windsurfen [v**i**nt-surfen]

salad der Salat [zal**aht**]

salad dressing die Salatsoße [zal**aht**-zohss-uh]

sale: for sale zu verkaufen [tsoo fairk**ow**fen]

salmon der Lachs [lacks]

salt das Salz [zalts]

same: the same derselbe [dairz**e**lb-uh]

the same man/woman

derselbe Mann/dieselbe
Frau [deezelb-uh]
the same as this dasselbe wie
das [dasselb-uh vee]
the same again, please
dasselbe nochmal, bitte
[noKHmahl bitt-uh]
it's all the same to me das ist
mir ganz egal [meer gants
aygahl]
sand der Sand [zant]
sandals die Sandalen
[zandahlen]
sandwich das belegte Brot
[belaykt-uh broht]
sanitary napkin (US) die
Damenbinde
[dahmenbind-uh]
sanitary towel die Damenbinde
[dahmenbind-uh]
sardines die Sardinen
[zardeenen]
Saturday der Samstag
[zamstahk]
sauce die Soße [zohss-uh]
saucepan der Kochtopf
[koKHtopf]
saucer die Untertasse [oonter-
tass-uh]
sauna die Sauna [zownah]
sausage die Wurst [voorst]
say: how do you say ... in
German? was heißt ... auf
Deutsch? [vass hyst ... owf
doytch]
what did he say? was hat er
gesagt? [gezahkt]
I said ... ich sagte ...
[zahkt-uh]

he said ... er sagte ...
could you say that again?
könnten Sie das
wiederholen? [kurnten zee
dass veeder-hohlen]
scarf (for neck) der Schal [shahl]
(for head) das Kopftuch
[kopftooKH]
scenery die Landschaft [lant-
shafft]
schedule (US) der Fahrplan
[fahrplahn]
scheduled flight der Linienflug
[leen-yenflook]
school die Schule [shool-uh]
scissors: a pair of scissors eine
Schere [shair-uh]
scotch der Scotch
Scotch tape der Tesafilm®
[tayzahfilm]
Scotland Schottland [shottlant]
Scottish schottisch [shottish]
I'm Scottish (man/woman) ich
bin Schotte [shott-uh]/
Schottin
scrambled eggs die Rühreier
[roor-ier]
scratch der Kratzer [kratser]
screw die Schraube
[shrowb-uh]
screwdriver der Schrau-
benzieher [shrowben-tsee-er]
scrubbing brush (for hands) die
Handbürste [hant-boorst-uh]
(for floors) die Scheuerbürste
[shoyer-boorst-uh]
sea das Meer [mair]
by the sea am Meer
seafood die Meeresfrüchte

[**mai**ress-fr**oo**sht-uh]
seafood restaurant das
Fischrestaurant [fish-
restorong]
seafront die Strandpromenade
[shtr**a**nt-promen**ah**d-uh]
seagull die Möwe [m**u**rv-uh]
search (verb) suchen [z**oo**KHen]
seashell die Muschel
[m**oo**shel]
seasick: I feel seasick ich bin
seekrank [ish bin z**ay**krank]
I get seasick ich werde leicht
seekrank [v**ai**rd-uh lysht]
seaside: by the seaside am
Meer [mair]
seat der Sitzplatz [z**i**tsplats]
is this anyone's seat? sitzt
hier jemand? [zitst heer
y**ay**mant]
seat belt der Sicherheitsgurt
[z**i**sherhites-goort]
seaweed der Tang
secluded abgelegen
[**a**p-gelaygen]
second (adj) zweiter [tsv**y**ter]
(of time) die Sekunde
[zek**oo**nd-uh]
just a second! Moment mal!
[mahl]
second class zweiter Klasse
[tsv**y**ter kl**a**ss-uh]
second-hand gebraucht
[gebr**ow**KHt]
see sehen [z**ay**-en]
can I see? kann ich mal
sehen?
have you seen ...? haben
Sie ... gesehen? [h**ah**ben

zee ... gez**ay**-en]
I saw him this morning ich
habe ihn h**eu**te m**o**rgen
gesehen
see you! bis später!
[shp**ay**ter]
I see (I understand) ich
verstehe [fairst**ay**-uh]
self-catering apartment die
Ferienwohnung [f**ay**ree-en-
vohnoong]
self-service die
Selbstbedienung [z**e**lpst-
bedeenoong]
sell verkaufen [fairk**ow**fen]
do you sell ...? haben Sie ...?
[h**ah**ben zee]
Sellotape® der Tesafilm®
[t**ay**zahfilm]
send senden [z**e**nden]
I want to send this to England
ich möchte dies nach
England senden [ish m**u**rsht-
uh deess]
senior citizen (man/woman) der
Rentner/die Rentnerin
separate getrennt
separated: I'm separated ich
lebe getrennt [ish l**ay**b-uh]
separately (pay, travel) getrennt
September der September
[zept**e**mber]
septic vereitert [fair-**ī**tert]
serious ernst [airnst]
service charge (in restaurant) die
Bedienung [bed**ee**noong]
service station die Tankstelle
(mit Werkstatt) [t**a**nkshtell-uh
mit v**ai**rkshtatt]

serviette die Serviette [zairvee-ett-uh]

set menu die Tageskarte [tahgess-kart-uh]

several mehrere [mairer-uh]

sew nähen [nay-en]

could you sew this back on? können Sie das wieder annähen? [kurnen zee dass veeder an-nay-en]

sex der Sex

sexy sexy

shade: in the shade im Schatten [shatten]

shake: let's shake hands geben wir uns die Hand [gayben veer oonss dee hant]

shallow (water) seicht [zysht]

shame: what a shame! wie schade! [vee shahd-uh]

shampoo das Shampoo

can I have a shampoo and set? können Sie mir die Haare waschen und legen? [kurnen zee meer dee hahr-uh vashen oont laygen]

share (room, table etc) sich teilen [zish tylen]

sharp (knife, taste) scharf [sharf]

(pain) stechend [shteshent]

shattered (very tired) todmüde [tohtmood-uh]

shaver der Rasierapparat [razeer-apparaht]

shaving foam die Rasierseife [razeer-zife-uh]

shaving point die Steckdose für Rasierapparate [shteckdohz-uh foor razeer-apparaht-uh]

she* sie [zee]

is she here? ist sie hier? [heer]

sheet (for bed) das Laken [lahken]

shelf das Brett

shellfish die Schaltiere [shahl-teer-uh]

sherry der Sherry

ship das Schiff [shiff]

by ship mit dem Schiff

shirt das Hemd [hemt]

shit! Scheiße! [shice-uh]

shock der Schock [shock]

I got an electric shock from ... ich habe einen elektrischen Schlag von ... bekommen [ish hahb-uh ine-en aylektrishen shlahk fon]

shock-absorber der Stoßdämpfer [shtohss-dempfer]

shocking (behaviour, prices) skandalös [skandalurss]

(custom etc) schockierend [shockeerent]

shoe der Schuh [shoo]

a pair of shoes ein Paar Schuhe [pahr shoo-uh]

shoelaces die Schnürsenkel [shnoor-zenkel]

shoe polish die Schuhcreme [shoo-kraym]

shoe repairer der Schuhmacher [shoo-maKHer]

shop das Geschäft [gesheft]

Shops generally open between 8.30 and 10 a.m. and close at 6.30 p.m. Mondays to Fridays. On Saturdays, shops close at 2 p.m. except for the first Saturday in each month when, at least in the town centres, shops do not close until 6 p.m. On Thursdays many shops remain open until about 8 p.m. (**langer Donnerstag**). Sunday opening is under debate, but do not expect to be able to do any shopping on a Sunday.

shopping: I'm going shopping ich gehe einkaufen [ish **gay**-uh **ine**-kowfen]

shopping centre das Einkaufszentrum [**ine**-kowfss-tsentroom]

shop window das Schaufenster [**show**fenster]

shore (of sea) der Strand [shtrant]

(of lake) das Ufer [**OO**fer]

short (time, journey) kurz [koorts]

(person) klein [kline]

shortcut die Abkürzung [**ap**-k**OO**rtsoong]

shorts die Shorts

should: what should I do? was soll ich machen? [vass zoll ish m**a**kHen]

he shouldn't be long er kommt sicher bald [air kommt z**i**sher balt]

you should have told me das hätten Sie mir sagen sollen [h**e**tten zee meer z**ah**gen zollen]

shoulder die Schulter [sh**oo**lter]

shout (verb) schreien [shr**y**-en]

show (in theatre) die Vorstellung [f**or**-shtelloong]

could you show me? könnten Sie mir das zeigen? [k**ur**nten zee meer dass ts**y**gen]

shower (in bathroom) die Dusche [d**OO**sh-uh]

with shower mit Dusche

shower gel das Duschgel [d**OO**sh-gayl]

shut (verb) schließen [shl**ee**ssen]

when do you shut? wann machen Sie zu? [vann m**a**kHen zee ts**OO**]

when do they shut? wann machen sie zu?

they're shut sie sind geschlossen [geshl**o**ssen]

I've shut myself out ich habe mich ausgesperrt [ish h**ah**b-uh mish **ow**ss-geshpairt]

shut up! halt den Mund! [dayn moont]

shutter (on camera) der Verschluß [fairshl**oo**ss]

shutters (on window) die Fensterläden [fenster-layden]

shy (person) schüchtern [sh**OO**shtern]

(animal) scheu [shoy]

sick (ill) krank

I'm going to be sick (vomit) ich muß mich übergeben [ish mooss mish ꝏbergayben]

side die Seite [zite-uh]
  the other side of town das
  andere Ende der Stadt
  [ander-uh end-uh dair shtatt]
side lights das Standlicht
  [shtantlisht]
side salad die Salatbeilage
  [zalaht-bylahg-uh]
side street die Seitenstraße
  [zyten-shtrass-uh]
sidewalk (US) der Bürgersteig
  [boorgershtike]
sight: the sights of ... die
  Sehenswürdigkeiten von ...
  [zay-ens-voordish-kyten fon]
sightseeing: we're going
  sightseeing wir machen eine
  Rundfahrt [veer maKHen ine-
  uh roont-fahrt]
  (on foot) wir machen einen
  Rundgang [ine-en roont-gang]
sightseeing tour die Rundfahrt
  [roont-fahrt]
sign das Schild [shilt]
  (roadsign) das Verkehrszeichen [fairkairs-tsyshen]
signal: he didn't give a signal
  (driver) er hat nicht geblinkt
  (cyclist) er hat keine Richtung
  angezeigt [kine-uh rishtoong
  an-getsykt]
signature die Unterschrift
  [oonter-shrift]
signpost der Wegweiser [vayk-
  vyzer]
silence die Ruhe [roo-uh]
silk die Seide [zyduh]
silly (person) albern [al-bairn]

(thing to do etc) dumm [doomm]

silver das Silber [zilber]
silver foil die Alufolie [ahloo-
  fohl-yuh]
similar ähnlich [aynlish]
simple (easy) einfach [ine-faKH]
since: since yesterday seit
  gestern [zite]
  since I got here seit ich hier
  bin [heer]
sing singen [zingen]
singer (man/woman) der Sänger
  [zenger]/die Sängerin
single (not married)
  unverheiratet [oon-fair-
  hyrahtet]
  a single to ... eine einfache
  Fahrt nach ... [ine-uh ine-
  faKH-uh fahrt naKH]
single bed das Einzelbett [ine-
  tsel-bett]
single room das Einzelzimmer
  [ine-tsel-tsimmer]
sink (in kitchen) die Spüle
  [shpool-uh]
sister die Schwester [shvester]
sister-in-law die Schwägerin
  [shvaygerin]
sit: can I sit here? kann ich
  mich hier hinsetzen? [ish
  mish heer hinzetsen]
  is anyone sitting here? sitzt
  hier jemand? [zitst heer
  yaymant]
sit down sich hinsetzen [zish
  hinzetsen]
  do sit down nehmen Sie Platz
  [naymen zee plats]
size die Größe [grurss-uh]

ENGLISH ❖ GERMAN | Si

ski der Ski [shee]
  (verb) skifahren [sheefahren]
  a pair of skis ein Paar Skier
  [pahr shee-er]
ski boots die Skistiefel [shee-
  shteefel]
skiing das Skifahren
  [sheefahren]
  we're going skiing wir gehen
  Skilaufen [veer gay-en shee-
  lowfen]
ski instructor (man/woman) der
  Skilehrer [shee-lairer]/die
  Skilehrerin
ski-lift der Skilift [sheelift]
skin die Haut [howt]
skinny dünn [dOOnn]
ski-pants die Skihose [shee-
  hohz-uh]
ski-pass der Skipaß [sheepas]
ski pole der Skistock
  [sheeshtock]
skirt der Rock
ski run die Skipiste [shee-
  pist-uh]
ski slope die Skipiste [shee-
  pist-uh]
ski wax das Skiwachs
  [sheevacks]
sky der Himmel
sleep schlafen [shlahfen]
  did you sleep well? haben Sie
  gut geschlafen? [hahben zee
  gOOt geshlahfen]
  I need a good sleep ich muß
  mich mal richtig
  ausschlafen [rishtish owss-
  shlahfen]
sleeper (on train) der

Schlafwagen [shlahfvahgen]
sleeping bag der Schlafsack
  [shlahfzack]
sleeping car der Schlafwagen
  [shlahfvahgen]
sleeping pill die Schlaftablette
  [shlahf-tablett-uh]
sleepy: I'm feeling sleepy ich
  bin müde [ish bin mOOd-uh]
sleeve der Ärmel [airmel]
slide (photographic) das Dia
  [dee-ah]
slip (under dress) der Unterrock
  [oonter-rock]
slippery glatt
Slovak (adj) slowakisch
  [slovahkish]
Slovak Republic die
  Slowakische Republik
  [slovahkish-uh repOObleek]
slow langsam [langzahm]
  slow down! etwas langsamer
  bitte [etvass]
slowly langsam [langzahm]
  could you say it slowly?
  könnten Sie das etwas
  langsamer sagen? [kurnten
  zee dass etvass langzahmer
  zahgen]
  very slowly ganz langsam
  [gants]
small klein [kline]
smell: it smells es stinkt
  [shtinkt]
smile (verb) lächeln [lesheln]
smoke der Rauch [rowKH]
  do you mind if I smoke?
  macht es Ihnen etwas aus,
  wenn ich rauche? [maKHt ess

een-en etvass owss venn ish
rowKH-uh]
I don't smoke ich bin
Nichtraucher [nishtrowKHer]
do you smoke? rauchen Sie?
[rowKHen zee]
snack: I'd just like a snack ich
möchte nur eine Kleinigkeit
[ish mursht-uh noor ine-uh
klynish-kite]
sneeze (verb) niesen [neezen]
snorkel der Schnorchel
[shnorshel]
snow der Schnee [shnay]
it's snowing es schneit
[shnite]
so: it's so good es ist so gut [zo
goot]
not so fast nicht so schnell
so am I ich auch [ish owKH]
so do I ich auch
so-so einigermaßen [ine-iger-
mahssen]
soaking solution (for contact
lenses) die Aufbewahrungslösung [owfbevahroongs-
lurzoong]
soap die Seife [zyfuh]
soap powder das Waschpulver
[vashpoolver]
sober nüchtern [nooshtern]
sock die Socke [zock-uh]
socket (electrical) die Steckdose
[shteck-dohz-uh]
soda (water) das Sodawasser
[zohda-vasser]
sofa das Sofa [zohfa]
soft (material etc) weich [vysh]
soft-boiled egg das

weichgekochte Ei [vysh-
gekoKHt-uh ī]
soft drink das alkoholfreie
Getränk [alkohohlfry-uh
getrenk], der Soft drink
soft lenses die weichen
Kontaktlinsen [vyshen
kontakt-linzen]
sole die Sohle [zohl-uh]
could you put new soles on
these? können Sie diese
Schuhe neu besohlen?
[kurnen zee deez-uh shoo-uh
noy bezohlen]
some: can I have some water/
rolls? kann ich etwas Wasser/
ein paar Brötchen haben?
[etvass vasser/ine pahr brurt-
shen hahben]
can I have some of those?
kann ich ein paar davon
haben? [da-fon]
somebody, someone jemand
[yaymant]
something etwas [etvass]
something to drink etwas zu
trinken
sometimes manchmal
[manshmahl]
somewhere irgendwo
[eergentvo]
son der Sohn [zohn]
song das Lied [leet]
son-in-law der Schwiegersohn
[shveeger-zohn]
soon bald [balt]
I'll be back soon ich bin bald
zurück [ish bin balt tsooroock]
as soon as possible so bald

wie möglich [vee **mur**glish]

sore: it's sore es tut weh [tOOt vay]

sore throat die Halsschmerzen pl [h**a**ls-shmairtsen]

sorry: (I'm) sorry tut mir leid [tOOt meer lite]

sorry? (didn't understand) wie bitte? [vee b**i**tt-uh]

sort: what sort of ...? welche Art von ...? [v**e**lsh-uh art fon]

soup die Suppe [z**OO**p-uh]

sour (taste) sauer [z**ow**er]

south der Süden [z**OO**den]

in the south im Süden

to the south nach Süden

South Africa Südafrika [zOOt-**a**frika]

South African (adj) südafrikanisch [zOOt-afrik**ah**nish]

I'm South African (man/woman) ich bin Südafrikaner [zOOt-afrik**ah**ner]/Südafrikanerin

southeast der Südosten [zOOt-**o**sten]

southwest der Südwesten [zOOt-**ve**sten]

souvenir das Souven**i**r

spa der Kurort [k**OO**r-ort]

spanner der Schraubenschlüssel [shr**ow**ben-shl**OO**sel]

spare part das Ersatzteil [airz**a**ts-tile]

spare tyre der Ersatzreifen [airz**a**ts-ryfen]

spark plug die Zündkerze [ts**OO**nt-kairts-uh]

speak: do you speak English? sprechen Sie Englisch? [shpr**e**shen zee **e**ng-lish]

I don't speak ... ich spreche kein ... [ish shpr**e**sh-uh kine]

•••••• DIALOGUE ••••••

can I speak to Wolfgang? kann ich Wolfgang sprechen?

who's calling? wer spricht bitte? [vair shprisht b**i**tt-uh]

it's Patricia Patricia

I'm sorry, he's not in, can I take a message? tut mir leid, er ist nicht da, kann ich etwas ausrichten? [tOOt meer lite, air ist nisht da, kann ish **e**tvass **ow**ss-rishten]

no thanks, I'll call back later nein danke, ich rufe später nochmal an [nine d**a**nk-uh, ish r**OO**f-uh shp**ay**ter n**o**KHmahl an]

please tell him I called bitte sagen Sie ihm, daß ich angerufen habe [z**ah**gen zee eem, dass ish **a**n-ger**oo**fen h**ah**b-uh]

speciality die Spezialität [shpets-yalit**ay**t]

spectacles die Brille [br**i**ll-uh]

speed die Geschwindigkeit [geshv**i**ndish-kite]

speed limit die Geschwindigkeitsbeschränkung [geshv**i**ndishkites-beshr**e**nkoong]

Speed limits are 50 km/h (31 mph) in towns and 100 km/h (62 mph) out of town, except on motorways (**Autobahnen**). →

There is still no nationwide speed limit on German motorways, although relatively few stretches are without any restrictions at all.

speedometer der Tachometer [taKHom**ay**ter]

spell: how do you spell it? wie schreibt man das? [vee shrypt man dass]

see **alphabet**

spend ausgeben [**ow**ssgayben] (time) verbringen [fairbr**i**ng-en]

spider die Spinne [shp**i**nn-uh]

spin-dryer die Schleuder [shl**oy**der]

splinter der Splitter [shpl**i**tter]

spoke (in wheel) die Speiche [shp**y**sh-uh]

spoon der Löffel [l**ur**fel]

sport der Sport [shport]

sprain: I've sprained my ... ich habe mein ... verstaucht [ish h**ah**b-uh mine ... fair-sht**ow**KHt]

spring (season) der Frühling [fr**oo**ling] (of car, seat) die Feder [f**ay**der]

square (in town) der Platz [plats]

stairs die Treppe [tr**e**pp-uh]

stale (bread) alt (drink) abgestanden [**a**p-geshtanden]

stall: the engine keeps stalling der Motor geht dauernd aus [dair m**oh**tohr gayt d**ow**ernt owss]

stamp die Briefmarke [br**ee**fmark-uh]

Stamps can be bought at post offices, from yellow vending machines (at post offices, stations, airports) and at some newspaper kiosks.

•••••• DIALOGUE ••••••

a stamp for England, please eine Marke nach England bitte [**ine**-uh m**a**rk-uh naKH]

what are you sending? was möchten Sie senden? [vass m**u**rshten zee z**e**nden]

this postcard diese Postkarte [d**ee**z-uh p**o**sstkart-uh]

standby: standby ticket das Standby-Ticket

star der Stern [shtairn] (in film) der Star

start der Anfang [**a**nfang] (verb) **a**nfangen

when does it start? wann fängt es an? [van fengt ess an]

the car won't start das Auto springt nicht an [dass **ow**to shpringt nisht an]

starter (of car) der **A**nlasser (food) die Vorspeise [for-shp**i**ze-uh]

state (in country) das Land [lant] **the States** (USA) die USA [oo-ess-**ah**]

station der Bahnhof [b**ah**nhohf]

statue die Statue [sht**ah**-too-uh]

stay: where are you staying? wo

wohnen Sie? [vo **voh**nen zee]
I'm staying at ... ich wohne
in ... [ish **voh**n-uh]
I'd like to stay another two
nights ich möchte gern noch
zwei Tage bleiben [m**ur**sht-uh
gairn noKH – **tah**g-uh bl**y**ben]
steak das Steak
steal stehlen [sht**ay**len]
my bag has been stolen
meine Tasche ist gestohlen
worden [gesht**oh**len v**or**den]
steep (hill) steil [sht**i**le]
steering die Lenkung [l**e**nkoong]
step: on the steps auf den
Stufen [owf dayn sht**oo**fen]
stereo die Stereoanlage
[sht**ay**ray-oh-anlahg-uh]
sterling das Pfund Sterling
[pf**oo**nt]
steward (on plane) der Steward
stewardess die Stewardeß
sticking plaster das
Heftpflaster
still: I'm still waiting ich warte
immer noch [v**a**rt-uh – n**o**KH]
is he still there? ist er noch
da?
keep still! stillhalten! [sht**i**ll-
halten]
sting: I've been stung ich bin
gestochen worden
[gesht**o**KHen v**or**den]
stockings die Strümpfe
[sht**roo**mpf-uh]
stomach der Magen [m**ah**gen]
stomach ache die
Magenschmerzen [m**ah**gen-
shmairtsen]

stone (rock) der Stein [sht**i**ne]
stop (verb) **a**nhalten
please, stop here (to taxi driver
etc) bitte halten Sie hier [b**i**tt-
uh h**a**l-ten zee heer]
do you stop near ...? halten
Sie in der Nähe von ...?
[n**ay**-uh]
stop doing that! hören Sie auf
damit! [h**ur**-ren zee owf damit]
stopover die Zwischenstation
[tsv**i**shen-shtats-yohn]
storm der Sturm [sht**oo**rm]
straight: it's straight ahead es ist
geradeaus [ger**ah**d-uh-**ow**ss]
a straight whisky ein Whisky
pur [p**oo**r]
straightaway sofort [z**o**fort]
strange (odd) seltsam [z**e**ltzahm]
stranger (man/woman) der/die
Fremde [fr**e**md-uh]
I'm a stranger here ich bin
hier fremd [heer fremt]
strap (on watch) das Band [bant]
(on dress) der Träger [tr**ay**ger]
(on suitcase) der Riemen
[r**ee**men]
strawberry die Erdbeere
[**a**irtbair-uh]
stream der Bach [baKH]
street die Straße [sht**rah**ss-uh]
on the street auf der Straße
[owf dair]
streetmap der Stadtplan
[sht**a**ttplahn]
string die Schnur [shn**oo**r]
strong (person, drink) stark
[sht**a**rk]
(taste) kräftig [kr**e**ftish]

stuck: the key's stuck der
Schlüssel steckt fest [shteckt]

student (male/female) der
Student/die Studentin
[shtoodent]

stupid dumm [doomm]

suburb die Vorstadt [for-shtatt]

subway (US) die U-Bahn
[oo-bahn]

suddenly plötzlich [plurtslish]

suede das Wildleder [vilt-
layder]

sugar der Zucker [tsoocker]

suit der Anzug [antsook]

it doesn't suit me (jacket etc) es
steht mir nicht [shtayt meer
nisht]

it suits you es steht Ihnen
[eenen]

suitcase der Koffer

summer der Sommer [zommer]

in the summer im Sommer

sun die Sonne [zonn-uh]

in the sun in der Sonne

out of the sun im Schatten
[shatten]

sunbathe sonnenbaden
[zonnen-bahden]

sunblock (cream) die Sun-
Block-Creme [-kraym]

sunburn der Sonnenbrand
[zonnen-brant]

sunburnt: to get sunburnt einen
Sonnenbrand bekommen
[ine-en zonnen-brant]

Sunday der Sonntag [zonntahk]

sunglasses die Sonnenbrille
[zonnen-brill-uh]

sun lounger der Ruhesessel

[roo-uh-zessel]

sunny: it's sunny die Sonne
scheint [dee zonn-uh shynt]

sun roof (in car) das
Schiebedach [sheeb-uh-daKH]

sunset der Sonnenuntergang
[zonnen-oontergang]

sunshade der Sonnenschirm
[zonnen-sheerm]

sunshine der Sonnenschein
[zonnen-shine]

sunstroke der Sonnenstich
[zonnen-shtish]

suntan die Sonnenbräune
[zonnen-broyn-uh]

suntan lotion die Sonnenmilch
[zonnen-milsh]

suntanned braungebrannt
[brown-gebrannt]

suntan oil das Sonnenöl
[zonnen-url]

super fantastisch [fantastish]

supermarket der Supermarkt
[zoopermarkt]

supper das Abendessen
[ahbent-essen]

supplement (extra charge) der
Zuschlag [tsooshlahk]

sure: are you sure? bist du/sind
Sie sicher? [bist doo/zint zee
zisher]

sure! klar!

surname der Nachname
[naKHnahm-uh]

swearword der Kraftausdruck
[kraft-owssdroock]

sweater der Pullover
[poolohver]

sweatshirt das Sweatshirt

Sweden Schweden [shvayden]
Swedish schwedisch
 [shvaydish]
sweet (taste) süß [zooss]
 (noun: dessert) der Nachtisch
 [naкнtish]
sweets die Süßigkeiten
 [zoossish-kyten]
swelling die Schwellung
 [shvelloong]
swim (verb) schwimmen
 [shvimmen]
 I'm going for a swim ich gehe
  schwimmen [gay-uh]
 let's go for a swim gehen wir
  schwimmen [gay-en veer]
swimming costume der
 Badeanzug [bahd-uh-antsook]
swimming pool das
 Schwimmbad [shvimmbaht]
swimming trunks die Badehose
 [bahd-uh-hohz-uh]
Swiss (man/woman) der
 Schweizer [shvytser]/die
 Schweizerin
 (adj) schweizerisch
 [shvytserish]
 the Swiss die Schweizer
Swiss Alps die Schweizer
 Alpen [shvytser]
switch der Schalter [shalter]
switch off (TV, lights)
 ausschalten [owss-shalten]
 (engine) abstellen [ap-shtellen]
switch on (TV, lights)
 einschalten [ine-shalten]
 (engine) anlassen
Switzerland die Schweiz
 [shvites]

swollen geschwollen
 [geshvollen]

T

table der Tisch [tish]
 a table for two ein Tisch für
  zwei Personen [foor tsvy
  pairzohnen]
tablecloth das Tischtuch
 [tishtooкн]
table tennis das Tischtennis
 [tishtennis]
table wine der Tafelwein
 [tahfelvine]
tailback (of traffic) der Rückstau
 [roock-shtow]
tailor der Schneider [shnyder]
take (lead) bringen
 (accept) nehmen [naymen]
 can you take me to the airport?
  können Sie mich zum
  Flughafen bringen? [kurnen
  zee mish tsoom]
 do you take credit cards?
  nehmen Sie Kreditkarten?
 fine, I'll take it gut, ich nehme
  es [goot, ish naym-uh ess]
 can I take this? (leaflet etc)
  kann ich das mitnehmen?
  [mitnaymen]
 how long does it take? wie
  lange dauert es? [vee lang-uh
  dowert ess]
 it takes three hours es dauert
  drei Stunden
 is this seat taken? ist dieser
  Platz besetzt? [deezer plats
  bezetst]

hamburger to take away
Hamburger zum Mitnehmen
[tsoom]

can you take a little off here?
(to hairdresser) können Sie hier
etwas kürzen? [**kur**nen zee
heer **e**tvass k**oo**rtsen]

talcum powder der
Körperpuder [**kur**per-p**oo**der]

talk (verb) sprechen [shpr**e**shen]

tall (person) groß [grohss]
(building) hoch [hohKH]

tampons die Tampons

tan die Bräune [br**oy**n-uh]
to get a tan braun werden
[brown **vai**rden]

tank (of car) der Tank

tap der Wasserhahn
[**va**sserhahn]

tape (for cassette) das Band
[bant]
(sticky) das Klebeband [kl**ay**b-
uh-bant]

tape measure das Bandmaß
[**ba**ntmahss]

tape recorder der
Kassettenrecorder

taste der Geschmack
[geshm**a**ck]
can I taste it? kann ich es
probieren? [prob**ee**ren]

taxi das Taxi
will you get me a taxi? können
Sie mir ein Taxi bestellen?
[**kur**nen zee meer]
where can I find a taxi? wo
bekomme ich ein Taxi? [vo
bek**o**mm-uh ish]

Taxis have a sign on the roof
which is illuminated when the
taxi is free. You can hail them
in the street, but Germans tend
to wait at taxi ranks (always to
be found at train stations and
near big hotels) or to phone.

•••••• DIALOGUE ••••••

to the airport/to Hotel ... please
zum Flughafen/zum Hotel ...
bitte [tsoom]

how much will it be? was kostet
das?

thirty marks dreißig Mark

that's fine right here thanks bis
hierhin, danke [heer-hin]

taxi-driver der Taxifahrer

taxi rank der Taxistand [t**a**ksi-
shtant]

tea (drink) der Tee [tay]
tea for one/two please Tee für
eine Person/zwei Personen
bitte [foor **ine**-uh pairz**oh**n/tsvy
pairz**oh**nen b**i**tt-uh]

teabag der Teebeutel
[**tay**boytel]

teach: could you teach me?
könnten Sie es mir
beibringen? [**kur**nten zee ess
meer b**y**bringen]

teacher (man/woman) der Lehrer
[**lai**rer]/die Lehrerin

team das Team

teaspoon der Teelöffel [**tay**-
lurfel]

tea towel das Geschirrtuch
[gesh**ee**r-t**oo**KH]

teenager der Teenager

telegram das Telegramm

telephone das Telefon
[telef**ohn**]
see **phone**

television das Fernsehen [f**airn**-zay-en]

tell: could you tell him ...?
können Sie ihm sagen ...?
[**kur**nen zee eem **zah**gen]

temperature (weather) die
Temperatur [temperat**oo**r]
(fever) das Fieber [**fee**ber]

tennis das Tennis

tennis ball der Tennisball
[**te**nnis-bal]

tennis court der Tennisplatz
[**te**nnis-plats]

tennis racket der Tennis-
schläger [**te**nnis-shlayger]

tent das Zelt [tselt]

term (at school) das Halbjahr
[**ha**lp-yar]
(at university) das Semester
[zem**e**ster]

terminus (rail) die Endstation
[**e**nt-shtats-yohn]

terrible furchtbar [**foo**rshtbar]

terrific sagenhaft [**zah**genhaft]

than* als [alss]
smaller than kleiner als

thanks, thank you danke
[**da**nk-uh]
thank you very much vielen
Dank [**fee**len]
thanks for the lift danke fürs
Mitnehmen [foors **mi**tnaymen]
no thanks nein danke [nine]

thanks danke

that's OK, don't mention it bitte
[b**i**tt-uh]

that: that man dieser Mann
[d**ee**zer]
that woman diese Frau
[d**ee**z-uh]
that one das da
I hope that ... ich hoffe,
daß ... [dass]
that's nice das ist schön
is that ...? ist das ...?
that's it (that's right) genau
[gen**ow**]

the* (singular) der/die/das [dair/
dee/dass]
(plural) die [dee]

theatre das Theater [tay**ah**ter]

their* ihr/ihre [eer/**ee**r-uh]

theirs* ihrer [**ee**r-er]

them* sie [zee]
for them für sie [f**oo**r]
with them mit ihnen [**ee**n-en]
I gave it to them ich habe es
ihnen gegeben [h**ah**b-uh]

then (at that time) damals
[d**ah**malss]
(after that) dann

there da, dort
over there dort drüben
[dr**oo**ben]
up there da oben
is there ...? gibt es ...? [geept]
are there ...? gibt es ...?
there is ... es gibt ...
there are ... es gibt ...
there you are (giving something)

bitte [bitt-uh]

thermometer das Thermometer [tairmo-**may**ter]

thermos flask die Thermosflasche [t**air**moss-flash-uh]

these*: these men diese Männer [d**ee**z-uh]

these women diese Frauen can I have these? kann ich diese hier haben? [heer]

they* sie [zee]

thick dick

(stupid) blöd [blurt]

thief der Dieb [deep]

thigh der Schenkel [sh**en**kel]

thin dünn [dꝏn]

thing das Ding

my things meine Sachen [m**ine**-uh za**KH**en]

think denken

I think so ich glaube ja [gl**ow**b-uh ya]

I don't think so ich glaube nicht [nisht]

I'll think about it ich werde darüber nachdenken [v**air**d-uh dar**ꝏ**ber na**KH**denken]

third party insurance die Haftpflichtversicherung [h**a**ft-pflisht-fairz**i**sheroong]

thirsty: I'm thirsty ich habe Durst [h**a**hb-uh doorst]

this: this man dieser Mann [d**ee**zer]

this woman diese Frau [d**ee**z-uh]

this one dieser/diese/dieses [d**ee**zess]

this is my wife das ist meine Frau [m**ine**-uh frow]

is this ...? ist das ...?

those: those men diese Männer [d**ee**z-uh]

those women diese Frauen which ones? – those welche? – diese [v**el**sh-uh]

thread der Faden [f**ah**den]

throat der Hals [halss]

throat pastilles die Halstabletten [h**a**lss-tabletten]

through durch [doorsh]

does it go through ...? (train, bus) fährt er über ...? [fairt air **ꝏ**ber]

throw (verb) werfen [v**air**fen]

throw away (verb) wegwerfen [v**e**kvairfen]

thumb der Daumen [d**ow**men]

thunderstorm das Gewitter [gev**i**tter]

Thursday der Donnerstag [d**o**nnerstahk]

ticket (train, bus, boat) die Fahrkarte [f**ah**rkart-uh]

(plane) das Ticket

(theatre, cinema) die Eintrittskarte [**ine**-trittskart-uh]

(cloakroom) die Garderobenmarke [garder**oh**ben-mark-uh]

•••••• DIALOGUE ••••••

a return ticket to Heidelberg eine Rückfahrkarte nach Heidelberg

coming back when? wann soll die Rückfahrt sein? [r**ꝏ**ck-fahrt]

today/next Tuesday heute/
nächsten Dienstag
that will be two hundred and ten
marks das macht
zweihundertzehn Mark

ticket office (bus, rail) der
Fahrkartenschalter
[**fahr**karten-shalter]
tide: high tide die Flut [fl00t]
low tide die Ebbe [**e**bb-uh]
tie (necktie) die Krawatte
[krav**a**tt-uh]
tight (clothes etc) eng
it's too tight es ist zu eng
[ts00]
tights die Strumpfhose
[shtr**oo**mpf-hohz-uh]
till (cash desk) die Kasse
[**ka**ss-uh]
time* die Zeit [tsite]
what's the time? wie spät ist
es? [vee shpayt ist ess]
this time diesmal [**dee**ssmahl]
last time letztes Mal [**le**tstess
mahl]
next time nächstes Mal
[**nay**kstess]
four times viermal [**fee**rmahl]
timetable der Fahrplan
[**fahr**plahn]
tin (can) die Dose [d**oh**z-uh]
tinfoil die Alufolie [**ah**l00-fohl-
yuh]
tin opener der Dosenöffner
[d**oh**zen-urfner]
tiny winzig [**vin**tsish]
tip (to waiter etc) das Trinkgeld
[tr**i**nkgelt]

Prices in pubs and restaurants
usually include a service charge,
but it is still customary to leave
a tip of around 5-10% if you are
happy with the service received.

tired müde [m**oo**d-uh]
I'm tired ich bin müde
tissues die Papiertücher
[pap**ee**r-t00sher]
to: to Freiburg/London nach
Freiburg/London [naKH]
to Germany/England nach
Deutschland/England
to the post office zum
Postamt [tsoom]
to the bank zur Bank [ts00r]
toast (bread) der Toast
today heute [h**oyt**-uh]
toe der Zeh [tsay]
together zusammen
[tsooz**a**mmen]
we're together (in shop etc) wir
sind zusammen [veer zint]
can we pay together? können
wir zusammen bezahlen?
[**kur**nen veer – bets**ah**len]
toilet die Toilette [twal**ett**-uh]
where is the toilet? wo ist die
Toilette? [vo]
I have to go to the toilet ich
muß zur Toilette [ts00r]

The signs on toilets are H
(= Herren) for men and D
(= Damen) for women. Public
conveniences are not especially
numerous.

toilet paper das
Toilettenpapier [twaletten-
papeer]
tomato die Tomate [tomaht-uh]
tomato juice der Tomatensaft
[tomahtenzaft]
tomato ketchup der
Tomatenketchup
tomorrow morgen
tomorrow morning morgen
früh [froo]
the day after tomorrow
übermorgen [OObermorgen]
toner (cosmetic) die
Tönungslotion [turnoongs-
lohts-yohn]
tongue die Zunge [tsoong-uh]
tonic (water) das Tonic
tonight heute abend [hoyt-uh
ahbent]
tonsillitis die Mandel-
entzündung [mandel-ent-
tsoondoong]
too (excessively) zu [tsoo]
(also) auch [owKH]
too hot zu heiß [hice]
too much zuviel [tsoofeel]
me too ich auch [ish]
tooth der Zahn [tsahn]
toothache die Zahnschmerzen
[tsahn-shmairtsen]
toothbrush die Zahnbürste
[tsahn-boorst-uh]
toothpaste die Zahnpasta
[tsahnpasta]
top: on top of ... oben auf...
[ohben owf]
at the top oben
top floor der oberste Stock

[ohberst-uh shtock]
topless oben ohne [ohben
ohn-uh]
torch die Taschenlampe
[tashenlamp-uh]
total die Endsumme
[entzoom-uh]
what's the total? was macht
das zusammen? [vass maKHt
dass tsoozammen]
tour (journey) die Reise [rize-uh]
is there a tour of ...? gibt es
eine Führung durch...?
[geept ess ine-uh fOOroong
doorsh]
tour guide der Reiseleiter [rize-
uh-lyter]
tourist (man/woman) der Tourist
[tOOrist]/die Touristin
tourist information office das
Fremdenverkehrsbüro
[fremden-fairkairs-bOOroh]
tour operator der
Reiseveranstalter [rize-uh-
fairanshtalter]
towards nach [naKH]
towel das Handtuch [hant-
tOOKH]
town die Stadt [shtatt]
in town in der Stadt [dair]
just out of town am Stadtrand
[shtattrant]
town centre die Innenstadt
[innen-shtatt]
town hall das Rathaus [raht-
howss]
toy das Spielzeug [shpeel-tsoyk]
track (US: at train station) der
Bahnsteig [bahnshtike]

tracksuit der Trainingsanzug [tra**i**nings-**a**ntsook]

traditional traditionell [tradits-yohn**e**ll]

traffic der Verkehr [fairk**a**ir]

traffic jam der Stau [shtow]

traffic lights die **A**mpel

trailer (for carrying tent etc) der Anhänger [**a**nheng-er] (US: caravan) der Wohnwagen [v**oh**nvahgen]

trailer park (US) der Wohnwagenplatz [v**oh**nvahgen-plats]

train der Zug [ts**oo**k]
  by train mit dem Zug [daym]

•••••• DIALOGUE ••••••

is this the train for ...? fährt dieser Zug nach ...? [fairt d**ee**zer tsook naKH]

sure ja [yah]

no, you want that platform there nein, gehen Sie zu dem Bahnsteig da [nine, g**ay**-en zee tsoo daym b**ah**nshtike]

trainers (shoes) die Turnschuhe [t**oo**rnsho-uh]

train station der Bahnhof [b**ah**nhof]

tram die Straßenbahn [shtr**ah**ssen-bahn]

translate übersetzen [oober-z**e**tsen]
  could you translate that? könnten Sie das übersetzen? [k**ur**nten zee]

translation die Übersetzung [oober-z**e**tsoong]

translator (man/woman) der Übersetzer [oober-z**e**tser]/die Übersetzerin

trash (waste) der Abfall [**a**p-fal] (poor quality goods) der Mist

trashcan (US) die Mülltonne [m**oo**lltonn-uh]

travel reisen [r**y**zen]
  we're travelling around wir machen eine Rundreise [veer ma**KH**en **ine**-uh r**oo**nt-rize-uh]

travel agent's das Reisebüro [r**ize**-uh-b**oo**ro]

traveller's cheque der Reisescheck [r**ize**-uh-sheck]

tray das Tablett

tree der Baum [bowm]

tremendous fantastisch [fant**a**stish]

trendy schick [shick]

trim: just a trim please (to hairdresser) nur etwas kürzen, bitte [noor etvass k**oo**rtsen b**i**tt-uh]

trip (excursion) der Ausflug [**ow**ssflook]
  I'd like to go on a trip to ... ich möchte gern eine Reise nach ... machen [m**u**rsht-uh gairn **ine**-uh r**ize**-uh naKH ... ma**KH**en]

trolley (in supermarket) der Einkaufswagen [**ine**-kowfs-v**ah**gen] (in station) der Kofferkuli [k**o**ffer-k**oo**lee]

trouble die Schwierigkeiten [shv**ee**rish-kyten]
  I'm having trouble with ... ich

ENGLISH ◆ GERMAN | Tr

habe Schwierigkeiten mit ...
[h**a**hb-uh]
sorry to trouble you tut mir
leid, Sie zu belästigen [toot
meer lite zee tsoo bel**e**stigen]
trousers die Hose [h**oh**z-uh]
true wahr [vahr]
that's not true das stimmt
nicht [shtimmt nisht]
trunk (US: of car) der
Kofferraum [k**o**ffer-rowm]
trunks (swimming) die Badehose
[b**a**h-uh-hohz-uh]
try (verb) versuchen
[fairz**OO**KHen]
can I have a try? kann ich es
versuchen?
try on: can I try it on? kann ich
es anprobieren?
[**a**n-probeeren]
T-shirt das T-Shirt
Tuesday der Dienstag
[d**ee**nstahk]
tuna der Thunfisch [t**OO**nfish]
tunnel der Tunnel [t**oo**nnel]
Turkey die Türkei [t**OO**rk-**ī**]
Turkish (adj) türkisch [t**OO**rkish]
(language) Türkisch
turn: turn left/right biegen Sie
links/rechts ab [b**ee**gen zee
links/reshts ap]
turn off: where do I turn off? wo
muß ich abbiegen? [vo mooss
ish **a**p-beegen]
can you turn the heating off?
können Sie die Heizung
abstellen? [k**u**rnen zee dee
h**y**tsoong **a**p-shtellen]
turn on: can you turn the heating

on? können Sie die Heizung
anstellen? [k**u**rnen zee dee
h**y**tsoong **a**n-shtellen]
turning (in road) die
Abzweigung [**a**p-tsvygoong]
TV das Fernsehen [f**ai**rnzay-en]
tweezers die Pinzette [pin-
ts**e**tt-uh]
twice zweimal [tsv**y**mahl]
twice as much zweimal soviel
[zof**ee**l]
twin beds zwei Einzelbetten
[tsvy **ine**-tsel-betten]
twin room das Zweibettzimmer
[tsv**y**bett-tsimmer]
twist: I've twisted my ankle ich
habe mir den Fuß vertreten
[ish h**a**hb-uh meer dayn f**oo**ss
fairtr**a**yten]
type die Art
a different type of ... eine
andere Art von ... [**ine**-uh
ander-uh]
typical typisch [t**OO**pish]
tyre der Reifen [r**y**fen]

U

ugly häßlich [hesslish]
UK das Vereinigte Königreich
[fair-**ine**-isht-uh k**u**rnish-rysh]
ulcer das Geschwür [geshv**OO**r]
umbrella der Schirm [sheerm]
uncle der Onkel
unconscious bewußtlos
[bev**oo**st-lohss]
under unter [**oo**nter]
underdone (meat) nicht gar
[nisht]

underground (railway) die
U-Bahn [**oo**-bahn]

underpants die Unterhose
[**oo**nter-hohz-uh]

understand: I understand ich
verstehe [ish fairsht**ay**-uh]
I don't understand das
verstehe ich nicht [nisht]
do you understand? verstehen
Sie? [fairsht**ay**-en zee]

unemployed arbeitslos [**a**rbites-
lohss]

United States die Vereinigten
Staaten [fair-**ine**-ishten
sht**ah**ten]

university die Universität
[**oo**nivairzi-t**ay**t]

unleaded petrol das bleifreie
Benzin [bly-fry-uh bents**ee**n]

unlimited mileage ohne
Kilometerbeschränkung
[ohn-uh keelo-m**ay**ter-
beshrenkoong]

unlock aufschließen [**owf**-
shleessen]

unpack auspacken [**ow**ss-
packen]

until bis [biss]

unusual ungewöhnlich [**oo**n-
gevurnlish]

up oben [**oh**ben]
up there da oben
he's not up yet (not out of bed)
er ist noch nicht auf [noKH
nisht owf]
what's up? (what's wrong?) was
ist los? [vass ist lohss]

upmarket (restaurant, hotel, goods
etc) anspruchsvoll

[**a**nshprooKHsfoll]

upset stomach die
Magenverstimmung
[m**ah**gen-fairsht**i**mmoong]

upside down verkehrt herum
[fairk**ai**rt hair**oo**m]

upstairs oben [**oh**ben]

urgent dringend [dr**i**ng-ent]

us* uns [oonss]
with us mit uns
for us für uns [f**oo**r]

USA die USA [oo-ess-**ah**]

use (verb) benutzen [ben**oo**tsen]
may I use ...? kann ich ...
benutzen?

useful nützlich [n**oo**tslish]

usual üblich [**oo**plish]
the usual (drink etc) dasselbe
wie immer [dass**e**lb-uh vee]

V

vacancy: do you have any
vacancies? (hotel) haben Sie
Zimmer frei? [h**ah**ben zee
ts**i**mmer fry]

vacation der Urlaub [**oo**rlowp]
(from university) die
Semesterferien [zem**e**ster-
fairee-en]

vaccination die Impfung
[**i**mpfoong]

vacuum cleaner der
Staubsauger [sht**ow**p-zowger]

valid (ticket etc) gültig [g**oo**ltish]
how long is it valid for? wie
lange ist es gültig? [vee
l**a**ng-uh]

valley das Tal [tahl]

valuable (adj) wertvoll [**vai**rtfol]
can I leave my valuables here?
kann ich meine Wertsachen
hierlassen? [m**ine**-uh
vairtzaKHen h**eer**lassen]

value der Wert [vairt]

van der Lieferwagen
[**lee**fervahgen]

vanilla die Vanille [van**ill**-uh]
a vanilla ice cream ein
Vanilleeis [van**ill**-uh-ice]

vary: it varies es ist
unterschiedlich [**oo**nter-
sheetlish]

vase die Vase [**vah**z-uh]

veal das Kalbfleisch [k**a**lp-flysh]

vegetables das Gemüse
[gem**oo**z-uh]

vegetarian (man/woman) der
Vegetarier [vegayt**ah**ree-er]/
die Vegetarierin

vending machine der Automat
[owtom**ah**t]

very sehr [zair]
very little for me nur eine
Kleinigkeit für mich [n**oo**r
ine-uh kl**ine**-ishkite f**oo**r mish]
I like it very much ich mag es
sehr gern [gairn]

vest (under shirt) das Unterhemd
[**oo**nterhemt]

via über [**oo**ber]

video (film) das Video
(recorder) der Videorecorder

Vienna Wien [veen]

view der Blick

villa die Villa

village das Dorf

vinegar der Essig [**e**ssish]

vineyard der Weinberg [**vine**-
bairk]

visa das Visum [**vee**zoom]

visit (verb) besuchen
[bez**oo**KHen]
I'd like to visit ... ich möchte
... besuchen [m**ur**sht-uh]

vital: it's vital that ... es ist
unbedingt notwendig,
daß ... [**oo**n-bedingt
n**oh**tvendish dass]

vodka der Wodka [**vo**dka]

voice die Stimme [sht**imm**-uh]

voltage die Spannung
[shp**a**nnoong]

The voltage is 240V. All sockets
are for plugs with two round pins
so a travel plug is useful.

---

vomit erbrechen [airb**re**shen]

W

waist die Taille [t**a**l-yuh]

waistcoat die Weste [v**e**st-uh]

wait warten [v**a**rten]
wait for me warten Sie auf
mich [zee owf mish]
don't wait for me warten Sie
nicht auf mich [nisht]
can I wait until my wife/partner
gets here? (eg as said to waiter)
kann ich warten, bis meine
Frau/Partnerin kommt?
can you do it while I wait?
kann ich darauf warten?
[dar**ow**f]
could you wait here for me? (eg

124

as said to taxi driver) **können Sie hier warten?** [kurnen zee heer]

waiter der Ober [ohber]
waiter! Herr Ober! [hair]

waitress die Kellnerin
waitress! Fräulein! [froyline]

wake: can you wake me up at 5.30? können Sie mich um 5.30 Uhr wecken? [kurnen zee mish oom – vecken]

wake-up call der Weckanruf [veck-anroof]

Wales Wales

walk: is it a long walk? geht man lange dorthin? [gayt man lang-uh]
it's only a short walk es ist nicht weit zu gehen [nisht vite tsoo gay-en]
I'll walk ich gehe zu Fuß [gay-uh tsoo fooss]
I'm going for a walk ich gehe spazieren [shpatseeren]

Walkman® der Walkman

wall die Wand [vant]
(external) **die Mauer** [mower]

wallet die Brieftasche [breeftash-uh]

wander: I like just wandering around ich wandere gern einfach so durch die Gegend [ish vander-uh gairn ine-faKH zo doorsh dee gaygent]

want: I want a ... ich möchte ein(e)... [ish mursht-uh ine (-uh)]
I don't want any ... ich möchte keinen ... [kine-en]
I want to go home ich will

nach Hause [vill]
I don't want to ich will nicht [nisht]
he wants to ... er will ...
what do you want? was wollen Sie? [vass vollen zee]

ward (in hospital) **die Station** [shtats-yohn]

warm warm [varm]
I'm so warm mir ist so warm [meer]

was*: it was ... es war ... [ess vahr]

wash (verb) **waschen** [vashen]
can you wash these? können Sie die für mich waschen? [kurnen zee]

washer (for bolt etc) **die Dichtung** [dishtoong]

washhand basin das Handwaschbecken [hantvash-becken]

washing (clothes) **die Wäsche** [vesh-uh]

washing machine die Waschmaschine [vashmasheen-uh]

washing powder das Waschpulver [vashpoolver]

washing-up liquid das Spülmittel [shpoolmittel]

wasp die Wespe [vesp-uh]

watch (wristwatch) **die Armbanduhr** [armbant-oor]
will you watch my things for me? könnten Sie auf meine Sachen aufpassen? [kurnten zee owf mine-uh zaKHen owfpassen]

watch out! **passen Sie auf!**

watch strap das Uhrarmband [**OO**r-armbant]

water das Wasser [**va**sser]
may I have some water? **kann ich etwas Wasser haben?** [**et**vass – **hah**ben]

waterproof (adj) **wasserfest** [**va**sserfest]

waterskiing Wasserskilaufen [**va**ssershee-lowfen]

wave (in sea) die Welle [**vell**-uh]

way: it's this way **es ist hier entlang** [heer]
it's that way **es ist dort entlang**
is it a long way to ...? **ist es weit bis nach ...?** [vite biss naKH]
no way! **auf keinen Fall!** [owf **kine**-en fal]

•••••• DIALOGUE ••••••

could you tell me the way to ...?
können Sie mir sagen, wie ich nach ... komme? [**kur**nen zee meer **zah**gen vee ish naKH ... **komm**-uh]
go straight on until you reach the traffic lights **fahren Sie geradeaus bis zur Ampel** [ge**rah**d-uh-owss]
turn left **biegen Sie links ab** [**bee**gen]
take the first on the right **nehmen Sie die erste Straße rechts** [**nay**men zee dee **airst**-uh **shtrahss**-uh reshts]
see also **where**

we* **wir** [veer]
weak **schwach** [shvaKH]

weather das Wetter [**v**etter]

•••••• DIALOGUE ••••••

what's the weather forecast? **wie ist die Wettervorhersage?** [vee ist dee vetter-for**hair**zahg-uh]
it's going to be fine **es gibt schönes Wetter** [geept sh**ur**ness]
it's going to rain **es gibt Regen** [**ray**gen]
it'll brighten up later **es wird sich später aufklären** [veert zish sh**payt**er owf-kl**air**en]

wedding die Hochzeit [h**o**KH-tsite]

wedding ring der Ehering [**ay**-uh-ring]

Wednesday der Mittwoch [**m**ittvoKH]

week die Woche [**vo**KH-uh]
a week (from) today **heute in einer Woche** [**hoyt**-uh in **ine**-er]
a week (from) tomorrow **morgen in einer Woche**

weekend das Wochenende [**vo**KHen-end-uh]
at the weekend **am Wochenende**

weight das Gewicht [ge**v**isht]

weird **seltsam** [**z**eltzahm]

weirdo der Verrückte [fair-r**OO**ckt-uh]

welcome: welcome to ...
willkommen in ... [vill**k**ommen]
you're welcome (don't mention it) **keine Ursache** [**kine**-uh **OO**rzaKH-uh]

well: I don't feel well ich fühle
mich nicht wohl [ish fool-uh
mish nisht vohl]
she's not well sie fühlt sich
nicht wohl [zee]
you speak English very well
Sie sprechen sehr gut
Englisch [shpreshen zair goot
eng-lish]
well done! gut gemacht!
[gemaKHt]
this one as well diesen auch
[deezen owKH]
well well! (surprise) na so was!
[zo vass]

•••••• DIALOGUE ••••••

how are you? wie geht es dir? [vee
gayt ess deer]
very well, thanks sehr gut, danke
[zair goot dank-uh]
and you? und dir? [oont deer]

well-done (meat) gut
durchgebraten [goot doorsh-
gebrahten]
Welsh walisisch [val-eezish]
I'm Welsh (man/woman) ich bin
Waliser [valleezer]/Waliserin
were*: I/you were ich war [var]/
du warst [varst]
we/they were wir/sie waren
[vahren]
west der Westen [vesten]
in the west im Westen
West Indian (adj) westindisch
[vestindish]
wet naß [nass]
what? was? [vass]
what's that? was ist das?

what should I do? was soll ich
tun? [zoll ish toon]]
what a view! was für ein
Blick! [vass foor ine]
what bus is it? welcher Bus
ist das? [velsher]
wheel das Rad [raht]
wheelchair der Rollstuhl [rol-
shtool]
when? wann? [van]
when's the train/ferry? wann
fährt der Zug/die Fähre? [van
fairt dair tsook/dee fair-uh]
when we get back wenn wir
zurückkommen [ven veer
tsooroock-kommen]
when we got back als wir
zurückkamen [alss]
where? wo? [vo]
I don't know where it is ich
weiß nicht, wo es ist [vice
nisht]

•••••• DIALOGUE ••••••

where is the cathedral? wo ist der
Dom?
it's over there er ist dort drüben
[drooben]
could you show me where it is on
the map? können Sie ihn mir auf
der Karte zeigen? [kurnen zee een
meer – tsygen]
it's just here er ist da
see also way

which: which bus? welcher
Bus? [velsher]
which house? welches Haus?
which bar? welche Bar?

which one? welcher?

that one dieser [**dee**zer]

this one? dieser?

no, that one nein, dieser [**nine**]

while: while I'm here während
ich hier bin [v**air**ent ish heer]

whisky der Whisky

white weiß [vice]

white wine der Weißwein
[**vice**-vine]

who? wer? [vair]

who is it? (reply to knock at door
etc) wer ist da?

the man who ... der Mann,
der ... [dair]

whole: the whole week die
ganze Woche [dee **ga**nts-uh
v**oKH**-uh]

the whole lot das Ganze

whose: whose is this? wem
gehört das? [vaym geh**urt**]

why? warum? [vahr**oo**m]

why not? warum nicht? [nisht]

wide breit [brite]

wife: my wife meine Frau
[m**ine**-uh frow]

will*: will you do it for me?
können Sie es für mich tun?
[k**ur**nen zee ess f**oo**r mish t**oo**n]

wind der Wind [vint]

window das Fenster

near the window am Fenster

in the window (of shop) im
Schaufenster [sh**ow**-fenster]

window seat der Fensterplatz

windscreen die
Windschutzscheibe [vint-

shoots-shybuh]

windscreen wiper der
Scheibenwischer [sh**y**ben-
visher]

windsurfing das Windsurfen
[**v**intzurfen]

windy: it's so windy es ist so
windig [zo **v**indish]

wine der Wein [vine]

can we have some more wine?
können wir noch etwas
Wein haben? [k**ur**nen veer
noKH **e**tvass – h**ah**ben]

The vast majority of German
wine is white. Like most EC
wine, German wine is divided
into two broad categories:
Tafelwein [**tah**fel-vine] (table
wine) and **Qualitäts-wein**
[kvalit**ay**ts-vine] (quality wine).
Landwein is a superior
Tafelwein. There are two basic
subdivisions of **Qualitätswein**:
QbA (Qualitätswein beson-
derer Anbaugebiete) and **QmP**
(Qualitätswein mit Prädikat).
QbA wines come from eleven
delimited regions and must pass
an official tasting and analysis.
QmP wines are further divided
into six grades:

Kabinett: the first and lightest
style.
Spätlese [sh**ay**t-layzuh]:
must come from a late grape
harvest, which gives riper
flavours.

→

Auslese [**ow**ss-layzuh]: made from a selected bunch of grapes, making a concentrated medium-sweet wine.

Beerenauslese [b**ai**ren-owss-layzuh]: wine made from late-harvested grapes; a rare wine, made only in the very best years, and extremely sweet.

Trockenbeerenauslese [tr**o**cken-bairen-owss-layzuh]: a very rare wine which is intensely sweet and concentrated.

Eiswein [**ice**-vine]: literally 'ice wine' a hard frost freezes the water content of the grape, concentrating the juice; the flavour of an Eiswein is remarkably fresh-tasting, due to its high acidity.

Some useful wine terms:
trocken dry
halbtrocken [h**a**lptrocken] semi-dry
lieblich [**lee**plish] mellow
süß [z**oo**ss] sweet
herb [hairp] very dry

If you are keen to try a local wine, ask for '**einen hiesigen Wein**' [**ine**-en h**ee**zigen vine].

wine list die Weinkarte [v**ine**-kart-uh]
winter der Winter [v**i**nter]
  in the winter im Winter
winter holiday der

Winterurlaub [v**i**nter-**oo**rlowp]
wire die Draht
  (electric) die Leitung [l**y**toong]
wish: best wishes mit b**e**sten
  Wünschen [v**oo**nshen]
with mit
  I'm staying with ... ich wohne
  bei... [v**oh**n-uh by]
without ohne [**oh**n-uh]
witness (man/woman) der Zeuge
  [ts**oy**g-uh]/die Zeugin
  will you be a witness for me?
  würden Sie für mich als
  Zeuge zur Verfügung
  stehen? [v**oo**rden zee
  f**oo**r mish – ts**oo**r fairf**oo**goong
  sht**ay**-en]
woman die Frau [frow]
wonderful wundervoll
  [v**oo**nder-fol]
won't*: it won't start es will
  nicht anspringen [vill nisht
  an-shpringen]
wood (material) das Holz [holts]
woods (forest) der Wald [valt]
wool die Wolle [v**o**ll-uh]
word das Wort [vort]
work die Arbeit [**a**rbite]
  it's not working es
  funktioniert nicht [foonkts-
  yohn**ee**rt nisht]
  I work in ... ich arbeite in ...
  [**a**rbite-uh]
world die Welt [velt]
worry: I'm worried ich mache
  mir Sorgen [ish m**a**KH-uh meer
  z**o**rgen]
worse: it's worse es ist
  schlimmer [shl**i**mmer]

worst am schlimmsten
[shl**i**mmsten]

worth: is it worth a visit? lohnt
sich ein Besuch dort? [zish
ine bez**OO**KH dort]

would: would you give this to ...?
könnten Sie dies ... geben?
[k**u**rnten zee – g**ay**ben]

wrap: could you wrap it up?
können Sie es einpacken?
[k**u**rnen zee ess **i**ne-packen]

wrapping paper das Packpapier
[p**a**ck-papeer]

wrist das Handgelenk
[h**a**ntgelenk]

write schreiben [shr**y**ben]

could you write it down?
könnten Sie es
aufschreiben? [k**u**rnten zee
ess **ow**f-shryben]

how do you write it? wie
schreibt man das? [vee shrypt]

writing paper das
Schreibpapier [shr**i**pe-papeer]

wrong: it's the wrong key es ist
der falsche Schlüssel [dair
f**a**lsh-uh]

this is the wrong train dies ist
der falsche Zug

the bill's wrong in der
Rechnung ist ein Fehler [dair
r**e**shnoong ist ine f**ay**ler]

sorry, wrong number tut mir
leid, falsch verbunden [t**oo**t
meer lite falsh fairb**oo**nden]

sorry, wrong room tut mir
leid, ich habe mich im
Zimmer geirrt [ish h**a**hb-uh
mish im ts**i**mmer guh-**ee**rrt]

there's something wrong with
... mit ... stimmt etwas nicht
[shtimmt **e**tvass nisht]

what's wrong? was ist los?
[vass ist lohss]

X

X-ray die Röntgenaufnahme
[**ru**rntgen-owfnahm-uh]

Y

yacht die Jacht [ya**KH**t]

yard* das Yard

year das Jahr [yahr]

yellow gelb [gelp]

yes ja [yah]

you don't smoke, do you? –
yes Sie rauchen nicht, oder?
– doch [zee r**ow**KHen nisht
ohder – do**KH**]

yesterday gestern

yesterday morning gestern
morgen

the day before yesterday
vorgestern [f**o**rgestern]

yet noch [no**KH**]

•••••• D I A L O G U E ••••••

is he here yet? ist er schon hier?
[air shohn heer]

no, not yet nein, noch nicht [nine
no**KH** nisht]

you'll have to wait a little longer yet
Sie müssen noch etwas warten
[zee m**OO**ssen]

yoghurt der Joghurt [y**oh**g-
hoort]

you* (familiar: singular) du [dOO]
(plural) ihr [eer]
(polite) Sie [zee]
this is for you das ist für dich/
euch [oych]/Sie
with you mit dir/euch/Ihnen
[**ee**nen]
young jung [yoong]
your* (familiar: singular) dein
[dine]
(plural) euer [**oy**er]
(polite) Ihr [eer]
your camera deine/Ihre
Kamera [**dine**-uh/**eer**-uh]
yours* (familiar: singular) deiner
[**dine**-er]
(plural) eurer [**oy**rer]
(polite) Ihrer [**ee**rer]
youth hostel die
Jugendherberge [y**OO**gent-
hairbairg-uh]

Z

zero null [nooll]
zip der Reißverschluß [**rice**-
fairshlooss]
could you put a new zip on?
könnten Sie einen neuen
Reißverschluß anbringen?
[**kurn**ten zee **ine**-en n**oy**-en]
zoo der Zoo [tsoh]

German-English

A

ab [ap] from; off; down

abbiegen [ap-beegen] to turn off

Abblendlicht n [ap-blent-lisht] dipped/dimmed headlights

Abend m [ahbent] evening
zu Abend essen to have dinner

Abendessen n [ahbent-essen] dinner

Abendkleid n [ahbent-klite] evening dress

abends [ahbents] in the evening

aber [ahber] but

Abf. (Abfahrt) dept, departure

Abfahrt f [ap-fahrt] departure(s)

Abfall m [ap-fal] litter; rubbish, garbage

Abfälle litter

Abfalleimer m [apfal-ime-er] rubbish bin, trashcan

Abfertigung f [ap-fairtigoong] check-in

Abflug m [ap-flook] departure(s)

Abführmittel n [ap-foor-mittel] laxative

abgefüllt in ... bottled in ...

abgezähltes Geld [ap-getsayltess gelt] exact fare

abheben [ap-hayben] to take off; to withdraw

Abhebung f [ap-hayboong] withdrawal

abholen [ap-hohlen] to pick up

Abkürzung f [ap-koortsoong]

abbreviation; shortcut

ablehnen [ap-laynen] to refuse

abnehmen [ap-naymen] to lift (the receiver); to remove; to lose weight

abreisen [ap-rize-en] to leave

abschließen [ap-shleessen] to lock

Absender m [ap-zender] sender

absichtlich [ap-zishtlish] deliberately

absolutes Halteverbot waiting strictly prohibited

absolutes Parkverbot parking strictly prohibited

absolutes Rauchverbot smoking strictly prohibited

Abstand m [ap-shtant] distance

Abtei f [ap-tī] abbey

Abteil n [ap-tile] compartment

Abteilung f [ap-tyloong] department

Abtreibung f [ap-tryboong] abortion

abtrocknen [ap-trocknen] to dry the dishes

Abwasch m [ap-vash] washing-up

abwaschen [ap-vashen] to do the dishes

Achse f [aks-uh] axle

ach so! [aKH zo] I see

acht [aKHt] eight

Achtung! [aKHtoong] look out!; attention

Achtung! Straßenbahn beware of trams

achtzehn [aKH-tsayn] eighteen

achtzig [aKH-tsish] eighty

134

ADAC (Allgemeiner Deutscher
Automobil-Club) [ah-day-ah-
ts**ay**] German motoring
organization
Adreßbuch n [adr**e**ssb**OO**KH]
address book
Affe m [**a**ff-uh] monkey
Agentur f [agent**OO**r] agency
ähneln [**ay**neln] to look like
ähnlich [**ay**nlish] similar
Aktentasche f [**a**kten-tash-uh]
briefcase
Aktie f [**a**ktsee-uh] share
Akzent m [akts**e**nt] accent
akzeptieren [aktsept**ee**ren] to
accept
albern silly
alle [**a**l-uh] all; everybody;
finished, all gone
allein [al**ine**] alone
alle Kassen all health
insurance schemes accepted
alle Rechte vorbehalten all
rights reserved
Allergie f [alairg**ee**] allergy
allergisch gegen [ala**i**rgish
g**ay**gen] allergic to
Allerheiligen n [allerh**y**ligen] All
Saints' Day (1 November)
alles [**a**l-ess] everything
alles Gute [**a**l-ess g**OO**t-uh] best
wishes; all the best
alles klar! [**a**l-ess klar] fine!,
great!
allgemein [al-gem**ine**] general;
generally
Alpen Alps
als [alss] when; than; as
also [**a**lzo] therefore

als ob [alss op] as if
alt [alt] old
Altbau m [altbow] old building
Altenheim n [**a**lten-hime] old
people's home
Alter n [**a**lter] age
Altersheim n [**a**lters-hime] old
people's home
altmodisch [**a**lt-mohdish] old-
fashioned
Altstadt f [**a**lt-shtatt] old (part
of) town
Alufolie f [**ah**l**OO**-fohlee-uh] silver
foil
a.M. (am Main) on the Main
am at the; on (the)
am schnellsten (the) fastest
am Apparat [am appar**ah**t]
speaking
Ambulanz f [amb**OO**lants] out-
patients
Ameise f [**ah**mize-uh] ant
Amerikaner m [amairee-**kah**ner],
Amerikanerin f American
amerikanisch [amairee-**kah**nish]
American
Ampel f traffic lights
amüsieren: sich amüsieren [zish
am**OO**z**ee**ren] to have fun
an at; to; on
anbieten [**a**nbeeten] to offer
Andenken n souvenir
andere [**a**nder-uh] other(s)
andere Orte other destinations
anderthalb [andert-h**a**lp] one
and a half
Änderung f [**e**nderoong] change;
alteration
Anfall m [**a**nfal] attack; fit

Anfang m beginning

anfangen to begin

Anfänger m [**a**nfenger], Anfängerin f beginner

Anfassen der Waren verboten do not touch the merchandise

Angeklagte m/f [**a**n-geklahkt-uh] defendant

Angeln m [**a**ng-eln] fishing

Angeln verboten no fishing

angenehm [**a**n-genaym] pleasant; pleased to meet you

Angestellte m/f [**a**n-geshtellt-uh] employee

Angst f fear

anhalten to stop

Anhalter: per Anhalter fahren to hitchhike

Anhänger m [**a**nhenger] trailer; pendant; follower

Ank. (Ankunft) arr, arrival

Ankauf ... we buy ...

ankommen to arrive

ankreuzen [**a**nkroytsen] to cross

Ankunft f [**a**nkoonft] arrival(s)

Ankunftshalle f [**a**nkoonfts-hal-uh] arrivals (area)

Anlieger frei residents only

Anmeldung f [**a**n-meldoong] reception

anprobieren [**a**nprobeeren] to try on

Anruf m [**a**nroof] call

anrufen [**a**nroofen] to phone, to ring

ans [anss] to the

anschalten [**a**n-shalten] to switch on

Anschluß m [**a**n-shlooss] connection

Anschluß an ... connects with ...

Anschrift f [**a**n-shrift] address

ansehen [**a**nzay-en] to look (at)

Ansicht f [**a**nzisht] view; opinion

Ansichtskarte f [**a**nzishts-kart-uh] picture postcard

anstatt [an-sht**a**tt] instead of

ansteckend [**a**n-shteckent] contagious

Antenne f [ant**e**nn-uh] aerial; antenna

Antiquitäten [anti-kvit**ay**ten] antiques

Antwort f [**a**ntvort] answer

antworten [**a**ntvorten] to answer

Anwalt m [**a**nvalt], Anwältin [**a**nveltin] f lawyer

Anwohner frei residents only

Anzahlung f [**a**n-tsahloong] deposit

anziehen [**a**ntsee-en] to dress sich anziehen [zish] to get dressed

Anzug m [**a**ntsook] suit

anzünden [**a**n-ts00nden] to light

AOK (Allgemeine Ortskrankenkasse) [ah-oh-k**ah**] German health insurance scheme

Apotheke f [apot**ay**k-uh] chemist's, pharmacy

Apparat m [appar**ah**t] telephone; apparatus

Appetit m [appet**ee**t] appetite

a.R. (am Rhein) on the Rhine

Arbeit f [**a**rbite] work; job

GERMAN ✤ ENGLISH | Ar

arbeiten [**a**rbite-en] to work

Arbeiter m [**a**rbyter], Arbeiterin f worker

arbeitslos [**a**rbites-lohss] unemployed

ARD (Arbeitsgemeinschaft der Rundfunkanstalten Deutschlands) [ah-air-d**ay**] first German television channel

Ärger m [**ai**rger] annoyance; trouble; hassle

ärgerlich [**ai**rgerlish] annoying

ärgern: sich ärgern [zish **ai**rgern] to be/get annoyed

arm poor

Arm m arm

Armaturenbrett n [armat**OO**renbrett] dashboard

Armband n [**a**rmbant] bracelet

Armbanduhr f [**a**rmbant-**OO**r] watch

Arschloch! [**a**rshlo**KH**] bastard!

Art f sort, kind

Arzt m [artst] doctor

Ärztin f [**ai**rtstin] doctor

Ärztlicher Notdienst m [**ai**rtstlisher n**oh**t-deenst] emergency medical service

Asche f [**a**sh-uh] ash

Aschenbecher m [**a**shenbesher] ashtray

Aschermittwoch m [ashermittvo**KH**] Ash Wednesday

aß [ahss], aßen [**ah**ssen], aßt [ahsst] ate

atmen [**ah**t-men] to breathe

Attentat n [atten-taht] assassination

Attest n certificate

auch [ow**KH**] too, also

auf [owf] on; to; open
auf deutsch in German

Aufbewahrungslösung f [owfbevahroongs-l**ur**zoong] soaking solution

Aufenthalt m [**ow**f-ent-halt] stay

Aufenthaltsraum m [**ow**f-enthalts-rowm] lounge

Aufführung f [**ow**f-fooroong] performance

aufgeben [**ow**f-gayben] to give up; to post, to mail

aufhören [**ow**f-hur-ren] to stop

aufpassen [**ow**f-passen] to pay attention

aufpassen auf [owf] to take care of; to watch out for

aufregend [**ow**f-raygent] exciting

aufs [owfs] on the; onto the

Aufsicht f [**ow**f-zisht] supervision

aufstehen [**ow**f-shtay-en] to get up

aufwachen [**ow**f-va**KH**en] to wake up

Aufzug m [**ow**f-ts**OO**k] lift, elevator

Auge n [**ow**g-uh] eye

Augenarzt m [**ow**gen-artst] ophthalmologist, optician

Augenblick m [**ow**genblick] moment

Augenbraue f [**ow**gen-brow-uh] eyebrow

Augenoptiker m [**ow**gen-optiker] optician

Augenzeuge m [**ow**gen-tsoyg-uh],

Augenzeugin f eye witness

aus [owss] from; off; out; out of; made of; finished

Ausfahrt f [owssfahrt] exit

Ausfahrt freihalten keep exit clear

Ausfahrt Tag und Nacht freihalten keep exit clear day and night

Ausflug m [owssflook] trip

ausfüllen [owssfoollen] to fill in

Ausgang m [owssgang] exit, way out; gate; departure

ausgeben [owssgayben] to spend

ausgenommen [owss-genommen] except

ausgezeichnet [owss-getsyshnet] excellent

Auskunft f [owsskoonft] information; information desk; directory enquiries

Ausland n [owsslant] international; overseas, abroad

Ausländer m [owsslender], Ausländerin f foreigner

ausländisch [owsslendish] foreign

ausländisches Erzeugnis foreign produce

ausländische Währungen fpl [owsslendish-uh vairoongen] foreign currencies

Ausland: im/ins Ausland [owsslant] abroad

Auslandsflüge international departures

Auslandsgespräche international calls

Auslandsporto n [owsslants-porto] overseas postage

Ausnahme f [owssnahm-uh] exception

auspacken [owsspacken] to unpack

Auspuff m [owsspooff] exhaust

ausruhen: sich ausruhen [zish owssroo-en] to relax; to take a rest

ausschalten [owss-shalten] to switch off

ausschl. (ausschließlich) excl., exclusive

aussehen [owss-zay-en] to look

Aussehen n look; appearance

außen [owssen] outside

außer [owsser] except

außer Betrieb out of order

außerhalb [owsser-halp] outside (of)

äußerlich anzuwenden not to be taken internally

außer sonntags Sundays excepted

Aussicht f [owss-zisht] view

Aussichtspunkt m [owss-zishts-poonkt] viewpoint

aussprechen [owss-shpreshen] to pronounce

aussteigen [owss-shtygen] to get off

Ausstellung f [owss-shtelloong] exhibition

Australien n [owstrahlee-en] Australia

australisch [owstrahlish] Australian

Ausverkauf m [**ow**ss-fairk**ow**f]
sale
ausverkauft [**ow**ss-fairk**ow**ft]
sold out
Auswahl f [**ow**ssvahl] choice;
selection
Ausweis m [**ow**ssvice] pass,
identity card; identification
Auszahlungen withdrawals;
cash desk, cashier
ausziehen: sich ausziehen [zish
owss-tsee-en] to undress
Auto n [**ow**to] car
mit dem Auto by car
Autobahn f [**ow**to-bahn]
motorway, highway,
freeway
Autobahndreieck motorway
junction; motorways merge
Autobahnkreuz motorway
junction
Autobahnraststätte service
station
Autobus m [**ow**tobooss] bus
Autofähre f [**ow**to-fair-uh] car-
ferry
Autofahrer m [**ow**tofahrer],
Autofahrerin f car driver,
motorist
Automat m vending machine
dieser Automat nimmt folgende
Banknoten an this machine
will accept the following
banknotes/bills
automatisch [owtom**ah**tisch]
automatic
Autoradio n [**ow**to-rahdee-o] car
radio
Autoreparaturen auto repairs

Autotelefon n [**ow**to-telef**oh**n]
car phone
Autounfall m [**ow**to-oonfal] car
accident
Autovermietung f [**ow**to-
fairm**ee**toong] car rental
Autowäsche f [**ow**tovesh-uh] car
wash

B

Babyartikel babywear, items
for babies
Bach m [baкн] stream
Bäcker m [becker] baker
Bäckerei f [becker-**ī**] baker's,
bakery
Bad n [baht] bath; bathroom
Badeanzug m [b**ah**d-uh-**a**ntsook]
swimming costume
Badehose f [b**ah**d-uh-hohz-uh]
swimming trunks
Bademantel m [b**ah**d-uh-mantel]
dressing gown
baden [b**ah**den] to have a bath
Badesalz n [b**ah**d-uh-zalts] bath
salts
Badewanne f [b**ah**d-uh-vann-uh]
bathtub
Badezimmer n [b**ah**d-uh-tsimmer]
bathroom
Badezimmerartikel bathroom
furniture and fittings
Badezimmerbedarf for the
bathroom
Bahnhof m [b**ah**n-hohf] station
Bahnhofsmission f [b**ah**nhohfs-
miss-y**oh**n] office providing
help for travellers in

difficulty

Bahnhofspolizei railway police

Bahnkilometer kilometres by rail

Bahnsteig m [b**a**hn-shtike] platform, (US) track

Bahnsteigkarte f [b**a**hn-shtike-kart-uh] platform ticket

Bahnübergang m [b**a**hn-oobergang] level crossing

bald [balt] soon

Balkangrill m [b**a**lkahn-grill] restaurant serving dishes from Balkan countries

Balkon m [balk**oh**n] balcony

Band n [bant] tape

Bank f bank; bench

Bankkonto n bank account

Bankleitzahl f [b**a**nklite-tsahl] sort code

Bankomat m [bankom**ah**t] cash dispenser, automatic teller

bar zahlen [ts**a**hlen] to pay cash

Bardame f [b**a**rdahm-uh] barmaid

Bargeld n [b**a**rgelt] cash

Barmann m [b**a**rmann] barkeeper

Bart m beard

Basel n [b**a**hzel] Basle

bat [baht], **baten** [b**a**hten] asked

Bauch m [bowKH] stomach; belly

Bauer m [b**ow**er] farmer

Bauernhof m [b**ow**ern-hohf] farm

Baum m [bowm] tree

Baumwolle f [b**ow**mvoll-uh] cotton

Baustelle f building site; roadworks

Baustellenausfahrt works exit; building site exit

Bayern [b**y**-ern] Bavaria

bayrisch [b**y**-rish] Bavarian

Beamter m [buh-**a**mter], **Beamtin** f civil servant; official

Bedarf m needs, requirements; demand

bedeuten [bed**oy**ten] to mean

bedeutend [bed**oy**tent] important

bedienen [bed**ee**nen] to serve

bedienen Sie sich! [zee zish] help yourself

Bedienung f [bed**ee**noong] service (charge)

Bedienung inbegriffen service included

Bedienungsanleitung instructions for use

Bedingung f [bed**i**ngoong] condition

beeilen: sich beeilen [zish buh-**i**len] to hurry

beeilen Sie sich! [zee zish] hurry up!

beenden [buh-**e**nden] to finish

Beerdigung f [buh-**air**digoong] funeral

Beerdigungsunternehmen undertaker, mortician

befehlen [bef**ay**len] to order

Beginn der Vorstellung um ... [dair f**o**rshtelloong oom] performance begins at ...

begleiten [begl**y**ten] to

accompany

behalten [behalten] to keep

behandeln to treat

Behandlung f [behantloong] treatment

behaupten [behowpten] to claim

Behauptung f [behowptoong] claim

behindert [behindert] disabled

Behinderte m/f [behindert-uh] handicapped person

bei [by] by; at; next to; near
bei Peter at Peter's

beide [bide-uh] both (of them)

Bei Frost Glatteisgefahr icy in cold weather

beim at the

Bein n [bine] leg

Beinbruch m [bine-brooKH] broken leg

Beispiel n [by-shpeel] example
zum Beispiel [tsoom] for example

Bei Störung Taste drücken press key in case of technical fault

bekannt known

Bekannte m/f [bekannt-uh] acquaintance

Bekleidung f [beklydoong] clothing

bekloppt [bekloppt] crazy

bekommen to get

belegt [belaykt] occupied, busy; no vacancies; full

beleidigen [belydigen] to offend

Beleuchtung f [beloyshtoong] lights

Beleuchtungsartikel lamps and lighting

Belgien n [belgee-en] Belgium

belgisch [belgish] Belgian

Belichtungsmesser m [belishtoongs-messer] light meter

bellen to bark

Belohnung f [belohnoong] reward

bemerken [bemairken] to notice; to remark

Bemerkung f [bemairkoong] remark

Benehmen n [benaymen] behaviour

benehmen: sich benehmen [zish benaymen] to behave

Benutzung f [benootsoong] use

Benutzung auf eigene Gefahr use at own risk

Benzin n [bentseen] petrol, gas(oline)

Benzinkanister m [bentseen-kanister] petrol/gasoline can

Benzinuhr f [bentseen-oor] fuel gauge

beobachten [buh-ohbaKHten] to watch

bequem [bekvaym] comfortable

bereit [berite] ready

Bereitschaftsdienst m [berite-shaftsdeenst] duty doctor; duty pharmacy

Berg m [bairk] mountain

Bergsteigen n [bairk-shtygen] mountaineering

Bergwacht f [bairk-vaKHt] mountain rescue

Bericht m [berisht] report

beruhigen: sich beruhigen [zish beroo-igen] to calm down

Beruhigungsmittel n [beroo-igoongs-mittel] tranquillizer

berühmt [beroomt] famous

berühren [berooren] to touch

Berühren der Waren verboten do not touch

Besatzung f [bezatsoong] crew

beschädigen [beshaydigen] to damage

Bescheid m [beshite] information

Bescheid sagen to tell

Bescheid wissen to know

Bescheinigung f [beshynigoong] certificate

bescheuert [beshoyert] crazy, daft

beschreiben [beshryben] to describe

Beschreibung f description

beschweren: sich beschweren [zish beshvairen] to complain

besetzt [bezetst] busy; engaged, occupied

Besetztzeichen n [besetst-tsyshen] engaged tone

Besichtigung f [bezishtigoong] tour

Besitzer m [bezitser] owner

besoffen [bezoffen] pissed, smashed

besonders [bezonders] especially

besorgt [bezorkt] worried

besser better

Bestandteile ingredients;

component parts

bestätigen [beshtaytigen] to confirm

Bestattungen funeral director's

beste [best-uh] best

Bestechung f [beshteshoong] bribery

Besteck n [beshteck] cutlery

bestellen [beshtellen] to order

Bestellung f [beshtelloong] order

Bestimmungsort m [beshtim-moongs-ort] destination

bestrafen [beshtrahfen] to punish

Besuch m [bezooKH] visit

besuchen [bezooKHen] to visit

Besuchszeit f [bezooKHs-tsite] visiting time

Besuchszeiten fpl [bezooKHs-tsyten] visiting hours

Betäubung f [betoyboong] anaesthetic

Beton m [baytong] concrete

Betrag m [betrahk] amount

Betreten auf eigene Gefahr enter at own risk, keep off/out

Betreten der Baustelle verboten no admission to building site

Betreten der Eisfläche verboten keep off the ice

Betreten des Rasens nicht gestattet keep off the grass

Betreten verboten keep out

Betrieb m [betreep] company, firm; operation, running; bustle

außer Betrieb out of order

betriebsbereit ready to use

GERMAN ◆ ENGLISH | Be

Betriebsferien [betr**ee**ps-fairee-en] works' holidays/vacation

Betrug m [betr**oo**k] fraud

betrunken [betr**oo**nken] drunk

Bett n bed

Bettdecken bedding

Betteln und Hausieren verboten no beggars, no hawkers

Bettwäsche f [b**e**ttvesh-uh] bed linen

Bettzeug n [b**e**tt-tsoyk] bedding

Be- und Entladen erlaubt loading and off-loading permitted

bevor [bef**o**r] before

bewegen: sich bewegen [zish be-v**ay**gen] to move

Beweis m [bev**i**ce] proof

Bewohner m [bev**oh**ner], Bewohnerin f inhabitant

bewölkt [bev**u**rlkt] cloudy

bezahlen [bets**ah**len] to pay

Bezahlung f [bets**ah**loong] payment

Bezahlung mit Kreditkarte möglich credit cards welcome

beziehungsweise or

Bf. (Bahnhof) station

BH (Büstenhalter) m [bay-h**ah**] bra

Bierkeller m [b**ee**r-keller] beer cellar

Bild n [bilt] picture

billig [b**i**llish] cheap, inexpensive

Billigpreise reduced prices

bin am

Bindemittel starch

Bio-Laden m [b**ee**-oh-lahden] health food shop

biologisch abbaubar biodegradable

Birne f [b**ee**rn-uh] light bulb; pear

bis until; by

bis morgen see you tomorrow

bis später [shp**ay**ter] see you later

Biß m [bis] bite

bißchen: ein bißchen [ine b**i**ss-shen] a little bit (of)

bist are

bitte [b**i**ttuh] please; you're welcome

bitte? pardon (me)?; can I help you?

bitte anschnallen fasten seat belt

bitte einordnen get in lane

bitte eintreten ohne zu läuten please enter without ringing

bitte einzeln eintreten please enter one at a time

bitte entwerten please stamp your ticket

bitte Karte einführen please insert card

bitte klingeln please ring

bitte klopfen please knock

bitten to ask

bitte nicht ... please do not ...

bitte nicht stören please do not disturb

bitte schließen please close the door

bitte schön/sehr [b**i**tt-uh shurn/

zair] here you are; you're welcome

bitte schön/sehr? what will it be; can I help you?

bitte Schuhe abtreten please wipe your shoes

bitte warten please wait

Blase f [blahz-uh] bladder; blister

blaß [blass] pale

Blatt n leaf

blau [blow] blue

blauer Fleck m [blower] bruise

Blei n [bly] lead

bleiben [blyben] to stay, to remain

bleiben Sie am Apparat [zee am apparaht] hold the line

Bleichmittel n [blysh-mittel] bleach

bleifrei [blyfry] unleaded

Bleistift m [bly-shtift] pencil

Blick m look; view

mit Blick auf ... [owf] overlooking ...

blieb [bleep], bliebst, blieben stayed

Blinddarmentzündung f [blint-darm-ent-tsoondoong] appendicitis

blinder Passagier m [blinnder passaJeer] stowaway

Blinker m indicator

Blitz m [blits] flash; lightning

blockiert [blockeert] blocked

Blödmann m [blurtmann] twit

Blödsinn [blurt-zinn] nonsense, rubbish

Blume f [bloom-uh] flower

Blumenhandlung f [bloomen-hantloong] florist

Bluse f [blooz-uh] blouse

Blut n [bloot] blood

Blutdruck m [bloot-droock] blood pressure

bluten [blooten] to bleed

Blutgruppe f [bloot-groopp-uh] blood group

Blutübertragung f [bloot-oobertrahgoong] blood transfusion

BLZ (Bankleitzahl) sort code

Boden m [bohden] bottom; floor

Bodenpersonal n [bohden-pairzonahl] ground crew

Bodensee: der Bodensee [bohdenzay] Lake Constance

Bohrer m drill

Boje f [boh-yuh] buoy

Bolzen m [boltsen] bolt

Boot n [boht] boat

Bootsverleih m [bohts-fairlī] boat hire/rental

Bordkarte f [bortkart-uh] boarding card

böse [burz-uh] angry

Botschaft f [bohtshaft] embassy

brachte [braKHt-uh], brachtest, brachten brought

Branchenverzeichnis n [brangshen-fairtsyshniss] yellow pages

Brand m [brant] fire

Brandstiftung f [brant-shtiftoong] arson

Bratpfanne f [braht-pfann-uh] frying pan

Bräu n [broy] brew

Brauch m [browKH] custom

brauchen [browKHen] to need

Brauerei f brewery

Brauereiabfüllung bottled in the brewery

braun [brown] brown

braungebrannt [brown-gebrannt] tanned

BRD (Bundesrepublik Deutschland) [bay-air-day] FRG (Federal Republic of Germany)

breit [brite] wide

Breite f [bryt-uh] width

Bremse f [bremz-uh] brake

bremsen [bremzen] to brake

Bremsflüssigkeit f [bremsflOOssishkite] brake fluid

brennbar combustible

brennen to burn

Brief m [breef] letter

Brieffreund m [breef-froynt], Brieffreundin f pen pal

Briefkasten m [breefkasten] letterbox, mailbox

Briefmarke f [breefmark-uh] stamp

Brieftasche f [breeftash-uh] wallet

Briefträger m [breeftrayger] postman

Briefträgerin f [breeftraygerin] postwoman

Brille f [brill-uh] glasses, eyeglasses

bringen to bring

Brosche f [brosh-uh] brooch

Broschüre f [broshOOr-uh]

brochure

Bruch m [brooKH] fracture

Brücke f [brOOck-uh] bridge

Bruder m [brOOder] brother

Brunnen m [brOOnnen] fountain

Brust f [broost] breast; chest

Buch n [bOOKH] book

buchen [bOOKHen] to book

Bücherei f [bOOsher-ī] library

Bücher und Zeitschriften books and magazines

Buchhandlung f [bOOKH-hantloong] bookshop, bookstore

Bucht f [bOOKHt] bay

Bügeleisen n [bOOgel-īzen] iron

Bügelfalte f [bOOgel-falt-uh] crease

bügeln [bOOgeln] to iron

Bühne f [bOOn-uh] stage

Bundesautobahn federal motorway/highway

Bundesgesundheitsminister m German Minister of Health

Der Bundesgesundheitsminister: Rauchen gefährdet Ihre Gesundheit government warning: smoking can damage your health

Bundeskanzler m [bOOndess-kantsler] chancellor

Bundesrepublik Deutschland f [bOOndess-repOObleek doytchlant] Federal Republic of Germany

Bundesstraße f [bOOndess-shtrahss-uh] major road, A-road

Bundestag m [bOOndess-tahk]

German parliament
Burg f [boork] castle
Bürgersteig m [bOOrger-shtike] pavement, sidewalk
Büro n [bOOro] office
Büroartikel office supplies
Bürste f [bOOrst-uh] brush
Busbahnhof m [booss-bahnhohf] bus station
Bushaltestelle f [booss-halt-uh-shtell-uh] bus stop
bzw. (beziehungsweise) or

C

Café n [kaffay] café, serving mainly cakes, coffee and tea etc
Campingbedarf camping equipment
Campingliege f [kemping-leeg-uh] campbed
Campingplatz m [kempingplats] campsite; caravan site, trailer park
CD-Spieler m [tsay-day-shpeeler] CD player
Charterflug m [charter-flOOk] charter flight
Chauvi m [shohvee] male chauvinist pig
Chef m [shef], **Chefin** f boss
chemische Reinigung f [shaymish-uh rynigoong] dry cleaner's
Chinarestaurant n [sheena-restorong] Chinese restaurant
chinesisch [sheenayzish] Chinese

Chirurg m [sheeroork], **Chirurgin** f surgeon
Coiffeur m [kwaffur] hairdresser

D

da there; as; since
Dach n [daKH] roof
Dachboden m [daKHbohden] attic
Dachgepäckträger m [daKH-gepeck-trayger] roof rack
dafür [dafOOr] for that; on that; in that; in favour; then again; considering
daher [dahair] from there; that's why
Dame f [dahm-uh] lady
Damen ladies' (toilet), ladies' room
Damenbinde f [dahmenbind-uh] sanitary towel/napkin
Damenkleidung f [dahmen-klydoong] ladies' clothing
Damenmoden ladies' fashions
Damensalon m [dahmen-zalong] ladies' hairdresser's
Damentoilette f [dahmen-twalett-uh] ladies' (toilet), ladies' room
Damenunterwäsche f [dahmen-oontervesh-uh] lingerie
damit so that; with it
Dampfer m steamer
danach [danaKH] after that; accordingly
Dänemark n [dayn-uh-mark] Denmark
dänisch [daynish] Danish
dankbar grateful

danke [d**a**nk-uh] thank you,
thanks
danke gleichfalls [gl**y**shfals] the
same to you
danken to thank
dann then
darf am allowed to; is allowed
to; may
darfst are allowed to; may
Darlehen n [d**ah**rlay-en] loan
darum [dar**oo**m] about it; that's
why
das the; who; that; which
daß [dass] that
Datum n [d**ah**toom] date
Dauerwelle f [d**o**wervell-uh]
perm
Daumen m [d**o**wmen] thumb
davon from there; of it; of
them; from it; from them
DB (Deutsche (Bundes)bahn)
German Railways
Decke f [d**e**ck-uh] blanket;
ceiling
Deckel m lid
defekt out of order; faulty
dein(e) [d**i**ne(-uh)] your
denken to think
Denkmal n [d**e**nkmahl]
monument
denn for, because; than
deprimiert [deprim**ee**rt]
depressed
der [dair] the; who; that
deshalb [d**e**ss-halp] therefore
Desinfektionsmittel n [desinfekts-
y**oh**ns-mittel] disinfectant
deutsch [d**oy**tch] German
Deutsche m/f [d**oy**tch-uh]

German
deutsches Erzeugnis made in
Germany
Deutschland n [d**oy**tchlant]
Germany
Deutschlandlied n [d**oy**tchlant-
leet] German national
anthem
d.h. (das heißt) i.e.
Dia n [d**ee**-ah] slide
Diabetiker m [dee-ah-b**ay**tiker],
Diabetikerin f diabetic
Diamant m [dee-ah-m**a**nt]
diamond
Diät f [dee-**ay**t] diet
dich [dish] you
Dichter m [d**i**shter] poet
dick fat; thick
die [dee] the; who; that; which
Dieb m [deep] thief
Diebstahl m [d**ee**p-shtahl] theft
Dienstag m [d**ee**nstahk] Tuesday
dienstbereit [d**ee**nst-berite] on
duty
dies [deess] this (one); that
(one); these (ones); those
(ones)
diese [d**ee**z-uh] this (one); that
(one); these (ones); those
(ones)
dieser [d**ee**zer] this (one); that
(one)
dieses [d**ee**zess] this (one);
that (one)
diesseits [d**ee**ss-zites] on this
side (of)
Ding n thing
dir [deer] (to) you
Direktflug m [d**ee**rekt-fl**oo**k] non-

stop flight

diskutieren [disk00t**ee**ren] to
discuss

DJH (Deutsche Jugendherberge)
German Youth Hostel
Association

**DLRG (Deutsche
Lebensrettungsgesellschaft)**
[day-el-air-g**ay**] German
lifeguards association

DM (Deutsche Mark) DM,
German mark

doch! [doKH] oh yes it is!; oh
yes I am! etc

Dolmetscher m [d**o**lmetcher],
Dolmetscherin f interpreter

Dom m [dohm] cathedral

Donau f [d**oh**now] Danube

Donner m thunder

Donnerstag m [d**o**nnerstahk]
Thursday

doof [dohf] stupid

Doppelbett n double bed

doppelt double

Doppelzimmer n [d**o**ppel-
tsimmer] double room

Dorf n village

dort there

dort drüben [dr**oo**ben] over
there; up there

dort oben [**oh**ben] over there;
up there

Dose f [d**oh**z-uh] can

Dosenöffner m [d**oh**zen-urfner]
tin opener

Dragees npl [dra**Jay**ss] sugar-
coated tablets

Draht m wire

Drahtseilbahn f [dr**ah**tzilebahn]

cable car

Dreck m dirt

drehen [dr**ay**-en] to turn

drei [dry] three

dreimal täglich einzunehmen to
be taken three times a day

dreißig [dr**y**ssish] thirty

dreizehn [dr**y**-tsayn] thirteen

dringend [dr**i**ng-ent] urgent

dritte(r,s) [dr**i**tt-uh,-er,-ess] third

Droge f [dr**oh**g-uh] drug

Drogerie f [drohger**ee**]
chemist's, toiletries shop

Druck m [dr**oo**ck] pressure

drücken [dr**oo**cken] to push

Drucker m [dr**oo**cker] printer

Drucksache f printed matter

**DSD (Duales System
Deutschland)** recycling
scheme

du [doo] you

du lieber Gott! [l**ee**ber gott] good
God!

du liebe Zeit! [l**ee**b-uh tsite]
struth!

Duft m [dooft] smell; fragrance

dumm [doomm] stupid

Dummheit f [d**oo**mmhite]
stupidity

Dummkopf m [d**oo**mmkopf] idiot

Dünen fpl [d**oo**nen] sand dunes

dunkel [d**oo**nkel] dark

Dunkelheit f [d**oo**nkelhite]
darkness

dünn [doonn] thin; skinny

durch [doorsh] through; by;
well-done

Durcheinander n [d**oo**rsh-ine-
ander] mess

Durchfall m [do**o**rshfal]
diarrhoea
Durchgang m [do**o**rshgang]
passage
Durchgangsverkehr through
traffic
durchgehend geöffnet open 24
hours
Durchschnitt m [do**o**rsh-shnitt]
average
durchstreichen [do**o**rsh-
shtryshen] to cross out, to
delete
Durchsuchung f [doorsh-
z**oo**KHoong] search
Durchwahl direct dialling
dürfen [do**o**rfen] to be allowed
to
Durst m [do**o**rst] thirst
Durst haben [h**ah**ben] to be
thirsty
Dusche f [do**o**sh-uh] shower
duschen [do**o**shen] to have a
shower
Düsenflugzeug n [d**oo**zen-
flooktsoyk] jet plane
Dutzend n [do**o**tsent] dozen
duzen: sich duzen [zish do**o**tsen]
to use the familiar 'du' form
D-Zug [d**ay**-tsook] express train

E

Ebbe f [**e**bb-uh] low tide
echt [esht] genuine
Ecke f [**e**ck-uh] corner
Edelstein m [**ay**del-shtine]
precious stone
EG (Europäische Gemeinschaft)

[ay-g**ay**] EC, European
Community
ehe [**ay**-uh] before
Ehe f [**ay**-uh] marriage
Ehefrau f [**ay**-uh-frow] wife
Ehemann m [**ay**-uh-man]
husband
ehrlich [**air**lish] honest; sincere
Ehrlichkeit f [**air**lishkite] honesty
Eiche f [**ī**sh-uh] oak
Eieruhr f [**ī**er-oor] egg timer
eifersüchtig [**ī**ferz**oo**shtish]
jealous
eigen [**ī**gen] own
eigenartig [**ī**gen-artish] strange
eigentlich [**ī**gentlish] actual;
actually
Eigentümer m [**ī**gent**oo**mer],
Eigentümerin f owner
Eilzug m [**ī**le-tsook] fast local
train
Eimer m [**ī**me-er] bucket
ein(e) [ine(-uh)] a; one
Einbahnstraße f [**ine**-bahn-
shtrahss-uh] one-way street
Einbrecher m [**ine**-bresher]
burglar
Einbruch m [**ine**-brooKH]
burglary
einchecken [**ine**-checken] to
check in
Eindruck m [**ine**-droock]
impression
eine [**ine**-uh] a
einfach [**ine**-faKH] simple;
single
einfache Fahrt one-way
journey; single; one way
Einfahrt f [**ine**-fahrt] entrance,

way in

Einfahrt freihalten keep entrance clear

Eingang m [**ine**-gang] entrance, way in

Eingang um die Ecke entrance round corner

eingeschränktes Halteverbot restricted parking

eingetragenes Warenzeichen registered trademark

Einheit f [**ine**-hite] unit

Einheitspreis flat rate

einige [**ine**-ig-uh] a few; some

Einkauf m [**ine**-kowf] shopping

einkaufen: einkaufen gehen [**ine**-kowfen g**ay**-en] to go shopping

Einkaufskorb m [**ine**-kowfss-korp] shopping basket

Einkaufstasche f [**ine**-kowfss-tash-uh] shopping bag

Einkaufswagen m [**ine**-kowfss-vahgen] shopping trolley

Einkaufszentrum n [**ine**-kowfss-tsentroom] shopping centre

einladen [**ine**-lahden] to invite

Einladung f [**ine**-lahdoong] invitation

Einlaß m [**ine**-lass] admission

einmal [**ine**-mahl] once
nicht einmal not even

einmalig [**ine**-mahlish] unique

einpacken [**ine**-packen] to wrap

einreiben [**ine**-ryben] to rub in

Einrichtung f [**ine**-rishtoong] furnishing; organization

eins [ine-ss] one

einsam [**ine**-zahm] lonely

einschalten [**ine**-shalten] to switch on

einschenken [**ine**-shenken] to pour

einschlafen [**ine**-shlahfen] to fall asleep

einschl. (einschließlich) incl., inclusive

einschließlich 15% Bedienung 15% service charge included

Einschreiben n [**ine**-shryben] registered letter

Einschreibsendungen registered mail

einsteigen [**ine**-shtygen] to get in

Einstieg hinten enter at the rear

Einstieg nur mit Fahrausweis obtain a ticket before boarding

Einstieg vorn enter at the front

eintreten in [**ine**-trayten] to enter

Eintritt m [**ine**-tritt] entry

Eintritt frei admission free

Eintrittskarte f [**ine**-tritts-kart-uh] ticket

Eintrittspreise admission

einverstanden! [**ine**-fairshtanden] OK!; agreed

einwerfen [**ine**-vairfen] to insert

Einzahlungen deposits

Einzelbett n [**ine**-tselbett] single bed

Einzelfahrkarte f [**ine**-tsel-fahrkart-uh] single/one-way ticket

Einzelhändler m [**ine**-tsel-hentler]

retailer
Einzelheit f [**ine**-tselhite] detail
Einzelpreis m [**ine**-tsel-price]
(unit) price
Einzelzimmer n [**ine**-tsel-
tsimmer] single room
Eiscafé n [**ice**-kaffay] ice cream
parlour (also serves coffee and
liqueurs)
Eisenbahn f [**ī**zenbahn] railway
Eisenwarenhandlung f
[**ī**zenvahren-hantloong]
hardware store
Eisstadion n [**ice**-shtahdee-on]
ice rink
Eiter m [**ite**-er] pus
Elektriker m [aylektriker]
electrician
Elektrizität f [aylektritsit**ayt**]
electricity
Elektroartikel mpl [aylektro-
arteekel] electrical goods
Elektrogeräte npl [aylektro-gerayt-
uh] electrical equipment
elf eleven
Elfmeter m [elfm**ay**ter] penalty
Ellbogen m [**ell**-bohgen] elbow
Eltern parents
Eltern haften für ihre Kinder
parents are responsible for
their children
Empfang m reception
Empfänger m [emp-f**e**nger]
addressee
empfehlen [emp-f**ay**len] to
recommend
Ende der Autobahn end of
motorway/highway
Ende der Vorfahrtsstraße end of

priority
endlich [entlish] at last; finally
Endstation f [ent-shtats-yohn]
terminus
eng narrow; tight
Engländer m [**eng**-lender]
Englishman
Engländerin f [**eng**-lenderin]
English girl/woman
englisch [**eng**-lish] English; rare
(meat)
Enkel m grandson
Enkelin f granddaughter
entdecken to discover
entfernt [entf**ai**rnt] away;
distant
Entfernung f [entf**ai**rnoong]
distance
entführen [entf**oo**ren] to kidnap,
to abduct
Entgleisung f [ent-gl**y**zoong]
derailment
enthält ... contains ...
entlang along(side)
entscheiden [ent-sh**y**den] to
decide
entschlossen [ent-shl**o**ssen]
determined
entschuldigen: sich
entschuldigen [zish
entsh**oo**ldigen] to apologize
entschuldigen Sie bitte [zee
bitt-uh] excuse me
Entschuldigung
[entsh**oo**ldigoong] sorry,
excuse me
entsetzlich [entz**e**tslish]
appalling
enttäuscht [ent-t**oy**sht]

disappointed

Enttäuschung f [ent-**toy**shoong] disappointment

entweder ... oder ... [e**n**tvayder **oh**der] either ... or ...

Entwerter m [entv**air**ter] ticket-stamping machine

entwickeln [entv**i**ckeln] to develop

Entzündung f [ent-ts**oo**ndoong] infection

er [air] he

Erde f [aird-uh] earth

Erdgeschoß n [**ai**rt-geshoss] ground floor, (US) first floor

Erfahrung f [airf**ah**roong] experience

Erfolg m [airf**o**llk] success

Erfrischung f [airfr**i**shoong] refreshment

ergibt die doppelte/dreifache Menge makes twice/three times as much

erhalten [airh**a**lten] to receive

erholen: sich erholen [zish airh**oh**len] to recover

Erholungsgebiet n [airh**oh**loongs-geb**ee**t] recreational area

erinnern: sich erinnern an [zish air-**i**nnern] to remember

Erinnerung f [air-**i**nneroong] memory

erkälten: sich erkälten [zish airk**e**lten] to catch cold

erkältet: erkältet sein [airk**e**ltet] to have a cold

Erkältung f [airk**e**ltoong] cold

erkennen [airk**e**nnen] to recognize

erklären [airkl**ai**ren] to explain

erlauben [airl**ow**ben] to allow

Erlaubnis f [airl**ow**pniss] permission

Erlebnis n [airl**ay**pniss] experience

Ermäßigte Preise reduced prices

Ermäßigungen reductions; concessions

ermorden [airm**o**rden] to murder

ernst [airnst] serious

Ersatzreifen m [airz**a**tz-ryfen] spare tyre

Ersatzteile npl [airz**a**tz-tile-uh] spare parts

erschießen [airsh**ee**ssen] to shoot (and kill)

Ersparnisse fpl [airshp**ah**rniss-uh] savings

erst [airst] only just; only

erstatten [airsht**a**tten] to refund

erstaunlich [airsht**ow**nlish] astonishing

erste(r,s) [**ai**rst-uh, -er, -es] first

Erste Hilfe f [**ai**rst-uh h**i**lf-uh] first aid

erste Klasse [**ai**rst-uh kl**a**ss-uh] first class

erstens [**ai**rstens] first; firstly

erster Stock m [**ai**rster shtock] first floor, (US) second floor

ersticken [airsht**i**cken] to suffocate

ertrinken [airtr**i**nken] to drown

Erwachsene m/f [airv**a**ksen-uh] adult

erwähnen [airv**ay**nen] to

mention

es [ess] it

eßbar [essbar] edible

essen to eat

Essen n food

Eßlöffel m [ess-lurffel]
tablespoon

Etage f [aytahJ-uh] floor, storey

Etagenbett n [aytahJen-bett]
bunk beds

Etat m [aytah] budget

Etikett n label

etwa [etvah] about; perhaps

etwas [etvass] something;
some; somewhat

etwas anderes [anderess]
something else

euch [oysh] you

euer [oyer] your

eure [oyr-uh] your

europäisch [oyro-pay-ish]
European

Euroscheck m [oyrosheck]
Eurocheque

ev. (evangelisch) Protestant

evangelisch [evangaylish]
Protestant

Explosionsgefahr f [eksplohz-
yohns-gefahr] danger of
explosion

F

Fabrik f [fabreek] factory

Fach n [faKH] subject;
pigeonhole

Facharzt m: Facharzt für ...
[faKHartst foor] specialist
for ...

Fachmann m [faKHmann]
specialist

Faden m [fahden] string;
thread

Fahne f [fahn-uh] flag

Fahrausweis m [fahr-owssvice]
ticket

Fahrausweise sind auf Verlangen
vorzuzeigen tickets must be
displayed on request

Fahrbahn f roadway

Fähre f [fair-uh] ferry

fahren to drive; to go

Fahrer m driver

Fahrgäste passengers

Fahrkarte f [fahrkart-uh] ticket

Fahrkartenautomat m
[fahrkarten-owtomaht] ticket
machine

Fahrkartenschalter m [fahrkarten-
shalter] ticket office

Fahrplan m [fahrplahn]
timetable, (US) schedule

Fahrpreise mpl [fahrprize-uh]
fares

Fahrrad n [fahr-raht] bicycle

Fahrräder bicycles

Fahrradkarte f [fahr-rahtkart-uh]
bicycle ticket

Fahrradverleih m [fahr-raht-fairlī]
bicycles for hire/to rent

Fahrradweg m [fahr-raht-vayk]
cycle path

Fahrschein m [fahr-shine] ticket

Fahrscheinkauf nur beim Fahrer
buy your ticket from the
driver

Fahrstuhl m [fahr-shtool] lift,
elevator

Fahrt f journey

Fahrtziele destinations

Fahrzeug n [**fahr**-tsoyk] vehicle

Fall m [fal] fall; case

fallen [**fal**-en] to fall

fallenlassen [**fal**-en-lassen] to drop

falls [falss] if

falsch [falsh] wrong; false

falten to fold

Familie f [fam**ee**lee-yuh] family

Familienpackung f family pack

fand [fant], fanden found

fangen to catch

Farbe f [**farb**-uh] colour; paint

Farben und Lacke paints

Farbfilm m [**farb**film] colour film

Fasching m [**fa**shing] annual carnival held in the pre-Lent period with fancy-dress processions and general celebrating

Fasse dich kurz! keep it brief!

fast [fasst] almost, nearly

faul [fowl] lazy; rotten

Feder f [**fay**der] feather; spring

Federbett n [**fay**derbett] quilt

Fehler m [**fay**ler] mistake; defect

fehlerhaft [**fay**ler-haft] faulty

Feierabend m [**fy**-erahbent] closing time; time to stop

Feiertag m [**fy**-ertahk] public holiday

Feinkostgeschäft n [**fine**-kost-gesheft] delicatessen

Feinschmecker m [**fine**-shmecker], Feinschmeckerin f gourmet

Feld n [felt] field

Felsen m [**fel**zen] rock

Fenster n window

Fensterläden mpl [**fe**nster-layden] shutters

Ferien fpl [**fai**ree-en] holidays, vacation

Ferienwohnung f [**fai**ree-en-vohnoong] holiday home

Ferngespräch n [**fair**n-geshpraysh] long-distance call

Fernlicht n [**fair**n-lisht] full beam

Fernschreiben n [**fair**n-shryben] telex

Fernsehen n [**fair**nzay-en] television

Fernsprecher m telephone

Ferse f [**fair**z-uh] heel

fertig [**fair**tish] ready; finished

fest fixed; firm; definite

festnehmen [**fe**stnaymen] to arrest

Fete f [**fay**t-uh] party

fett greasy

Fett n fat

Fettgehalt fat content

feucht [foysht] damp

Feuchtigkeitscreme f [**foy**shtish-kites-kraym] moisturizer; cold cream

Feuer n [**foy**er] fire

Feuergefahr f [**foy**er-gefahr] fire hazard

Feuerlöscher m [**foy**erlursher] fire extinguisher

Feuertreppe f [**foy**ertrepp-uh] fire escape

Feuerwehr f [**foy**ervair] fire

GERMAN ❖ ENGLISH | Fe

brigade

Feuerwehrausfahrt fire brigade exit

Feuerwerk n [**foy**ervairk] fireworks

Feuerzeug n [**foy**er-tsoyk] lighter

Fieber n [**fee**ber] fever

Filmmusik f [film-moo**zeek**] soundtrack

Filzstift m [filts-shtift] felt-tip pen

finden [**fin**-den] to find

Fingernagel m [**fing**-er-nahgel] fingernail

Firma f [**feer**mah] company

Fischgeschäft n [fish-ge**sheft**] fishmonger's

FKK [ef-kah-**kah**] nudism

flach [flakH] flat

Flasche [**fla**sh-uh] bottle

Flaschenöffner m [**fla**shen-urfner] bottle-opener

Fleck m stain; spot

Fleischerei f [flysher-**ī**] butcher's

Fliege f [**flee**g-uh] fly; bow tie

fliegen [**flee**gen] to fly

fließend [**flee**ssent] fluent

Flitterwochen fpl [**fli**ttervoKHen] honeymoon

Flucht f [flooKHt] escape

flüchten [**floo**shten] to escape

Flug m [flook] flight

Flugdauer f [**flook**-dower] flight time

Flügel m [**floo**gel] wing

Fluggast m [**floo**k-gast] air passenger

Fluggeschwindigkeit f [**floo**k-geshwindish-kite] flight speed

Fluggesellschaft f [**floo**k-gezellshafft] airline

Flughafen m [**floo**k-hahfen] airport

Flughafenbus m [**floo**k-hahfen-booss] airport bus

Flughöhe f [**floo**k-hur-uh] altitude

Flugkarte f [**floo**k-kart-uh] flight ticket

Fluglinie f [**floo**k-leen-yuh] airline

Fluglotse m [**floo**k-lohts-uh] air traffic controller

Flugplan m [**floo**kplahn] timetable, (US) schedule

Flugsteig m [**floo**k-shtike] gate

Flugzeug n [**floo**k-tsoyk] (aero)plane

Flugzeugabsturz m [**floo**ktsoyk-**a**pshtoorts] plane crash

Flur m [floor] corridor

Fluß m [flooss] river

Flut f [floot] high tide

fl.W. (fließendes Wasser) running water

folgen [fol-gen] to follow

folgende [folgend-uh] next

Fön® m [furn] hair dryer

fönen: sich fönen lassen [zish **fur**nen] to have a blow-dry

fordern to demand

Formular n [formool**ahr**] form

Foto n [**foto**] photo(graph)

Fotoartikel mpl [**foto**-arte**ek**el] photographic equipment

Fotograf m [foto**grahf**] photographer

fotografieren [foto-grafe**ee**ren] to

photograph

Fotografin f [fotograhfin] photographer

Fr. (Frau) Mrs; Ms

Frage f [frahg-uh] question

fragen [frahgen] to ask

Frankreich n [frank-rysh] France

Franzose m [frantsohz-uh] Frenchman

Französin f [frantsurzin] French girl; French woman

französisch [frantsurzish] French

Frau f [frow] woman; wife; Mrs; Ms

Frauenarzt m [frowen-artst] gynaecologist

Fräulein n [froyline] Miss

frech [fresh] cheeky

frei [fry] free, vacant

frei von Konservierungsstoffen contains no preservatives

frei von künstlichen Aromastoffen contains no artificial flavouring

Freibad n [frybaht] outdoor swimming pool

freigegeben ab ... Jahren suitable for those over ... years of age

Freikörperkultur f [fry-kurper-kooltoor] nudism

Freitag m [frytahk] Friday

freiwillig [fry-villish] voluntary; voluntarily

Freizeichen n [fry-tsyshen] ringing tone

Freizeit f [fry-tsite] spare time; leisure

Freizeitzentrum n [fry-tsite-tsentroom] leisure centre

fremd [fremt] strange; foreign

Fremde m/f [fremd-uh] stranger; foreigner

Fremdenzimmer npl [fremden-tsimmer] room(s) to let/rent

freuen: sich freuen [zish froyen] to be happy

Freund m [froynt] friend; boyfriend

Freundin f [froyndin] friend; girlfriend

freundlich [froyntlish] kind; friendly

freut mich! [froyt mish] pleased to meet you!

Frieden m [freeden] peace

Friedhof m [freet-hohf] cemetery

frisch [frish] fresh

frisch gestrichen wet paint

Frischhaltepackung f airtight pack

Friseur m [frizzur] barber; hairdresser

Frisur f [frizzoor] hairstyle

Frittenbude f [fritten-bood-uh] chip shop

Frl. (Fräulein) Miss

froh glad

frohes neues Jahr [froh-ess noy-ess yahr] happy New Year!

frohe Weihnachten! [froh-uh vynakHten] happy Christmas!

Frostschaden m [frost-shahden] frost damage

Frostschutzmittel n [frost-shoots-mittel] antifreeze

früh [froo] early

Frühling m [frooling] spring

Frühstück n [frooshtoock] breakfast

frühstücken [frooshtoocken] to have breakfast

fühlen: (sich) fühlen [(zish) foolen] to feel

fuhr [foor], fuhren drove; went; travelled

führen [fooren] to lead
wir führen ... we stock ...

Führer m [foorer] guide; guidebook

Führerin f [foorerin] guide

Führerschein m [foorer-shine] driving licence

fuhrst [foorst] drove; went

Führung f [fooroong] guided tour

füllen [foollen] to fill

Fundbüro n [foont-booro] lost property office

fünf [foonf] five

fünfzehn [foonf-tsayn] fifteen

fünfzig [foonf-tsish] fifty

Fünfzigmarkschein m [foonftsish-mark-shine] fifty-mark note/bill

Funktaxi n [foonk-taksee] radio taxi

funktionieren [foonkts-yohneeren] to work

für [foor] for

Furcht f [foorsht] fear

furchtbar [foorshtbar] terrible

fürchten: sich fürchten [zish foorshten] to be afraid

fürs [foorss] for the

Fuß m [fooss] foot

zu Fuß on foot

Fußball m [foossbal] football

Fußballplatz m [foossbal-plats] football ground

Fußballstadion n [foossbal-shtahdee-on] football stadium

Fußgänger m [fooss-geng-er], Fußgängerin f pedestrian

Fußgänger bitte andere Straßenseite benutzen pedestrians please use other side of road

Fußgängerüberweg m [foossgeng-er-oobervayk] pedestrian crossing

Fußgängerzone f [foossgeng-er-tsohn-uh] pedestrian precinct

G

gab [gahp] gave

Gabel f [gahbel] fork; hook

gaben [gahben], gabst [gahpst] gave

gähnen [gaynen] to yawn

Gang m corridor; gear; walk; course

ganz [gants] whole; quite; very
den ganzen Tag all day
ganz gut [goot] pretty good

Garderobe f [garderohb-uh] cloakroom
für Garderobe wird nicht gehaftet the management accepts no liability for items left here

Garten m garden

Gaspedal n [gahss-pedahl] accelerator

Gast m guest

Gastarbeiter m [gast-arbyter], Gastarbeiterin f foreign worker

Gästebuch n [gest-uh-bookh] visitors' register

Gastfreundschaft f [gastfroynt-shafft] hospitality

Gastgeber m [gast-gayber] host

Gastgeberin f [gast-gayberin] hostess

Gasthaus n [gast-howss] inn

Gasthof m [gast-hohf] restaurant, inn

Gaststätte f [gast-shtett-uh] restaurant; pub; inn

Gastwirtschaft f [gast-veert-shafft] pub

geb. (geboren) born, née

Gebäude n [geboyd-uh] building

geben [gayben] to give

Gebiß n [gebiss] dentures

geblieben [gebleeben] stayed

geboren: geboren sein [gebohren zine] to be born

gebracht [gebrakht] brought

Gebrauch m [gebrowkh] use; custom

vor Gebrauch schütteln shake before using

gebrauchen [gebrowkhen] to use

Gebrauchsanleitung instructions for use

Gebrauchsanweisung beachten follow instructions for use

gebraucht [gebrowkht] second-hand

gebrochen [gebrokhen] broken

gebt [gaypt] give

Gebühren fpl [gebooren] charges

gebührenpflichtig liable to charge

Geburt f [geboort] birth

Geburtsort m [geboorts-ort] place of birth

Geburtstag m [geboorts-tahk] birthday

Gedächtnis n [gedeshtnis] memory

Gedanke m [gedank-uh] thought

Gefahr f [gefahr] danger

gefahren travelled; gone; driven

gefährlich [gefairlish] dangerous

Gefährliche Einmündung dangerous junction; danger: concealed exit

Gefährliche Kurve dangerous bend

gefallen: das gefällt mir [dass gefellt meer] I like it

Gefangene m/f [gefangen-uh] prisoner

Gefängnis n [gefengniss] prison

Gefriertruhe f [gefreer-troo-uh] freezer

gefroren [gefrohren] frozen

Gefühl n [gefool] feeling

gefunden [gefoonden] found

gegangen [gegang-en] gone

gegeben [gegayben] given

gegen [gaygen] against

Gegenanzeige contra-indications

Gegend f [gaygent] area

Gegenstand m [gaygenshtant] object

Gegenteil n [gaygen-tile] opposite

gegenüber [gaygen-oober] opposite

Gegenverkehr hat Vorfahrt oncoming traffic has right of way

gegessen eaten

Gegner m [gaykner], **Gegnerin** f opponent

gehabt [gehapt] had

geheim [gehime] secret

Geheimnis n [gehymnis] secret

Geheimzahl eingeben enter personal number

gehen [gay-en] to go; to walk
geht das? is that OK?
das geht nicht that's not on

Gehirn n [geheern] brain

Gehirnerschütterung f [geheern-airshootteroong] concussion

Gehör n [gehur] hearing

gehören [ge-hur-ren] to belong (to)

Geisel f [gyzel] hostage

Geistlicher m [gystlisher] priest

gekommen come

gekonnt been able to; masterly

gekühlt haltbar bis ... if chilled will keep until ...

gelassen relaxed; left

gelb [gelp] yellow

Gelbe Seiten [gelb-uh zyten] yellow pages

Geld n [gelt] money

Geldautomat m [gelt-owtomaht] cash dispenser, automatic teller

Geld einwerfen insert money

Geldeinwurf insert money

Geldrückgabe returned coins

Geldschein m [geltshine] banknote, (US) bill

Geldstrafe f [geltshtrahf-uh] fine

Geldwechsel m [geltveksel] bureau de change

Gelegenheitskauf m [gelaygen-hites-kowf] bargain

Gelenk n joint

Gemälde n [gemayld-uh] painting

gemocht [gemoKHt] liked

Gemüsehändler m [gemooz-uh-hentler] greengrocer

gemußt [gemoosst] had to

genau [genow] exact; exactly

Genf [genf] Geneva

genommen taken

genug [genook] enough
genug haben (von) to be fed up (with)

geöffnet [guh-urfnet] open; opened

geöffnet von ... bis ... open from ... to ...

Gepäck n [gepeck] luggage, baggage

Gepäckaufbewahrung f [gepeck-owf-bevahroong] left luggage, (US) baggage check

Gepäckausgabe f [gepeck-owssgahb-uh] baggage claim

Gepäckkontrolle f [gepeck-kontrol-uh] baggage check

Gepäckschließfach n [gepeck-shleessfaKH] luggage locker

Gepäckträger m [gepeck-trayger] porter

gepflegt [gepflaykt] well looked
after; refined

gerade [gerahd-uh] just;
straight

geradeaus [gerahd-uh-**owss**]
straight on

Gerät n [gerayt] device

gerecht [geresht] fair

Gericht n [gerisht] court; dish

gern(e) [gairn(uh)] gladly
etwas gern(e) tun to like
doing something

Geruch m [gerOOKH] smell

Gesamtpreis m [gezamt-price]
total

Geschäft n [gesheft] shop;
business

Geschäftsfrau f [gesheftsfrow]
businesswoman

Geschäftsführer m [gesheftes-
fOOrer] manager

Geschäftsführerin f [gesheftes-
fOOrerin] manageress

Geschäftsmann m [gesheftsmann]
businessman

Geschäftsreise f [gesheftes-rize-uh]
business trip

Geschäftszeiten hours of
business

geschehen [geshay-en] to
happen

Geschenk n [geshenk] present,
gift

Geschenkartikel gifts

Geschichte f [geshisht-uh] story;
history

geschieden [gesheeden]
divorced

Geschirr n [gesheerr] crockery

Geschirrtuch n [gesheerr-tOOKH]
tea towel

Geschlecht n [geshlesht] sex

Geschlechtskrankheit f
[geshleshts-krank-hite] VD

geschlossen closed

geschlossen von ... bis ... closed
from ... to ...

Geschmack m [geshmack] taste;
flavour

geschrieben [geshreeben]
written

Geschwindigkeit f [geshvindish-
kite] speed

Geschwindigkeitsbeschränkung f
[geshvindish-kites-
beshrenkoong] speed limit

Geschwindigkeitsbeschränkung
beachten observe speed limit

geschwollen [geshvollen]
swollen

gesehen [gezay-en] seen

Gesellschaft f [gezellshafft]
society; company

Gesetz n [gezets] law

Gesicht n [gezisht] face

Gesichtcreme f [gezishts-kraym]
face cream

gesperrt closed; no entry

Gesperrt für Fahrzeuge aller Art
closed to all vehicles

Gespräch n [geshpraysh] call;
conversation

Gestalt f [geshtalt] figure

gestattet [geshtattet] allowed

gestern [gestern] yesterday

gestorben [geshtorben] died

gesund [gezoont] healthy

Gesundheit f [gezoont-hite]

health

Gesundheit! bless you!

getan [get**ah**n] done

Getränkekarte f [getr**e**nk-uh-kart-uh] drinks list

getrennt [getr**e**nnt] separate; separately

Getriebe n [getr**ee**b-uh] gearbox

getrunken [getr**oo**nken] drunk

Gewehr n [gev**ai**r] gun

gewesen [gev**ay**zen] been

Gewicht n [gev**i**sht] weight

Gewichtsverlust durch Erhitzen weight loss through heating

Gewinn m [gev**i**nn] prize; profit

gewinnen [gev**i**nnen] to win

Gewitter n [gev**i**tter] thunderstorm

Gewohnheit f [gev**oh**nhite] habit

gewöhnlich [gev**ur**nlish] usual; usually

geworden [gev**o**rden] become

gewünschten Betrag wählen select required amount

gewünschte Rufnummer wählen dial number required

gewußt [gev**oo**sst] known

Gezeiten [gets**y**ten] tides

gibst [geepst] give

gibt [geept] gives

gibt es ...? is/are there ...?

es gibt ... there is/are ...

Gift n poison

giftig [g**i**ftish] poisonous

ging, gingen [g**i**ng-en], gingst went

Gips m plaster (of Paris)

Gipsverband m [g**i**ps-fairbant] plastercast

Girokonto n [J**ee**ro-konto] current account

Giroverkehr m [J**ee**ro-fairkair] giro transactions

Gitarre f [git**a**rr-uh] guitar

Glas n [glahss] glass

glatt slippery; smooth

Glatteis n [gl**a**tt-ice] black ice

Glatteisgefahr black ice

Glatze f [gl**a**ts-uh] bald head

glauben [gl**ow**ben] to believe

gleich [glysh] equal; same; in a moment

Gleis n [glice] platform, (US) track

zu den Gleisen to the platforms/tracks

Glocke f [gl**o**ck-uh] bell

Glück n [gl**oo**ck] luck; happiness

zum Glück [tsoom] fortunately

glücklich [gl**oo**cklish] lucky; happy

Glücksbringer m [gl**oo**cks-bring-er] lucky charm

Glühbirne f [gl**oo**beern-uh] light bulb

GmbH (Gesellschaft mit beschränkter Haftung) [gay-em-bay-h**ah**] Ltd, limited company

Gott n God

Gottesdienst m [g**o**ttes-deenst] church service; mass

Grab n [grahp] grave

Grammatik f grammar

Gras n [grahss] grass

gratis [gr**ah**tiss] free

grau [grow] grey

grausam [gr**ow**zahm] cruel

Grenze f [grents-uh] border

Grenzkontrolle f [grents-kontroll-uh] border checkpoint

Griechenland n [greeshenlant] Greece

griechisch [greeshish] Greek

Griff m handle

grinsen [grinzen] to grin

Grippe f [gripp-uh] flu

Groschen m [groshen] 10 pfennig piece

groß [grohss] big, large; tall

Großbritannien n [grohss-britannee-en] Great Britain

Größe f [grurss-uh] size

Großmutter f [grohss-mootter] grandmother

Großpackung f [grohss-packoong] large size

Großvater m [grohss-fahter] grandfather

grün [groon] green
   der grüne Punkt suitable for recycling

Grund m [groont] cause

Grundierungscreme f [groondeeroongs-kraym] foundation cream

Grundschule f [groont-shool-uh] primary school

Gruppe f [groopp-uh] group; party

Gruppenreise f [grooppen-rize-uh] group excursion

Gruß m [grooss] greeting
   schöne Grüße an ... [shurn-uh grooss-uh] give my regards to ...

grüßen [groossen] to greet; to say hello to

grüß Gott [grooss] hello (South German)

gültig [gooltish] valid

Gummi n [goommee] rubber

Gummiband n [goommeebant] rubber band

günstig [goonstish] favourable; convenient; inexpensive

Gürtel m [goortel] belt

gut [goot] good; well

gutaussehend [goot-owss-zay-ent] handsome; good-looking

gute Besserung! [goot-uh besseroong] get well soon!

guten Abend [gooten ahbent] good evening

gute Nacht [goot-uh naKHt] good night

guten Appetit! [gooten appeteet] enjoy your meal!

guten Morgen [gooten] good morning

guten Tag [gooten tahk] hello

guten Tag, freut mich [gooten tahk froyt mish] how do you do, nice to meet you

gute Reise [goot-uh rize-uh] have a good trip

Güterzug m [gooter-tsook] goods train

gutmütig [gootmootish] good-natured

Gutschein m [goot-shine] voucher

Gymnasium n [goom-nahzee-oom] secondary school

H

H (Haltestelle) bus/tram stop

Haar n [hahr] hair

Haarfestiger m [hahrfestiger] conditioner

Haarschnitt m [hahrshnitt] haircut

Haarstudio n [hahr-shtoodee-oh] hairdressing studio

haben [hahben] to have

Hafen m [hahfen] harbour, port

Hafenpolizei f [hahfen-polits-ī] harbour police

Hafenrundfahrt f [hahfen-roontfahrt] boat trip round the harbour

Haft f custody

Häftling m [heftling] prisoner

Hagel m [hahgel] hail

Haken m [hahken] hook

halb [halp] half

halbe Stunde f [halb-uh shtoond-uh] half an hour

Halbpension f [halp-pangz-yohn] half board

Hälfte f [helft-uh] half

Hallenbad n [hallenbaht] indoor swimming pool

Hals n [halss] neck

Halskette f [halsskett-uh] necklace

Hals-Nasen-Ohren-Arzt m [halss-nahzen-ohren-artst] ear, nose and throat specialist

Halsschmerzen [halss-shmairtsen] sore throat

Halstabletten fpl [halss-tabletten] throat pastilles

halt! [hallt] stop!

Haltbar bis … best before …

Haltbarkeitsdatum best before date

Halte deine Stadt sauber keep your city clean

halten to hold; to stop

Haltestelle f [hallt-uh-shtell-uh] stop

Halteverbot no stopping; no waiting

hält nicht in … does not stop in …

Handarbeit f [hant-arbite] needlework

Handbremse f [hantbremz-uh] handbrake

Handel m deal; commerce

Handelsgesellschaft f (trading) company

Handelsbank f merchant bank

Handgelenk n [hant-gelenk] wrist

Handgepäck n [hant-gepeck] hand luggage/baggage

Handlung f [hantloong] shop; action

Handschuhe mpl [hant-shoo-uh] gloves

Handtasche f [hant-tash-uh] handbag, (US) purse

Handtuch n [hant-tooKH] towel

Handwerk n [hantvairk] crafts

Handzettel m [hant-tsettel] leaflet

Hansaplast® n [hanzaplast] Elastoplast®, (US) Band-Aid

hart hard

Hase m [hahz-uh] hare; rabbit

Haß m [hass] hatred

hassen to hate

häßlich [hesslish] ugly

hast have

hat has

hatte [hatt-uh] had

hätte [hett-uh] would have; had

hatten, hattest had

Haupt- [howpt] main

Hauptbahnhof m [howpt-bahnhohf] central station

Hauptpost f [howpt-posst] main post office

Hauptprogramm n [howpt-programm] main feature

Hauptsaison f [howpt-zaysong] high season

Hauptstraße f [howpt-shtrahss-uh] main road; high street

Haus n [howss] house

zu Hause [tsoo howz-uh] at home

nach Hause gehen [naKH – gay-en] to go home

Haushaltsgeräte npl [howss-hallts-gerayt-uh] household equipment

Haushaltwaren fpl [howss-hallt-vahren] household goods

Hausmeister m [howss-myster] caretaker, janitor

Hausnummer f [howss-noommer] street number

Hausordnung f [howss-ortnoong] house rules

Hausschuhe mpl [howss-shoo-uh] slippers

Haustier n [howsteer] pet

Hauswirt m [howssveert] landlord

Hauswirtin f [howss-veertin] landlady

Haut f [howt] skin

Hautreiniger m [howt-ryniger] skin cleanser

Hbf (Hauptbahnhof) central station

Heft n exercise book

Heftzwecke f [heft-tsveck-uh] drawing pin

Heißlufttrockner m [hice-looft-trockner] hot-air hand-drier

heilen [hylen] to cure

Heiligabend m [hylish-ahbent] Christmas Eve

Heimwerkerbedarf DIY supplies

Heirat f [hyraht] marriage

heiraten [hyrahten] to get married

heiß [hice] hot

heißen [hyssen] to be called

wie heißen Sie? [vee] what's your name?

Heißwachs m [hice-vaks] hot wax

Heizdecke f [hites-deck-uh] electric blanket

Heizgerät n [hites-gerayt] heater

Heizung f [hytsoong] heating

helfen to help

hell light; bright

Hemd n [hemt] shirt

herabgesetzt reduced

zu stark herabgesetzten Preisen prices slashed

Herbergsmutter f [hairbairks-mootter] warden

Herbergsvater m [hairbairks-fahter] warden

Herbst m [hairpst] autumn, (US) fall

herein! [hair-**ine**] come in!

hergestellt in ... made in ...

Herr m [hair] Mr; gentleman

Herren gents' (toilet), men's room

Herrenkleidung f [h**ai**ren-kl**y**doong] menswear

Herrenmoden men's fashions

Herrensalon m [h**ai**ren-zalong] men's hairdresser

Herrentoilette f [h**ai**ren-twalett-uh] gents' (toilet), men's room

herrlich [h**ai**rlish] lovely

Hersteller m manufacturer

Herz n [hairts] heart

Herzinfarkt m [h**ai**rts-inf**a**rkt] heart attack

herzlich willkommen [h**ai**rtslish villk**o**mmen] welcome

herzlichen Glückwunsch! [h**ai**rtslishen gl**oo**ckvoonsh] congratulations!; happy birthday!; happy anniversary!

Heufieber n [h**oy**feeber] hay fever

heute [h**oy**t-uh] today

heute abend [**ah**bent] tonight

heute geschlossen closed today

hier [heer] here

hier abreißen tear off here

hier abschneiden cut off here

hier einreißen tear off here

hier einsteigen enter here

hierher [h**ee**rhair] here

hierhin here

hier öffnen open here

hier Parkschein lösen buy parking permit here

Hilfe f [h**i**lf-uh] help

Himmel m sky; heaven

hinlegen: sich hinlegen [zish h**i**nlaygen] to lie down

hinsichtlich [h**i**nzishtlish] with regard to

hinten at the back

hinter behind

Hintergrund m [h**i**ntergroont] background

Hinterhof m [h**i**nterhohf] back yard

Hintern m bottom

Hinterrad n [h**i**nter-raht] back wheel

Hirsch m [heersh] stag

Hitzewelle f [h**i**ts-uh-vell-uh] heat wave

hoch [hohKH] high

Hochschule f [h**o**hKH-sh**oo**l-uh] college; university

höchste [h**u**rkst-uh] highest

Höchstgeschwindigkeit maximum speed

Hochzeit f [h**o**KH-tsite] wedding

Hochzeitstag m [h**o**KH-tsites-tahk] wedding anniversary

hoffen to hope

hoffentlich [h**o**ffentlish] hopefully

Hoffnung f [h**o**ffnoong] hope

höflich [h**u**rflish] polite

Höhe f [h**u**r-uh] height

höher [h**u**r-er] higher

höhere Schule f [h**u**rer-uh sh**oo**l-uh] secondary school

Höhle f [h**ur**l-uh] cave
holen [h**oh**len] to fetch, to get
holländisch [h**o**llendish] Dutch
Holz n [holts] wood
hören [h**ur**-ren] to hear
Hörer m [h**ur**-rer] receiver;
listener
Hörer abnehmen lift receiver
Hörer einhängen replace
receiver
Hörerin f [h**ur**-rerin] listener
Hörgerat n [h**ur**-gerayt] hearing
aid
Höschen n [h**ur**ss-shen] panties
Hose f [h**oh**z-uh] trousers, (US)
pants
Hr. (Herr) Mr
hübsch [h**oo**psh] pretty
Hubschrauber m [h**oo**p-shrowber]
helicopter
Hüfte f [h**oo**ft-uh] hip
Hügel m [h**oo**gel] hill
Hund m [hoont] dog
Hunde bitte anleinen dogs must
be kept on a lead
hundert [h**oo**ndert] hundred
Hundertmarkschein m [h**oo**ndert-
m**a**rk-shine] hundred-mark
note/bill
Hunde sind an der Leine zu
führen dogs must be kept on
a lead
Hunger: Hunger haben [h**oo**ng-er
h**ah**ben] to be hungry
Hupe f [h**oo**p-uh] horn
Hupen verboten sounding horn
forbidden
Husten m [h**oo**sten] cough
Hut f [hoot] hat

Hypothek f [h**oo**pot**ay**k]
mortgage

I

i.A. (im Auftrag) pp
ich [ish] I; me
Idee f [eed**ay**] idea
i.d.T. (in der Trockenmasse) dry
measure
ihm [eem] him; to him
ihn [een] him
ihnen them; to them
Ihnen [**ee**nen] you; to you
ihr [eer] you; her; to her; their
Ihr [eer] your
ihre [**ee**r-uh] her; their
Ihre [**ee**r-uh] your
Illustrierte f [illoostr**ee**rt-uh]
magazine
im in (the)
immer always
Immobilienmakler m [immob**ee**l-
yen-mahkler] estate agent
Impfung f [**i**mpfoong]
vaccination
indem [ind**ay**m] as; by
Industriegebiet n [indoostr**ee**-
gebeet] industrial zone
infolge [in-f**o**lg-uh] as a result of
Infopostsendung f [**i**nfo-posst-
zendoong] printed matter
Informationsschalter m
[informats-y**oh**ns-shalter]
information desk
Inh. (Inhaber) proprietor
Inhalt contents
Initialen fpl [inits-y**ah**len] initials
Inland domestic

Inlandsflüge domestic flights

Inlandsgespräch n [**i**nlants-gespr**ays**h] inland call

Inlandsporto n [**i**nlants-porto] inland postage

innen (im/in) inside

innerhalb [**i**nner-halp] within

ins into the; to the

Insektenschutzmittel n [inz**e**kten-shoots-mittel] insect repellent

Insel f [**i**nzel] island

insgesamt altogether

Installateur m [inshtalat**ur**] plumber

Intensivstation f [intenz**ee**f-shtats-y**oh**n] intensive care unit

interessant interesting

Interesse n [inter**e**ss-uh] interest

irgend etwas [**ee**rgent **e**tvass] something; anything

irgend jemand [**ee**rgent y**ay**mant] somebody; anybody

irgendwo [**ee**rgent-vo] somewhere

irisch [**ee**rish] Irish

ißt [isst] eat; eats

ist is

Italien n [it**ah**lee-en] Italy

italienisch [ital-y**ay**nish] Italian

J

ja [yah] yes

Jacht f [ya**KH**t] yacht

Jachthafen m [ya**KH**t-hahfen] marina

Jacke f [y**a**ck-uh] jacket; cardigan

Jahr n [yahr] year

Jahreszeit f [y**ah**ress-tsite] season

Jahrhundert n [yahr-h**oo**ndert] century

Jahrmarkt m [y**ah**rmarkt] fair

Jalousie f [Jal**oo**z**ee**] Venetian blind

Jausenstation f [y**ow**zen-shtats-yohn] snack bar

je [yay] ever

jede [y**ay**d-uh] each; every

jeden Tag [y**ay**den tahk] every day

jeder [y**ay**der] everyone; each

jedes [y**ay**dess] each

jedesmal [y**ay**dessmahl] every time

je ... desto ... [yay d**e**sto] the ... the ...

jemals [y**ay**mahlss] ever

jemand [y**ay**mant] somebody

jenseits [y**ay**n-zites] on the other side (of); beyond

jetzt [yetst] now

JH (Jugendherberge) youth hostel

joggen: joggen gehen [dJ**o**ggen g**ay**-en] to go jogging

Jucken n [y**oo**cken] itch

jüdisch [y**oo**dish] Jewish

Jugendherberge f [y**oo**gent-hairbairg-uh] youth hostel

Jugendklub m [y**oo**gent-kl**oo**p] youth club

Jugendliche: für Jugendliche ab ... Jahren for young people over the age of ...

Juli m [y**oo**lee] July

jung [yoong] young

Junge m [y**oo**ng-uh] boy

junge Leute [y**oo**ng-uh l**oy**t-uh] young people

Junge Mode fashions for the young

Junggeselle m [y**oo**ng-gezell-uh] bachelor

Juni m [y**oo**nee] June

Juwel n [yoov**ay**l] jewel

Juwelier m [yoov-uh-l**eer**] jeweller's

K

Kabel n [k**ah**bel] cable

Kabine f [kabee**n**-uh] cabin

Kaffeefilter m [k**a**ffay-filter] coffee filter

Kaffeehaus n [k**a**ffay-howss] café

kahl bald

Kai m [kī] quay

Kalender m calendar; diary

kalt cold

kam [kahm], kamen came

Kamin m [kam**ee**n] chimney; fireplace

Kamm m comb

Kampf m fight

kämpfen [k**e**mpfen] to fight

kamst [k**ah**mst] came

Kanadier m [kan**ah**dee-er], Kanadierin f Canadian

kanadisch [kan**ah**dish] Canadian

Kanal m [kan**ah**l] canal; Channel

Kaninchen n [kan**ee**nshen] rabbit

kann can

Kännchen [k**e**nnshen] pot

Kanne f [k**a**nn-uh] (tea/coffee) pot

kannst can

Kanu n [k**ah**n∞] canoe

Kapitän m [kapit**ay**n] captain

Kappe f [k**a**pp-uh] cap

kaputt [kap**oo**tt] broken

Karfreitag m [karfr**y**tahk] Good Friday

Karneval m [k**a**rn-uh-val] annual carnival held in the pre-Lent period with fancy-dress processions and general celebrating

Karte f [k**a**rt-uh] card; ticket

Karten tickets

Kartenleser m [k**a**rten-layzer] card reader

Kartenspiel n [k**a**rtenshpeel] card game

Kartentelefon n [k**a**rten-telefohn] cardphone

Kasse f [k**a**ss-uh] cashdesk, till, cashier; box office

Katalysator m [katal∞z**ah**tohr] catalytic converter

Kater m [k**ah**ter] hangover; tomcat

kath. (katholisch) Catholic

Katze f [k**a**ts-uh] cat

kaufen [k**ow**fen] to buy

Kaufhaus n [k**ow**fhowss] department store

kaum [kowm] hardly

Kaution f [k**ow**ts-yohn] deposit

Kehle f [k**ay**l-uh] throat

Keilriemen m [**kile**-reemen] fan belt

kein(e) ... [**kine**(-uh)] no ...; not ...

keine Ahnung [**kine**-uh **ah**noong] no idea

ich habe keine [ish h**ah**b-uh **kine**-uh] I don't have any

keine ... mehr [**kine**-uh mair] no more ...

kein ... mehr [**kine** mair] no more ...

kein Ausstieg no exit

keine heiße Asche einfüllen do not put hot ashes in this container

kein Einstieg no entry

keine Selbstbedienung no self-service

keine Zufahrt no entry

kein Trinkwasser not drinking water

kein Verkauf an Jugendliche unter ... Jahren sales forbidden to minors under the age of ...

kein Zugang no entry

kein Zutritt no admittance; no entrance

kein Zutritt fur Jugendliche unter ... Jahren no admission to minors under the age of ...

Keller m cellar

Kellner m waiter

Kellnerin f waitress

kennen to know

Keramik f [kair**ah**mik] china

Kerze f [**kairts**-uh] candle

Kette f [kett-uh] chain

Keuchhusten m [**koysh**-h**oo**sten] whooping cough

Kiefer m [**kee**fer] jaw; pine

Kind n [kint] child

Kinder npl children

für Kinder ab ... Jahren for children from the age of ...

Kinderarzt m [kinder-artst], Kinderärztin f pediatrician

Kinderbett n cot

Kinderkleidung f [kinder-klydoong] children's clothing

Kindermoden children's fashions

Kindersitz m [kinder-zits] child seat

Kinderspielplatz m [kinder-shpeelplats] children's playground

Kindervorstellung f [kinder-forshtelloong] children's performance

Kinderwagen m [kindervahgen] pram

Kinn n chin

Kino n [**kee**no] cinema, movie theater

Kinocenter n [**kee**no-senter] multiplex cinema/movie theater

Kirche f [**keersh**-uh] church

Klang m sound

klar clear; OK, sure

Klasse f [kl**ass**-uh] class

klebrig [kl**ay**brish] sticky

Kleid n [klite] dress

Kleider [kl**y**der] clothes

Kleiderbügel m [kl**y**der-b**oo**gel] (coat)hanger

klein [kline] small

Kleinbus m [kline-booss] van

Kleingeld n [kline-gelt] change

Klempner m plumber

Klima n [kleemah] climate

Klimaanlage f [kleemah-anlahg-uh] air-conditioning

klimatisiert [klimateezeert] air-conditioned

Klingel f bell

klingeln to ring

Klippe f [klipp-uh] cliff

Klo n loo

Kloster n [klohster] convent; monastery

klug [klook] clever

Kneipe f [k-nipe-uh] pub, bar

Knie n [k-nee] knee

Knöchel m [k-nurshel] ankle

Knochen m [k-noKHen] bone

Knopf m [k-nopf] button

Knoten m [k-nohten] knot

Koch m [koKH] cook

Kochgeschirr n [koKH-gesheerr] cooking utensils

Köchin f [kurshin] cook

Kochnische f [koKHneesh-uh] kitchenette

Kochtopf m [koKHtopf] saucepan

Koffer m bag; suitcase

Kofferkuli m [kofferkOOlee] luggage/baggage trolley

Kofferraum m [koffer-rowm] boot, (US) trunk

Kohle f [kohl-uh] coal

Kollege m [kollayg-uh], Kollegin f colleague

Köln [kurln] Cologne

Kölnisch Wasser [kurlnish vasser] eau de Cologne

komisch [kohmish] funny

kommen to come

das kommt darauf an [dahrowf] it depends

Komödie f [komurdee-uh] comedy

kompliziert [komplitseert] complicated

Konditorei f [kondeetor-ī] cake shop

Kondom n [kondohm] condom

König m [kurnish] king

Königin f [kurnigin] queen

Konkurrenz f [konkoorents] competition

können [kurnen] to be able to; can

können Sie ...? [zee] can you ...?

könnte [kurnt-uh], könnten, könntest could

konnte [konnt-uh], konnten, konntest could

Konservierungsstoffe preservatives

Konsulat n [konzOOlaht] consulate

Kontaktlinsen fpl [kontakt-linzen] contact lenses

Konto n account

Kontrolle f [kontrol-uh] control

kontrollieren [kontrolleeren] to control

Konzert n [kontsairt] concert

Kopf m head

Kopfkissen n pillow

Kopfschmerzmittel n [kopfshmairts-mittel] aspirin

Kopfstütze f [kopf-shtOOts-uh]

headrest
Kopftuch n [k**o**pft**oo**KH] scarf
Kopfweh n [k**o**pf-vay] headache
Kopie f [k**o**p**ee**] copy
kopieren [kop**ee**ren] to copy
Korb m [korp] basket
Korkenzieher m [k**o**rken-tsee-er] corkscrew
Körper m [k**u**rper] body
Körperpuder m [k**u**rper-p**oo**der] talcum powder
Kosmetika npl [kosm**a**ytikah] cosmetics
kostbar [k**o**st-bar] precious
kosten to cost
kostenlos [k**o**sten-lohss] free of charge
köstlich [k**u**rstlish] delicious
Kostüm n [kost**oo**m] ladies' suit
Kragen m [kr**ah**gen] collar
Krampf m cramp
krank ill, (US) sick
Kranke m/f [kr**a**nk-uh] sick person
Krankenhaus n [kr**a**nken-howss] hospital
Krankenkasse f [kr**a**nkenkass-uh] medical insurance
Krankenpfleger m [kr**a**nken-pflayger] male nurse
Krankenschein m [kr**a**nken-shine] health insurance certificate
Krankenschein nicht vergessen don't forget your health insurance certificate
Krankenschwester f [kr**a**nken-shvester] nurse
Krankenwagen m [kr**a**nkenvahgen] ambulance

Krankheit f [kr**a**nk-hite] disease
Krawatte f [krav**a**tt-uh] tie, necktie
Krebs m [krayps] cancer
Kreditabteilung accounts department
Kredite mpl [krayd**ee**t-uh] loans
Kreditkarte f [krayd**ee**tkart-uh] credit card
Kreis m [krice] circle
Kreisverkehr m [kr**i**ce-fairkair] roundabout
Kreuz n [kr**oy**ts] cross
Kreuzfahrt f [kr**oy**tsfahrt] cruise
Kreuzung f [kr**oy**tsoong] junction; crossroads, intersection
Kreuzworträtsel n [kr**oy**tsvortraytsel] crossword puzzle
Kriechspur crawler lane
Krieg m [kreek] war
kriegen [kr**ee**gen] to get
Krücken fpl [kr**oo**cken] crutches
Krug m [kr**oo**k] jug
Küche f [k**oo**sh-uh] cooking, cuisine; kitchen
Küchenbedarf for the kitchen
Kugel f [k**oo**gel] ball
Kugelschreiber m [k**oo**gel-shryber] biro®
Kuh f [k**oo**] cow
kühl [k**oo**l] cool
Kühler m [k**oo**ler] radiator (on car)
kühl lagern keep in a cool place
Kühlschrank m [k**oo**l-shrank] fridge
kühl servieren serve chilled

Kultur f [kooltoor] culture

Kulturbeutel m [kooltoor-boytel] toiletry bag

Kumpel m [koompel] pal

Kunde m [koond-uh], Kundin f customer

Der Kunde ist König the customer is always right

Kundenparkplatz customer car park/parking lot

Kunst f [koonst] art

Kunstgalerie f [koonst-galeree] art gallery

Kunsthalle f [koonst-hal-uh] art gallery

Künstler m [koonstler], Künstlerin f artist

künstlich [koonstlish] artificial

Kupplung f [kooploong] clutch

Kurbelwelle f [koorbel-vell-uh] crankshaft

Kurort m [koor-ort] spa

Kurs m [koorss] rate; exchange rate; course

Kurswagen m [koors-vahgen] through coach

Kurve f [koorv-uh] bend

Kurvenreiche Strecke bends

kurz [koorts] short

kurz nach [naKH] just after

kurz vor [for] just before

kurzsichtig [koorts-zishtish] shortsighted

Kurzstrecke f [koorts-shtreck-uh] short journey

Kurzwaren fpl [koortsvahren] haberdashery

Kusine f [koozeen-uh] cousin

Kuß m [kooss] kiss

küssen [koossen] to kiss

Küste f [koost-uh] coast

Küstenwacht f [koosten-vaKHt] coastguard

L

l (Liter) litre

Labor n [labohr] laboratory

lächeln [lesheln] to smile

Lächeln n smile

lachen [laKHen] to laugh

lächerlich [lesherlish] ridiculous

Laden m [lahden] shop

Ladenstraße f [lahdenshtrahss-uh] shopping street

Laken n [lahken] sheet

Lampe f [lamp-uh] lamp

Land n [lant] country

landen to land

Länder npl [lender] administrative districts of Germany, each with its own parliament

Landeskennzahl f [landess-kenntsahl] country dialling code

Landkarte f [lantkart-uh] map

Landschaft f [lantshafft] countryside; landscape; scenery

Landstraße f [lant-shtrahss-uh] country road

Landtag m [lant-tahk] regional parliament

Land- und forstwirtschaftlicher Verkehr frei agricultural and forestry vehicles only

lang long

lange [lang-uh] for a long time

Länge f [leng-uh] length

langsam [langzahm] slow; slowly

Langsam fahren drive slowly

langweilig [langvile-ish] boring

Lärm m [lairm] noise

lassen to let; to leave

lässig [lessish] relaxed

Laster m lorry, truck

Lastwagen m [lasst-vahgen] lorry, truck

Latzhose f [lats-hohz-uh] dungarees

laufen [lowfen] to run

Läufer m [loyfer] runner; rug

laut [lowt] loud; noisy

lauwarm [low-varm] lukewarm

Lawine f [laveen-uh] avalanche

Lawinengefahr danger of avalanches

Leben n [layben] life

leben to live

lebendig [lebendish] alive

Lebensgefahr f [laybens-gefahr] danger

Lebenshaltungskosten pl [laybens-haltoongs-kosten] cost of living

Lebenslauf m [laybens-lowf] CV, résumé

Lebensmittel npl [laybens-mittel] groceries

Lebensmittelhandlung f [laybensmittel-hantloong] grocer's

Lebensmittelvergiftung f [laybensmittel-fairgiftoong] food poisoning

Leber f [layber] liver

Leck n leak

lecker tasty

Leder n [layder] leather

Lederwaren leather goods

ledig [laydish] single

leer [lair] empty

Leerung f [lairoong] collection

Nächste Leerung next collection

legen [laygen] to put

Lehrer m [lairer], Lehrerin f teacher; instructor

leicht [lysht] easy; light

leicht verderblich will not keep, perishable

leiden [lyden] to suffer

leider [lyder] unfortunately

leid: tut mir leid [toot meer lite] I'm sorry

leihen [ly-en] to borrow; to lend

Leihgebühr f [ly-geboor] rental

Leim m [lime] glue

Leiter f [lyter] ladder

Leiter m, Leiterin f leader; manager

Lenkrad n [lenkraht] steering wheel

Lenkung f [lenkoong] steering

lernen [lairnen] to learn

lesen [layzen] to read

Leser m [layzer], Leserin f reader

letzte(r,s) [letst-uh,-er,-ess] last

Leute pl [loyt-uh] people

Licht n [lisht] light

Licht einschalten turn on lights

Lichtspiele cinema, movie

theater
Lidschatten m [leet-shatten] eye
  shadow
Liebe f [leeb-uh] love
lieben [leeben] to love
lieber [leeber] rather
Liebhaber m [leep-hahber],
  Liebhaberin f lover
Lieblings- [leeplings] favourite
Lied n [leet] song
Lieferant m [leeferant] supplier
liefern to deliver
liegen [leegen] to lie; to be
  situated
Liegestuhl f [leeg-uh-shtool]
  deckchair
Liegewagen f [leeg-uh-vahgen]
  couchette
lila [leelah] purple
Limousine f [limoozeen-uh]
  saloon car
Linie f [leen-yuh] line; airline
Linienflug m [leen-yen-flook]
  scheduled flight
links left
links (von) [fon] on the left (of)
Linksabbieger left filter
Links halten keep left
linkshändig [links-hendish] left-
  handed
Linse f [linz-uh] lens
Lippe f [lipp-uh] lip
Lippenstift m [lippen-shtift]
  lipstick
Liste f [list-uh] list
Lkw m [el-kah-vay] lorry, truck;
  heavy goods vehicle, HGV
Loch n [loKH] hole
Locke f [lock-uh] curl

Lockenwickler m [locken-vickler]
  curler
Löffel m [lurfel] spoon
los [lohss] loose
  los! come on!
  was ist los? what's up?
Löwe m [lurv-uh] lion
Lücke f [loock-uh] gap
Luft f [looft] air
luftdicht verpackt airtight pack
Luftdruck m [looft-droock] air
  pressure
Luftkissenboot n [looftkissen-
  boht] hovercraft
Luftpost: per Luftpost [pair
  looftposst] by airmail
Luftpostsendungen airmail
lügen [loogen] to lie
Lunge f [loong-uh] lung
Lungenentzündung f [loongen-
  ent-tscondoong] pneumonia
Lust haben auf [loost hahben
  owf] to feel like
Luxus m [looksoos] luxury

M

machen [maKHen] to make; to
  do
mach schon! [maKH shohn] get
  on with it!
mach's gut [goot] take care
Mädchen n [mayt-shen] girl
Mädchenname m [mayt-shen-
  nahm-uh] maiden name
mag [mahk] like; likes; may
Magen m [mahgen] stomach
Magenschmerzen mpl [mahgen-
  shmairtsen] stomach ache

Magenverstimmung f [m**ah**gen-
fairshtimmoong] indigestion

magst [mahkst] like

Mahlzeit f [m**ah**l-tsite] meal

nach den Mahlzeiten
einzunehmen to be taken
after meals

vor den Mahlzeiten
einzunehmen to be taken
before meals

Mai m [my] May

Mal n [mahl] time

zum ersten Mal [tsoom **ai**rsten]
for the first time

malen [m**ah**len] to paint

man one; you

man spricht Englisch English
spoken

manchmal [m**a**nshmahl]
sometimes

Mandelentzündung f [mandel-
ent-ts∞ndoong] tonsillitis

Mandeln fpl tonsils

Mangel m shortage

Mann m man; husband

Mann! boy!

männlich [m**e**nnlish] male

Mannschaft f [m**a**nnshafft] team;
crew

Mantel m coat

Markt m market

Markthalle f [m**a**rkt-hal-uh]
indoor market

März m [mairts] March

Masern [m**ah**zern] measles

Massenmedien npl [m**a**ssen-
mayd-yen] mass media

Matratze f [matrats-uh] mattress

Mauer f [m**ow**er] wall

Maus f [mowss] mouse

maximale Belastbarkeit
maximum load

Mechaniker m [mesh**ah**neeker]
mechanic

Medikament n medicine

Meer n [mair] sea

mehr [mair] more

mehrere [m**ai**rer-uh] several

Mehrfachstecker m [m**ai**rfaKH-
shtecker] adaptor

Mehrfahrtenkarte f [m**ai**rfahrten-
kart-uh] multi-journey ticket

Mehrheit f [m**ai**rhite] majority

Mehrwertsteuer f [m**ai**rvairt-
shtoyer] Value Added Tax,
VAT

mein [mine], meine [m**i**ne-uh]
my

Meinung f [m**y**noong] opinion

meiste: das meiste (von) [m**y**st-
uh (fon)] most (of)

Melone f [mel**oh**n-uh] melon;
bowler hat

Menge f [meng-uh] crowd

Mensch m [mensh] person

Mensch! wow!

Menschen people

menschlich [m**e**nshlish] human

Messe f [m**e**ss-uh] (trade) fair

Messegelände n [m**e**ssuh-
gelenduh] fair (site)

Messer n knife

Meter m [m**a**yter] metre

Metzger m [m**e**tsger] butcher's

Metzgerei f [metsger-**i**] butcher's

mich [mish] me

Mietauto [m**ee**t-owto] hire car,
rental car

Miete f [meet-uh] rent

mieten [meeten] to rent

Mietkauf m [meetkowf] lease
purchase

Militärisches Sperrgebiet keep
off: military zone

Milliardär m [mill-yardair],
Milliardärin f billionaire

Millionär m [mill-yonair],
Millionärin f millionaire

min. (Minute) minute

Minderheit f [minderhite]
minority

mindestens at least

Mindestens haltbar bis ... will
keep at least until ...

Mineralölsteuer f [minerahl-url-
shtoyer] oil tax

Minirock m miniskirt

mir [meer] me; to me
mir geht's gut [gayts goot] I'm
OK

Mischung f [mishoong] mixture

Mißbrauch strafbar penalty for
misuse

Mißgeschick n [miss-geshick]
mishap

Mißverständnis n [miss-
fairshtentnis] misunder-
standing

Mist! bugger!, shit!

Miststück n [mist-shtoock] bitch

mit with

Mitbringen von Hunden nicht
gestattet no dogs allowed

Mitfahrzentrale f [mitfahr-
tsentrahl-uh] agency for
arranging lifts

Mitleid n [mit-lite] pity

mitnehmen [mit-naymen] to
take; to give a lift to
zum Mitnehmen to take away,
(US) to go

Mittag m [mittahk] midday

Mittagessen n [mittahk-essen]
lunch

mittags [mittahks] at midday

mittags geschlossen closed at
lunchtime

Mitte f [mitt-uh] middle

Mitteilung f [mit-tyloong]
message

Mittel n means

Mittelalter n [mittel-alter] Middle
Ages

mittelgroß [mittel-grohss]
medium-sized

Mittelmeer n [mittel-mair]
Mediterranean

Mitternacht f [mitternaKHt]
midnight

Mittwoch m [mittvoKH]
Wednesday

Möbel pl [murbel] furniture

möbliert [mur-bleert] furnished

möchte [mursht-uh] would like
to
ich möchte gern [gairn] I
would like

Mode f [mohd-uh] fashion

Modeartikel fashions

modisch [mohdish] fashionable

Mofa n [mohfah] small moped

mögen [murgen] to like

möglich [murklish] possible

Möglichkeit f [murklishkite]
possibility

Monat m [mohnaht] month

Monatskarte f [mohnats-kart-uh] monthly ticket

Monatsraten fpl [mohnahts-rahten] monthly instalments

Mond m [mohnt] moon

Montag m [mohntahk] Monday

Mord m [mort] murder

Mörder m [murder], Mörderin f murderer

morgen tomorrow

Morgen m morning

morgens in the morning

Motor abstellen switch off engine

Motorboot n [mohtorboht] motorboat

Motorhaube f [mohtohr-howb-uh] bonnet, (US) hood

Motorrad n [motohr-raht] motorbike

Möwe f [murv-uh] seagull

müde [mood-uh] tired

Mühe f [moo-uh] trouble

Müll abladen verboten no tipping (rubbish/garbage)

Mülltonne f [mooll-tonn-uh] dustbin, trashcan

München [moonshen] Munich

Mund m [moont] mouth

Münzeinwurf insert coin here

Münzen fpl [moontsen] coins

Münztank m [moonts-tank] coin-operated pump

Muschel f [mooshel] shell; mussel

Muskel m [mooskel] muscle

muß [mooss] must

müssen [moossen] to have to

mußt [moosst], müßt [moosst]

must

mußte [moosst-uh], mußten, mußtest had to

Muster n [mooster] pattern; specimen

mutig [mootish] brave

Mutter f [mootter] mother; nut

Mutti f [moottee] mum

Mütze f [moots-uh] cap

MWSt (Mehrwertsteuer) VAT

N

nach [naKH] after; to; according to

Nachbar m [naKHbar], Nachbarin f neighbour

nachdem [naKHdaym] after; afterwards

nachher [naKH-hair] afterwards

Nachmittag m [naKHmittahk] afternoon

Nachmittags geschlossen closed in the afternoons

Nachname m [naKHnahm-uh] surname

Nachricht f [naKHrisht] message

Nachrichten fpl [naKHrishten] news

nachsenden [naKHzenden] to forward

nächste [naykst-uh] next; nearest

nächstes Jahr next year

Nacht f [naKHt] night

Nachtdienst m [naKHt-deenst] late night chemist's/ pharmacy

Nachteil m [naKHtile]

disadvantage

Nachthemd n [na**ĸ**Ht-hemt] nightdress

Nachtportier m [na**ĸ**Ht-port-yay] night portier

Nachtruhe f [na**ĸ**Htroo-uh] sleep

nachts [na**ĸ**Hts] at night

Nacken m nape of the neck

nackt naked

Nadel f [na**h**del] needle; pin

Nagel m [na**h**gel] nail

Nagelfeile f [na**h**gelfile-uh] nailfile

Nagellack m [na**h**gel-lack] nail polish

Nagellackentferner m [na**h**gel-lack-entf**air**ner] nail polish remover

Nagelschere f [na**h**gel-shair-uh] nail clippers

nah(e) [na**h**(-uh)] near

Nähe: in der Nähe [in dair na**y**-uh] near here

nähen [na**y**-en] to sew

nahm, nahmen, nahmst took

Nahschnellverkehrszug local train

Nahverkehrszug m [na**h**-fairkairs-ts00k] local train

Narkose f [nark**oh**z-uh] anaesthetic

Nase f [na**h**z-uh] nose

Nasenbluten n [na**h**zenbl00ten] nosebleed

naß [nass] wet

natürlich [nat**oo**rlish] natural; of course

Naturprodukt natural produce

Nebel m [na**y**bel] fog

Nebelschlußleuchte f [naybel-shl**oo**ss-loysht-uh] rear fog light

neben [na**y**ben] next to

Nebenstraße f [na**y**ben-shtrahss-uh] minor road

nee [nay] nope

Neffe m [n**e**ff-uh] nephew

nehmen [na**y**men] to take

Neid m [nite] envy

neidisch [n**y**dish] envious

nein [nine] no

Nerven mpl [n**air**fen] nerves

Nervenzusammenbruch m [n**ai**rfen-ts00zammenbrooĸH] nervous breakdown

nervös [nairv**ur**ss] nervous

nett nice

Nettogewicht net weight

Nettoinhalt net contents

Netz n [nets] net; network

Netzkarte f [n**e**tskart-uh] travelcard, runabout ticket

neu [noy] new

Neubau m [n**oy**bow] new building

Neujahr n [n**oy**-yar] New Year

neulich [n**oy**lish] recently; the other'day

neun [noyn] nine

neunzehn [n**oy**n-tsayn] nineteen

neunzig [n**oy**n-tsish] ninety

nicht [nisht] not

nicht ... do not ...

nicht berühren do not touch

nicht betriebsbereit not ready

nicht bügeln do not iron

Nichte f [n**i**sht-uh] niece

Nichtgefallen: bei Nichtgefallen

Geld zurück money back if not satisfied

nicht hinauslehnen do not lean out

nicht hupen sounding horn forbidden

nicht in der Maschine waschen do not machine wash

nicht rauchen no smoking

Nichtraucher non-smokers

Nichtraucherabteil n [nishtrowKHer-apt**ile**] non-smoking compartment

nichts [nishts] nothing

nicht schleudern do not spin-dry

nicht stürzen fragile

nicht zur innerlichen Anwendung not for internal use

Nichtzutreffendes bitte streichen please delete as appropriate

nie [nee] never

Niederlage f [n**ee**derlahg-uh] defeat

Niederlande pl [n**ee**der-land-uh] Netherlands

niederländisch [n**ee**der-lendish] Dutch

niemals [n**ee**malss] never

niemand [n**ee**mant] nobody

Niere f [n**ee**r-uh] kidney

niesen [n**ee**zen] to sneeze

nimmst take

nimmt takes

nirgends [n**ee**rgents] nowhere

noch [noKH] still; even; more

noch ein(e) ... [ine(-uh)] another ...

noch nicht [nisht] not yet

nochmal [noKHmahl] again

Norden m north

Nordfriesische Inseln fpl [n**o**rtfreezish-uh **i**nzeln] North Frisian Islands

nordirisch [nort-**ee**rish] Northern Irish

Nordirland n [nort-**ee**rlant] Northern Ireland

nördliche Stadtteile city north

nördlich von [n**u**rtlish fon] north of

Nordsee f [n**o**rtzay] North Sea

Normal n [norm**ah**l] two-star petrol, regular gas

Norwegen n [n**o**rvaygen] Norway

norwegisch [n**o**rvaygish] Norwegian

Notarzt m [n**o**ht-artst] emergency doctor

Notaufnahme f [n**o**ht-owfnahm-uh] casualty department, A&E

Notausgang m [n**o**ht-owssgang] emergency exit

Notausstieg m [n**o**ht-owss-shteek] emergency exit

Notbremse f [n**o**htbremz-uh] emergency brake

Notfall m [n**o**htfal] emergency im Notfall Scheibe einschlagen smash glass in case of emergency

Notfälle mpl [n**o**ht-fell-uh] emergencies

nötig [n**u**rtish] necessary

Notizbuch n [not**ee**ts-booKH] notebook

Notruf m [n**o**ht-roof] emergency

call

Notrufsäule f [no**h**t-roof-zoyl-uh] emergency telephone

notwendig [nohtv**e**ndish] necessary

Nr. (Nummer) No., number

nüchtern einzunehmen to be taken on an empty stomach

null [nooll] zero

Nummer f [n**oo**mmer] number

Nummernschild n [n**oo**mmern-shilt] number plate

nun [n**oo**n] now

nur [n**oo**r] only; just

nur begrenzt haltbar will keep for a limited period only

nur für Anlieger access for residents only

nur für Bedienstete staff only

nur für Busse buses only

nur für Erwachsene adults only

nur für Gäste (hotel) patrons only

nur gegen Voranmeldung by appointment only

nur im Notfall benutzen emergency use only

nur mit der Hand waschen hand wash only

nur solange der Vorrat reicht only as long as stocks last

nur werktags weekdays only

nur zur äußerlichen Anwendung for external use only

nützlich [n**oo**tslish] useful

O

ob [op] whether; if

oben [**oh**ben] top; at the top; upstairs

Obergeschoß upper floor; top floor

Oberweite bust measurement, chest measurement

Obst und Gemüse fruit and vegetables

obwohl [opv**oh**l] although

oder [**oh**der] or

oder? isn't it?; don't you?; aren't I? etc; OK?

offen open

offensichtlich [offenz**i**shtlish] obvious

öffentlich [**ur**fentlish] public

Öffentlichkeit f [**ur**fentlish-kite] public

öffnen [**ur**fnen] to open

Öffnung [**ur**fnoong] opening Nach Öffnung nur beschränkt haltbar will keep for a limited period only after opening

Öffnungszeiten [**ur**fnoongs-tsyten] opening times

oft often

ohne [**oh**n-uh] without

ohne Konservierungsstoffe no preservatives

ohne künstliche Aromastoffe no artificial flavouring

Ohnmacht: in Ohnmacht fallen [**oh**n-maKHt] to faint

Ohr n [ohr] ear

Oktoberfest n [okt**oh**berfest] Munich beer festival (held in

September)
Ölstand m [**ur**lshtant] oil level
Ölwechsel sofort oil change
  while you wait
Oma f [**oh**mah] granny
Omnibus m [**o**mneebooss] bus
Onkel m uncle
Opa m [**oh**pah] grandad
Oper f [**oh**per] opera
Operationssaal m [opairats-
  yohns-zahl] operating theatre
Opfer n victim
Optiker m optician
Ordner m [**o**rtner] folder;
  steward
Ordnung f [**o**rtnoong] order
  in Ordnung all right
Ort m town; place
örtliche Betäubung f [**ur**tlish-uh
  bet**oy**boong] local anaesthetic
Ortsgespräch n [**o**rts-geshpr**ay**sh]
  local call
Ortsnetz n [**o**rtsnets] local
  network
Ortszeit f [**o**rts-tsite] local time
Ossi m [**o**ssee] East German
Osten m east
Ostern n [**oh**stern] Easter
Österreich n [**ur**ster-rysh] Austria
Österreicher m [**ur**ster-rysher]
  Austrian
Österreicherin f [**ur**ster-rysherin]
  Austrian (woman)
österreichisch [**ur**ster-ryshish]
  Austrian
Ostfriesische Inseln fpl
  [**o**stfreezish-uh **i**nzeln] East
  Frisian Islands
östliche Stadtteile city east

östlich von [**ur**stlish fon] east of
Ostsee f [**o**stzay] Baltic

P

Paar n [pahr] pair
paar: ein paar ... a few ...
Päckchen n(pl) [**p**eckshen] small
  parcel(s)
packen to pack
Packung f [**p**ackoong] pack
Paket n [pak**ay**t] parcel,
  package
Paketannahme f [pak**ay**t-an-
  nahm-uh] parcels counter
Palast m palace
Panne f [**p**ann-uh] breakdown
Pannendreieck n [**p**annen-dry-eck]
  emergency triangle
Pannenhilfe f [**p**annen-hilf-uh]
  breakdown services
Papier n [pap**ee**r] paper; litter
Papier(hand)tücher npl [pap**ee**r-
  (hant-)t**oo**sher] paper
  handkerchiefs, tissues
Pappe f [**p**app-uh] cardboard
Parfüm n [parf**oo**m] perfume
Parkausweis m [park-**o**wssvice]
  parking permit
Parkbucht f [**p**arkbookHt]
  parking space
Parkdauer parking allowed
  for ...
parken to park
Parken nur mit Parkscheibe
  parking disc holders only
Parken nur mit Parkschein
  parking only with parking
  permit

Parken verboten no parking

Parkett n stalls

Parkhaus n [parkhowss] multistorey car park/ parking garage

Parkplatz m [parkplats] car park, parking lot

Parkscheinautomat m [parkshine-owtomaht] car park/parking lot ticket vending machine

Parkschein entnehmen take a ticket

Parkuhr f [park-oor] parking meter

Parkverbot no parking

Paß m [pas] passport; pass

Passagier m [passah-Jeer] passenger

Paßkontrolle f [pas-kontrol-uh] passport control

Pauschalreise f [powshahl-rize-uh] package tour

Pause f [powz-uh] interval, intermission; rest

Pech n [pesh] bad luck

peinlich [pine-lish] embarrassing

Pelz m [pelts] fur

Pelzmantel m [peltsmantel] fur coat

Pension f [pangz-yohn] guesthouse

Personalausweis m [pairzonahl-owssvice] identity card

Personaleingang staff entrance

Personenzug m [pairzohnen-tsook] passenger train, stopping train

Perücke f [perOOck-uh] wig

Pf. (Pfennig) pfennig

Pfandleihe f [pfant-ly-uh] pawnbroker

Pfanne f [pfann-uh] frying pan

Pfd. (Pfund) pound (German pound = 500g)

Pfeife f [pfife-uh] pipe

Pferd n [pfairt] horse

Pferderennbahn f [pfaird-uh-rennbahn] race course

Pferdeschwanz m [pfaird-uh-shvants] ponytail

Pfingsten n Whitsun

Pflanze f [pflants-uh] plant

Pf. (Pfennig) pfennig (German unit of currency, 100 pf = DM 1)

Pfund n [pfoont] pound (German pound = 500g); pound (Sterling)

Phonoartikel hi-fi equipment

Pickel m spot

pikant savoury; spicy

Pille f [pill-uh] pill

Pinsel m [pinzel] paint brush

Pinzette f [pintsett-uh] tweezers

Pistole f [pistohl-uh] gun

Pkw m [pay-kah-vay] private car

Plakat n [plakaht] poster

Plakate ankleben verboten stick no bills

Plastik n plastic

Plastiktüte f [plastik-toot-uh] plastic bag

platt flat

Plattenspieler m [platten-shpeeler] record player

Platz m [plats] seat; square; place; space

Platzanweiserin f [plats-

anv**y**zerin] usherette
Platzkarte f [pl**a**ts-kart-uh] seat reservation
pleite [pl**ite**-uh] broke
Plombe f [pl**o**mb-uh] filling
plötzlich [pl**ur**tslish] suddenly
PLZ (Postleitzahl) postcode, zipcode
Pokal m [pohk**ah**l] cup
Polen n [p**oh**len] Poland
Politik f [polit**ee**k] politics
Politiker m [pol**ee**ticker], Politikerin f politician
politisch [pol**ee**tish] political
Polizei f [polits-**ī**] police
Polizeipräsidium n [polits-**ī**-prayz**ee**dee-oom] police headquarters
Polizeiwache f [polits-**ī**-vaKH-uh] police station
Polizist m [polits**i**st] policeman
Polizistin f [polits**i**st] policewoman
polnisch [p**o**l-nish] Polish
Pony m [p**o**nnee] fringe
Portemonnaie n [port-monn**ay**] purse
Portier m [port-y**ay**] porter
Porto n postage
portugiesisch [portoo-g**ee**zish] Portuguese
Porzellan n [portsell**ah**n] porcelain; china
Post f [posst] mail; post office
Postamt n [p**o**sst-amt] post office
Postanweisung f [p**o**sst-anvyzoong] postal/money order
Postanweisungen money orders
Postkarte f [p**o**sstkart-uh] postcard
postlagernd [p**o**sst-lahgernt] poste restante
postlagernde Sendungen poste restante
Postleitzahl f [p**o**sst-lite-tsahl] postcode, zip code
Postscheckkonto n [p**o**sst-sheck-konto] (post office) giro account
Postsparkasse f [p**o**sst-shparkass-uh] post office savings bank
Postwertzeichen n(pl) [p**o**sst-vairt-tsyshen] postage stamp(s)
Postwertzeichen in kl. Mengen stamps in small quantities
praktisch [pr**a**ktish] practical
praktische Ärztin f [pr**a**ktish-uh **ai**rtstin] GP
praktischer Arzt m [pr**a**ktisher artst] GP
Präservativ n [prezairvat**ee**f] condom
Praxis f [pr**a**ksis] doctor's surgery; practice
Preis m [price] price
zum halben Preis half price
preisgünstig [pr**ice**-gōōnstish] cheap; inexpensive
Preis reduziert price reduced
Preissenkung reduction
preiswert bargain price, inexpensive
prima! [pr**ee**mah] good!
Prinz m [prints] prince

Prinzessin f [printsessin]
princess
Privateigentum private
property
Privatgrundstück private
property
Privatparkplatz private car
park/parking lot
pro: pro Woche [voKH-uh] per
week
Probe f [prohb-uh] rehearsal;
sample
probieren [probeeren] to taste;
to try
Programmkino n [programm-
keeno] arts cinema
Prospekt m brochure
prost! [prohst] cheers!
Prozent n [prohtsent] per cent
Prozeß m [proh-tsess] trial;
process
prüfen [prOOfen] to check
Publikum n [pOOblikoom]
audience
Puder m [pOOder] powder
Pumpe f [poomp-uh] pump
Punkt m [poonkt] point; dot; full
stop
pünktlich [pOOnktlish] punctual
Puppe f [poopp-uh] doll
putzen [pootsen] to clean
Putzfrau f [pootsfrow] cleaning
lady

Q

Qualität f [kvalitayt] quality
Qualitätsware quality goods
Qualle f [kvall-uh] jellyfish

Quatsch m [kvatsh] nonsense
Quelle f [kvell-uh] spring;
source
Quittung f [kvittoong] receipt

R

Rabatt m reduction, discount
Rad n [raht] wheel
Radfahren n [raht-fahren]
cycling
Radfahrer m [raht-fahrer] cyclist
Radfahrer frei cyclists only
Radfahrerin f [raht-fahrerin]
cyclist
Radiergummi n [radeer-
goommee] rubber, eraser
Radweg m [raht-vayk] cycle
path
Radweg kreuzt cycle track
crossing
Rand m [rant] edge; rim
Rang m [rang] row; stalls; grade
Rasen m [rahzen] lawn
Rasierapparat m [razeer-
apparaht] razor
Rasiercreme f [razeer-kraym]
shaving cream
rasieren: sich rasieren [zish
razeeren] to shave
Rasierklinge f [razeerkling-uh]
razor blade
Rasierpinsel m [razeer-pinzel]
shaving brush
Rasierseife f [razeerzife-uh]
shaving foam
Rasierwasser n [razeervasser]
aftershave
Raststätte f [rast-shtett-uh]

services area

Rat m [raht] advice; council

Rate f [raht-uh] instalment; rate

raten [rahten] to guess; to advise

Ratenzahlung f [rahten-tsahloong] hire purchase, installment plan

Ratenzahlung möglich credit terms available

Rathaus n [raht-howss] town hall

Rätsel n [raytsel] puzzle

Ratskeller m [rahtskeller] restaurant and bar close to town hall

Ratte f [ratt-uh] rat

Rattengift n [rattengift] rat poison

Raub m [rowp] robbery

Raubüberfall m [rowp-oober-fal] armed robbery

Rauch m [rowкн] smoke

rauchen [rowкнen] to smoke

Rauchen einstellen no smoking

Rauchen und offenes Feuer verboten no smoking or naked lights

Rauchen verboten no smoking

Raucher smokers

Raucherabteil n [rowкнer-aptile] smoking compartment

rauh [row] rough

raus! [rowss] get out!

Rechner m [reshner] calculator; computer

Rechnung f [reshnoong] bill, (US) check

rechts [reshts] right

Rechtsabbieger right filter lane

Rechtsanwalt m [reshts-anvalt] lawyer

Rechtsanwältin f [reshts-anveltin] lawyer

rechts fahren keep to the right

rechts halten keep right

rechtshändig [reshts-hendish] right-handed

rechts (von) [reshts (fon)] on the right (of)

rechtzeitig [resht-tsytish] on time

reduziert reduced

Reformhaus n [reform-howss] health food shop

Reformkost f health food

Regen m [raygen] rain

Regenmantel m [raygen-mantel] raincoat

Regenschirm m [raygen-sheerm] umbrella

Regierung f [regeeroong] government

regnen [rayknen] to rain

es regnet [ess rayk-net] it's raining

regnerisch [rayknerish] rainy

Reh n [ray] roe deer

Reibe f [ribe-uh] grater

reich [rysh] rich

reichen: das reicht [rysht] that's enough

reif [rife] ripe

Reifen m [ryfen] tyre

Reifendruck m [ryfendroock] tyre pressure

Reifenpanne f [ryfenpann-uh] puncture

Reihe f [ry-uh] row; series

reine Baumwolle pure cotton

reine Schurwolle pure wool

reine Seide pure silk

reine Wolle pure wool

reinigen [rynigen] to clean

Reinigung f [rynigoong] laundry

Reinigungscreme f [rynigoongs-kraym] cleansing cream

Reise f [rize-uh] journey

Reiseandenken souvenirs

Reiseapotheke f [rize-uh-apotayk-uh] first aid kit

Reiseauskunft f [rize-uh-owsskoonft] travel information

Reisebedarf m [rize-uh-bedarf] travel requisites

Reisebüro n [rize-uh-booro] travel agency

Reiseführer m [rize-uh-foorer] guide; guidebook

reisen [rize-en] to travel

Reisende [ryzend-uh] passengers

Reisepaß m [rize-uh-pas] passport

Reiseproviant m [rize-uh-prohvee-ant] food for the journey

Reisescheck m [rize-uh-sheck] travellers' cheque/check

Reißverschluß m [rice-fairshlooss] zip

Reitsport m [rite-shport] horse riding

Reitweg m [rite-vayk] bridle path

Reklamationen complaints

Reklame f [reklahm-uh] advertising; advertisement

Rennbahn f race track

Rentner m, Rentnerin f old-age pensioner

Reparaturen repairs

Reparaturwerkstatt f [reparatoor-vairkshtatt] garage, repairs

reparieren [repareeren] to mend, to repair

Reportage f [reportahJ-uh] report

reservieren [rezairveeren] to reserve

reserviert [rezerveert] reserved

Reservierung f [rezairveeroong] reservation

Restgeld wird zurückgegeben change will be given

Rettungsring m [rettoongs-ring] lifebelt

Rezept n [retsept] recipe; prescription

rezeptpflichtig sold on prescription only

Rhein m [rine] Rhine

Rheuma n [roymah] rheumatism

Richter m [rishter] judge

Richterin f [rishterin] judge

richtig [rishtish] right; correct

Richtung f [rishtoong] direction

riechen [reeshen] to smell

Riegel m [reegel] bolt

Risiko n [reezeeko] risk

Rock m skirt; rock music

Rodelbahn f [rohdelbahn] toboggan run

Rohr n [rohr] pipe

Rolle f [rol-uh] role; part

Rollsplit loose chippings

Rollstuhl m [rol-shtool] wheelchair

Rolltreppe f [rol-trepp-uh] escalator

Roman m [romahn] novel

Röntgenaufnahme f [rurntgen-owfnahm-uh] X-ray

rosa [rohza] pink

Rosenmontagszug m [rohzen-mohntaks-tsook] carnival procession held on the Monday before Ash Wednesday (public holiday)

rot [roht] red

Röteln [rurteln] German measles

rothaarig [roht-hahrish] red-headed

Rubin m [roobeen] ruby

Rücken m [roocken] back

Rückenschmerzen mpl [roockenshmairtsen] backache

Rückfahrkarte f [roockfahrkart-uh] return/round trip ticket

Rücklichter npl [roocklishter] rear lights

Rückseite f [roockzite-uh] back; reverse

rücksichtslos [roockzishts-lohss] reckless

Rücksitz m [roockzits] back seat

Rückspiegel m [roock-shpeegel] rearview mirror

rückwärts [roockvairts] backwards

Rückwärtsgang m [roockvairts-gang] reverse gear

Ruderboot n [rooderboht]

rowing boat

Ruf m [roof] call

ruf doch mal an somebody somewhere wants a phonecall from you

rufen [roofen] to call; to shout

Rufnummer f [roofnoommer] telephone number

Rufsäule f [roofzoyl-uh] emergency telephone

Ruhe f [roo-uh] quiet; rest

ruhestörender Lärm disturbance of the peace

Ruhetag closed all day

ruhig [roo-ish] quiet

ruhige Lage peaceful, secluded spot

rund [roont] round

Rundfahrt f [roontfahrt] guided tour

Rundgang m guided tour (on foot)

Rundreise f [roont-ryzuh] guided tour

russisch [roossish] Russian

Rußland n [roosslant] Russia

S

Sache f [zaKH-uh] thing; matter; affair

Sachsen n [zakzen] Saxony

Sackgasse f [zack-gass-uh] cul-de-sac, dead end

sagen [zahgen] to say

man sagt, daß ... [zahkt dass] they say that ...

sagenhaft [zahgenhaft] terrific

sah [zah], sahen, sahst saw

Salbe f [zalb-uh] ointment

Salon m [zalong] lounge

salzig [zaltsish] salty

Sammelkarte f [zammel-kart-uh] multi-journey ticket

sammeln [zammeln] to collect

Sammlung f [zamloong] collection

Samstag m [zamstahk] Saturday

samstags [zamstahks] on Saturdays

Sandstrand m [zant-shtrant] sandy beach

Sanitäter m [zanee-tayter] ambulanceman

Sanitätsdienst m [zanitayts-deenst] ambulance service

Sanitätsstelle f [zanitayts-shtell-uh] first aid centre

Satz m [zats] sentence; rate

sauber [zowber] clean

säubern [zoybern] to clean

sauer [zower] sour; pissed off

Sauerstoff m [zowershtoff] oxygen

SB (Selbstbedienung) self service

S-Bahn f [ess-bahn] local urban railway

SB-Tankstelle f [ess-bay-tankshtell-uh] self-service petrol/gas station

Schachtel f [shaкHtel] box; packet

schade: das ist schade [shahd-uh] it's a pity

Schädel m [shaydel] skull

Schaden m [shahden] damage

Schaf n [shahf] sheep

Schaffner m [shaffner] conductor

schal [shahl] stale

Schal m [shahl] scarf

Schallplatte f [shallplatt-uh] record

Schalter m [shalter] counter; switch

Schalterstunden hours of business

Schaltknüppel m [shaltk-nooppel] gear lever

schämen: sich schämen [zish shaymen] to be ashamed

scharf [sharf] sharp; hot

Schatten m [shatten] shade

Schauer m [shower] shower

Schaufenster n [show-fenster] shop window

Scheck m [sheck] cheque, (US) check

Scheckheft n [sheck-heft] cheque book

Scheckkarte f [sheck-kart-uh] cheque card

Scheibe f [shibe-uh] slice

Scheibenwischer m [shyben-visher] windscreen wiper

Schein m [shine] note, bill; appearance

Scheineingabe insert banknote

scheinen [shynen] to shine; to seem

Scheinwerfer mpl [shine-vairfer] headlights

Scheiße! [shice-uh] shit!

Scheißkerl m [shice-kairl] bastard

Schenkel m [shenkel] thigh

Schere f [shair-uh] scissors

scheu [shoy] shy

Schiedsrichter m [sheets-rishter] referee

Schiff n [shiff] ship; boat

Schild n [shilt] sign

Schirm m [sheerm] umbrella; screen

Schlafanzug m [shlahf-antsook] pyjamas

schlafen [shlahfen] to sleep

Schlaflosigkeit f [shlahf-flohzish-kite] insomnia

Schlafmittel n [shlahf-mittel] sleeping drug

Schlafraum m [shlahf-frowm] dormitory

Schlafsaal m [shlahf-zahl] dormitory

Schlafsack m [shlahf-zack] sleeping bag

Schlaftablette f [shlahf-tablett-uh] sleeping pill

Schlafwagen m [shlahf-vahgen] sleeper, sleeping car

Schlafzimmer n [shlahf-tsimmer] bedroom

Schlafzimmerbedarf for the bedroom

schlagen [shlahgen] to hit

Schläger m [shlayger] racket; hooligan

Schlange f [shlang-uh] snake; queue

Schlange stehen [shtay-en] to queue

schlank [shlank] slim

Schlauch m [shlowKH] inner tube

schlecht [shlesht] bad; badly; unwell

Schlechte Fahrbahn bad road surface

schlechter [shleshter] worse

schlechteste [shleshtest-uh] worst

Schleudergefahr danger of skidding

schleudern [shloydern] to skid

Schleuderpreise prices slashed

schließen [shleessen] to close

Schließfach n [shleessfakH] left luggage locker

Schließfächer luggage lockers

schloß [shloss] shut

Schloß n castle; lock

Schluckauf m [shloock-owf] hiccups

schlucken [shloocken] to swallow

Schluß m [shlooss] end

Schlüssel m [shlOOssel] key; spanner; wrench

schmackhaft [shmack-haft] tasty

schmecken [shmecken] to taste; to taste good

Schmerz m [shmairts] pain

schmerzen [shmairtsen] to hurt

schmerzhaft [shmairts-haft] painful

Schmerzmittel n [shmairts-mittel] painkiller

schminken: sich schminken [zish shminken] to do one's make-up

Schmuck m [shmoock] jewellery

schmutzig [shmootsish] dirty

schnarchen [shnarshen] to snore

Schnauze! [shnowts-uh] shut

your mouth!

Schnee m [shnay] snow

schneebedeckt snow-covered

Schneeketten fpl snow chains

Schneeverhältnisse fpl [shnay-fair-heltniss-uh] snow conditions

Schneeverwehung f [shnay-fairvayoong] snow drift

schneiden [shnyden] to cut

sich schneiden to cut oneself

Schneiderei f [shnyder-ī] tailor's

schneien [shny-en] to snow

schnell [shnell] fast

Schnellimbiß m [shnell-imbiss] snackbar

Schnellzug m [shnell-tsook] express train

Schnupfen m [shnoopfen] cold

Schnurrbart m [shnoorrbart] moustache

schön [shurn] beautiful; fine; nice

schon [shohn] already

Schönheitspflege f [shurnhites-pflayg-uh] beauty care

Schönheitssalon m [shurnhites-zalong] beauty salon

Schornstein m [shorn-shtine] chimney

Schotte m [shott-uh] Scotsman

Schottin f [shottin] Scotswoman

Schrank m [shrank] cupboard

Schranke f [shrank-uh] barrier

Schraube f [shrowb-uh] screw

Schraubenschlüssel m [shrowben-shloossel] spanner, wrench

Schraubenzieher m [shrowben-tsee-er] screwdriver

schreiben [shryben] to write

Schreibmaschine f [shripe-masheen-uh] typewriter

Schreibpapier n [shripe-papeer] writing paper

Schreibtisch m [shripe-tish] desk

Schreibwaren pl [shripe-vahren] stationery

Schreibwarenladen m [shripe-vahren-lahden] stationer's

schreien [shry-en] to scream

schrieb [shreep], **schriebst**, **schrieben** wrote

Schriftsteller m [shrift-shteller], **Schriftstellerin** f writer

Schritt m [shritt] step

Schritt fahren drive at walking speed

schüchtern [shooshtern] shy

Schuhcreme f [shoo-kraym] shoe polish

Schuhe mpl [shoo-uh] shoes

Schuhmacher m [shoomaкнer] shoe repairer

Schuhreparaturen shoe repairs, heelbar

Schulbedarf school items

Schulden fpl [shoolden] debts

schuld: er ist schuld [air ist shoolt] it's his fault

schuldig [shooldish] guilty

Schule f [shool-uh] school

Schüler und Studenten school children and students

Schulhof m [shool-hohf] school playground

Schulter f [shoolter] shoulder

Schüssel f [shoossel] bowl

Schutt abladen verboten no tipping

schützen [shOOtsen] to protect

Schützenfest n [shOOtsenfest] local carnival

Schwaben n [shvahben] Swabia

schwach [shvaKH] weak

Schwachkopf [shvaKH-kopf] idiot, wally

Schwachsinn [shvaKH-zin] rubbish

Schwager m [shvahger] brother-in-law

Schwägerin f [shvaygerin] sister-in-law

Schwamm m [shvamm] sponge

schwanger [shvang-er] pregnant

Schwanz m [shvants] tail

schwarz [shvartz] black

Schwarzes Brett n [shvartsess] noticeboard

Schwarzwald m [shvartsvalt] Black Forest

schwarz-weiß [shvarts-vice] black and white

Schwein n [shvine] pig

Schweiz f [shvites] Switzerland

Schweizer m [shvytser] Swiss

Schweizerin f [shvytserin] Swiss woman

schwer [shvair] heavy; difficult

Schwerlastverkehr heavy vehicles

Schwester f [shvester] sister

Schwiegermutter f [shveeger-mootter] mother-in-law

Schwiegersohn m [shveegerzohn] son-in-law

Schwiegertochter f [shveeger-toKHter] daughter-in-law

Schwiegervater m [shveegerfahter] father-in-law

schwierig [shveerish] difficult

Schwimmbad n [shvimmbaht] swimming pool

Schwimmen n [shvimmen] swimming

schwimmen to swim

schwimmen gehen [gay-en] to go swimming

Schwimmen verboten no swimming

Schwimmer m [shvimmer], Schwimmerin f swimmer

Schwimmweste f [shvimmvest-uh] life jacket

schwindlig [shvintlish] dizzy

schwitzen [shvitsen] to sweat

schwul [shvOOl] gay

sechs [zeks] six

sechzehn [zesh-tsayn] sixteen

sechzig [zesh-tsish] sixty

See m [zay] lake

See f sea

seekrank [zaykrank] seasick

Segelboot n [zaygelboht] sailing boat

Segeln n [zaygeln] sailing

Segler m [zaygler] yachtsman

Seglerin f [zayglerin] yachtswoman

sehen [say-en] to see

Sehenswürdigkeit f [zay-ens-vOOrdishkite] sight

sehr [zair] very

sei [zy] be

seid [zite] are

seien Sie [zy-en zee] be

Seide f [z**ide**-uh] silk
Seife f [z**ife**-uh] soap
Seil n [zile] rope
sein [zine] to be; his; its
seine [z**ine**-uh] his; its
seit [zite] since
seitdem [zite-d**aym**] since
Seite f [z**ite**-uh] side; page
Seitenstreifen nicht befahrbar
  soft verges, keep off
Sekunde f [zek**oo**nd-uh] second
selbe [z**e**lb-uh] same
selbst [zelpst] even
  er/sie selbst himself/herself
Selbstbedienung f [zelpst-
  bedeenoong] self-service
selbstverständlich [zelpst-
  fairsht**e**ntlish] of course
Selbstwählferndienst direct
  long-distance dialling
seltsam [z**e**ltzahm] strange
senden [z**e**nden] to send
Sender m [z**e**nder] (radio/TV)
  station
Sendung f [z**e**ndoong]
  programme
sensibel [zenz**ee**bel] sensitive
Serviervorschlag serving
  suggestion
Sessellift m [z**e**ssel-lift] chairlift
setzen [z**e**tsen] to put
  sich setzen to sit down
sexistisch [seks**i**stish] sexist
sicher [z**i**sher] sure; safe
Sicherheitsgurt m [z**i**sherhites-
  goort] seat belt
Sicherheitsnadel f [z**i**sherhites-
  n**ah**del] safety pin
Sicherung f [z**i**sheroong] fuse

Sicht f [zisht] visibility
sie [zee] she; her; they; them
Sie you
sieben [z**ee**ben] seven
siebzehn [z**ee**p-tsayn]
  seventeen
siebzig [z**ee**p-tsish] seventy
Sieg m [zeek] victory
siehe ... see ...
siehst [zeest] see
sieht [zeet] sees
siezen [z**ee**tsen] to use the
  more formal 'Sie' form
Silber n [z**i**lber] silver
silbern [z**i**lbern] silver
Silvester n [zilvester] New Year's
  Eve
sind [zint] are
singen [z**i**ng-en] to sing
sinken [z**i**nken] to sink
Sitz m [zits] seat
Sitz für Schwerbehinderte seat
  for handicapped
Sitzplätze seats
skifahren [sh**ee**fahren] to ski
Skifahren n skiing
Skigebiet n [sh**ee**-gebeet] skiing
  area
Skihose f [sh**ee**-hohzuh] ski
  pants
Skilehrer m [sh**ee**-lairer],
  Skilehrerin f ski instructor
Skipiste f [sh**ee**pist-uh] ski slope
Skistiefel mpl [sh**ee**-shteefel] ski
  boots
Skistock m [sh**ee**-shtock] ski
  pole
Smoking m dinner jacket
so [zo] so; this way

so ... wie [vee] as ... as
sobald [zohbalt] as soon as
Socke f [zock-uh] sock
Sodbrennen n [zohtbrennen] heartburn
sofort [zofort] immediately
Sohn m [zohn] son
solange [zohlang-uh] as long as
Sommer m [zommer] summer
Sommerfahrplan m [zommerfahrplahn] summer timetable/schedule
Sommerferien fpl [zommer-fairee-en] summer holidays/ vacation
Sommerschlußverkauf summer sale
Sonderangebot n [zonder-angeboht] special offer
Sonderflug m [zonderflook] special flight
sondern [zondern] but
Sonderpreis m [zonder-price] special price
Sondervorstellung f [zonderforshtelloong] special performance
Sonnabend m [zonnahbent] Saturday
Sonne f [zonn-uh] sun
sonnenbaden [zonnenbahden] to sunbathe
Sonnenbrand m [zonnenbrant] sunburn
Sonnenbrille f [zonnenbrill-uh] sunglasses
Sonnenöl n [zonnen-url] suntan lotion; suntan oil
Sonnenschein m [zonnen-shine]

sunshine
Sonnenstich m [zonnen-shtish] sunstroke
Sonnenuntergang m [zonnen-oontergang] sunset
sonnig [zonnish] sunny
Sonntag m [zonntahk] Sunday
Sonntagsfahrer [zonntahks-fahrer] roadhog, Sunday driver
sonn- und feiertags on Sundays and public holidays
sonst [zonst] otherwise
Sorge f [zorg-uh] worry
sich Sorgen machen (um) [zish zorgen maкнen (oom)] to worry (about)
Sorte f [zort-uh] kind; sort
Souterrain [zootereng] basement
soweit [zovite] as far as
sowieso [zoveezoh] anyway
sowohl ... als auch ... [zovohl alss owкн] both ... and ...
Spanien n [shpahnee-en] Spain
sparen [shpahren] to save
Sparguthaben n [shpahrgoot-hahben] savings account
Sparkasse f [shpahrkass-uh] savings bank
Spaß m [shpahss] fun; joke
spät [shpayt] late
wie spät ist es? [vee] what time is it?
Spaten m [shpahten] spade
Spätschalter m [shpayt-shalter] night counter
Spätvorstellung f [shpaytforshtelloong] late

performance

spazieren gehen [shpats**ee**ren g**ay**-en] to go for a walk

Spaziergang m [shpats**ee**rgang] walk

Speiche f [shp**y**sh-uh] spoke

Speisegaststätte f [shp**ize**-uh-gast-shtett-uh] restaurant

Speiseraum m [shp**ize**-uh-rowm] dining room

Speisesaal m [shp**ize**-uh-zahl] restaurant, dining room

Speisewagen m [shp**ize**-uh-vahgen] restaurant car

Speisezimmer n [shp**ize**-uh-tsimmer] dining room

Sperrgebiet prohibited area

Spiegel m [shp**ee**gel] mirror

Spiel n [shpeel] game; match

spielen [shp**ee**len] to play

Spielende Kinder children at play

Spieler m [shp**ee**ler], **Spielerin** f player; gambler

Spielkasino n [shp**ee**l-kazeeno] casino

Spielplatz m [shp**ee**lplats] playground

Spielwaren fpl [shp**ee**l-vahren] toys

Spielzeug n [shp**ee**ltsoyk] toy

Spinne f [shp**inn**-uh] spider

spinnen: du spinnst wohl! [doo shpinnst wohl] you've got to be joking!, you're out of your mind!

Spion m [shpee-**ohn**] spy

Spirale f [shpeer**ahl**-uh] spiral; IUD

Spitze f [shp**its**-uh] fantastic, magic

Spitzenqualität top quality

Spitzname m [shp**its**nahm-uh] nickname

Sportartikel sports goods

Sportplatz m [shp**ort**-plats] sports ground

Sporttauchen n [shp**ort**-towKHen] skin-diving

Sportverein m [shp**ort**-fair-ine] sports club

Sportwagen m [shp**ort**-vahgen] sports car; buggy

Sportzentrum n [shp**ort**-tsentroom] sports centre

Sprache f [shpr**ah**KH-uh] language

Sprachenschule f [shpr**ah**KHen-shool-uh] language school

Sprachführer m [shpr**ah**KH-foorer] phrase book

sprechen [shpr**e**shen] to speak; to talk

Sprechstunde f [shpr**e**sh-shtoond-uh] surgery

Sprechzimmer n [shpr**e**sh-tsimmer] surgery (room)

spricht [shprisht] speaks **wer spricht, bitte?** [vair – b**i**tt-uh] who's calling please?

springen [shpr**i**ngen] to jump

Spritze f [shpr**its**-uh] injection

Sprungschanze f [shpr**oo**ng-shants-uh] ski jump

Spüle f [shp**oo**l-uh] sink

spülen [shp**oo**len] to do the dishes; to rinse

Spülmittel n [shp**oo**l-mittel]

washing-up liquid

Staat m [shtaht] state

Staatsangehörigkeit f [shtahts-an-gehur-rish-kite] nationality

Staatsanwalt m [shtahts-anvalt] public prosecutor

Stadion n [shtahdee-on] stadium

Stadt f [shtatt] town; city

Stadthalle f [shtatt-hal-uh] city hall

Stadtmitte f [shtatt-mitt-uh] city centre

Stadtplan m [shtatt-plahn] map

Stadtzentrum n [shtatt-tsentroom] city centre

Stammgast m [shtammgast] regular customer

Stammtisch m [shtammtish] table for regulars

stand [shtant], standen [shtanden] stood

Standesamt n [shtandess-amt] registry office

Standlicht n [shtantlisht] sidelights

starb [shtarp], starben [shtarben] died

stark [shtark] strong; great

Starkes Gefälle steep gradient

Start m [shtart] start; take-off

Station f [shtats-yohn] (hospital) ward; stop

statt [shtatt] instead of

Stau m [shtow] tailback, traffic jam

Staub m [shtowp] dust

Staubsauger m [shtowp-zowger] vacuum cleaner

Std. (Stunde) hour

St

stechen [shteshen] to sting

Stechmücke f [shtesh-mook-uh] mosquito

Steckdose f [shteck-dohz-uh] socket

Stecker m [shtecker] plug

stehen [shtay-en] to stand

das steht mir [shtayt meer] it suits me

stehlen [shtaylen] to steal

Stehplätze mpl [shtayplets-uh] standing room

steil [shtile] steep

Stein m [shtine] stone

Steinschlag falling rocks

Steinschlaggefahr danger of falling rocks

Stelle f [shtell-uh] place

stellen [shtellen] to put

Steppdecke f [shteppdeck-uh] continental quilt

sterben [shtairben] to die

Stereoanlage f [shtayray-oh-anlahg-uh] stereo system

Stern m [shtairn] star

Steuer f [shtoyer] tax

Steuer n steering wheel

Stiefel m [shteefel] boot

Stift m [shtift] pen

Stil m [shteel] style

Stille f [shtill-uh] silence

stillen [shtillen] to breastfeed

Stimme f [shtimm-uh] voice; vote

stimmt [shtimmt] that's right

Stimmung f [shtimmoong] mood

Stirn f [shteern] forehead

Stock m [shtock] floor, storey; stick

Stockwerk n [shtockvairk] floor, storey

Stoff m [shtoff] material; fabric

stolz [shtolts] proud

Stöpsel m [shturpsel] plug

stören [shtur-ren] to disturb
stört es Sie, wenn ich ...?
[shturt ess zee venn ish] do you mind if I ...?

Störungsstelle f [shtur-roongs-shtell-uh] faults service

Stoßdämpfer m [shtohss-dempfer] shock-absorber

Stoßstange f [shtohss-shtang-uh] bumper, fender

Str. (Straße) street

Straßenbauarbeiten roadworks

Straßenkilometer kilometres by road

Strafe f [shtrahf-uh] penalty; punishment

Strand m [shtrant] beach

Strandgut n [shtrant-goot] flotsam and jetsam

Strandkorb m [shtrantkorp] wicker beach chair

Strandpromenade f [shtrant-promenahd-uh] promenade

Straße f [shtrahss-uh] street; road

Straßenbahn f [shtrahssenbahn] tram

Straßenbauarbeiten fpl [shtrahssenbow-arbyten] roadworks

Straßenschild n [shtrahssen-shilt] road sign

Straßenverkehrsordnung f [shtrahssen-fairkairs-ortnoong]

highway code

Strecke f [shtreck-uh] route; stretch

streichen [shtryshen] to paint; to cancel

Streichholz n [shtrysh-holts] match

strengstens untersagt strictly prohibited

Streugut grit

stricken [shtricken] to knit

Strickwaren knitwear

Strom m [shtrohm] electricity; stream

Stromausfall m [shtrohm-owss-fal] power cut

Stromkosten [shtrohm-kosten] electricity costs

Strömung f [shtrurmoong] current

Strümpfe mpl [shtroompf-uh] stockings

Strumpfhose f [shtroompf-hohz-uh] tights, pantyhose

Stück n [shtook] piece; play

Student m [shtoodent], Studentin f student

Stuhl m [shtool] chair

Stunde f [shtoond-uh] hour; lesson

Stundenplan m [shtoonden-plahn] timetable, (US) schedule

stündlich [shtoontlish] hourly

Sturm m [shtoorm] storm

stürmisch [shtoormish] stormy

Sturz m [shtoorts] fall

suchen [zOOKHen] to look for

Sucher m [zOOKHer] viewfinder

Süden m [zooden] south
südliche Stadtteile city south
südlich von [zootlish fon] south of
Summe f [zoomm-uh] sum
Super n [zooper] four-star petrol, premium (gas)
super [zooper] great
Suppenteller m [zooppenteller] soup plate
süß [zooss] sweet

T

Tabak m [tahbak] tobacco
Tabakwaren tobacconist's
Tabelle f [tabell-uh] (league) table
Tablett n tray
Tablette f [tablett-uh] pill, tablet
Tacho m [taKHo] speedometer
Tafel f [tahfel] plate; blackboard
Tag m [tahk] day
Tag der Deutschen Einheit Day of German Unity, 3rd October, a public holiday
Tagebuch n [tahg-uh-booKH] diary
Tagesdecke f [tahgess-deck-uh] bedspread
Tageskarte f [tahgess-kart-uh] day ticket; menu of the day
Tageszeitung f [tahgess-tsytoong] daily newspaper
täglich [tayklish] daily
täglich frisch fresh every day
Taille f [tal-yuh] waist
Taillenweite f [tal-yen-vite-uh] waist measurement
Tal n [tahl] valley
Talsperre f [tahlshpair-uh] dam
Tankstelle f [tankshtell-uh] petrol/gas station
Tankwart m [tankvart] petrol/gas pump attendant
Tanne f [tann-uh] fir tree
Tante f [tant-uh] aunt
Tanz m [tants] dance
Tanzcafé n [tants-kaffay] café with dancing
tanzen [tantsen] to dance
Tapete f [tapayt-uh] wallpaper
tapezieren [tapaytseeren] to wallpaper
tapfer brave
Tasche f [tash-uh] pocket; bag
Taschendieb m [tashen-deep] pickpocket
Taschenlampe f [tashen-lamp-uh] torch
Taschenmesser n [tashen-messer] penknife
Taschenrechner m [tashen-reshner] calculator
Taschentuch n [tashentooKH] handkerchief
Tasse f [tass-uh] cup
tat [taht], tatst, taten did
taub [towp] deaf
tauchen [towKHen] to dive
Tauchen verboten no diving
tauschen [towshen] to exchange
tausend [towzent] thousand
Tauwetter n [tow-vetter] thaw
Taxistand m [taksi-shtant] taxi rank

TEE m [tay-ay-**ay**] Trans-Europe Express

Teekanne f [**tay**kann-uh] teapot

Teelöffel m [**tay**-lurfel] teaspoon

Teestube f [**tay**shtOOb-uh] tea room

Teich m [tysh] pond

Teil m [tile] part

teilen [**ty**len] to share

teils ... teils ... [tiles] partly ... partly ...

Teilzahlung möglich credit available

Telefax n fax

Telefonbuch n [telef**ohn**-bOOKH] phone book

Telefonieren ohne Münzen cardphone

Telefonkarte f [telef**ohn**kart-uh] phonecard

Telefonnummer f [telef**ohn**-noommer] phone number

Telefonzelle f [telef**ohn**-tsell-uh] phone box

Teller m plate

Teppich m [t**e**ppish] carpet

Teppichboden fitted carpet

Termin m [tairm**ee**n] appointment

Terrasse f [tair**a**ss-uh] patio

Tesafilm® m [**tay**zah-film] Sellotape®, Scotch tape®

teuer [t**oy**er] dear; expensive

Theaterstück n [tay-**ah**tershtOOck] play

tief [teef] deep; low

Tiefe f [t**ee**f-uh] depth

Tiefgeschoß lower floor, basement

Tiefkühlkost frozen food

Tier n [teer] animal

Tierarzt m [t**ee**r-artst] vet

Tiergarten m [t**ee**rgarten] zoo

Tierpark m [t**ee**rpark] zoo

Tinte f [t**i**nt-uh] ink

Tisch m [tish] table

Tischdecke f [t**i**shdeck-uh] tablecloth

Tischtennis n [t**i**sh-tennis] table tennis

Tochter f [t**o**KHter] daughter

Tod m [toht] death

Todesgefahr! danger of death!

Toilettenpapier n [twal**e**tten-pap**ee**r] toilet paper

toll! tremendous!, brilliant!

Tollwutgefahr danger of rabies

Ton m [tohn] sound; clay

Topfpflanzen fpl [t**o**pf-pflantsen] pot plants

Tor n goal; gate

tot [toht] dead

Tote m/f [t**o**ht-uh] dead man/woman

töten [t**ur**ten] to kill

Trage f [tr**ah**g-uh] stretcher

tragen [tr**ah**gen] to carry

Tragödie f [trag**ur**dee-uh] tragedy

Trainingsanzug m [tr**ay**nings-antsOOk] tracksuit

trampen [tr**e**mpen] to hitchhike

Trampen n [tr**e**mpen] hitchhiking

trank, trankst, tranken drank

Trauer f [tr**o**wer] sorrow

Traum m [trowm] dream

träumen [tr**oy**men] to dream

traurig [tro**w**rish] sad

Trauring m [tro**w**ring] wedding ring

treffen to meet

Treffen n meeting

Treffpunkt m [tr**e**ffpoonkt] meeting place

Treibstoff m [tr**ipe**-shtoff] fuel

Treppe f [tr**e**pp-uh] stairs

Treppenhaus n [tr**e**ppen-howss] stairs; staircase; stairwell

treu [troy] faithful

Trikot n [treek**oh**] jersey

Trimm-dich-Pfad jogging track; keep-fit track

trinken to drink

Trinkgeld n [tr**i**nk-gelt] tip

trocken dry

trocknen to dry

Tropfen m drop

trotz [trots] in spite of

trotzdem [trots-daym] in spite of that; all the same; nonetheless

tschüs [chœss] cheerio

Tuch n [tooKH] cloth

tun [toon] to do; to put

Tür f [toor] door

Türkei f [toor-ky] Turkey

Turm m [toorm] tower

Turnschuhe mpl [t**oo**rnshoo-uh] trainers

TÜV m [tooff] (Technischer Überwachungs-Verein) MOT

Typ m [toop] guy, bloke

U

U-Bahn f [**oo**-bahn] underground, (US) subway

U-Bahnhof m [**oo**-bahnhohf] underground/subway station

über [**oo**ber] over; above

überall [oober-**a**l] everywhere

überfahren [ooberf**a**hren] to run over

Überfall m [**oo**ber-fal] attack

übergeben [oober-g**ay**ben] to hand over

sich übergeben to be sick

Übergewicht n [**oo**bergevisht] overweight; excess baggage

überholen [ooberh**oh**len] to overtake

Überholen verboten no overtaking

Überholverbot no overtaking

Überlebende m/f [ooberl**ay**bend-uh] survivor

übermorgen [**oo**bermorgen] the day after tomorrow

Übernachtung f [oobern**a**KHtoong] night

Übernachtung mit Frühstück f [mit fr**oo**shtœck] bed and breakfast

überqueren [oober-kv**ai**ren] to cross

überraschend [oober-r**a**shent] surprising

Überraschung f [oober-r**a**shoong] surprise

überreden [oober-r**ay**den] to persuade

Überschwemmung f
[ɔɔbershvemmoong] flood
übersetzen [ɔɔberzetsen] to
translate
Übersetzer m [ɔɔberzetser],
Übersetzerin f translator
übertreiben [ɔɔbertryben] to
exaggerate
Überweisung f [ɔɔber-vyzoong]
transfer
überzeugen [ɔɔber-tsoygen] to
convince
üblich [ɔɔplish] usual
Ufer n [ɔɔfer] shore
Uhr f [ɔɔr] clock; o'clock
Uhrmacher m [ɔɔrmaKHer]
watchmaker
UKW (Ultrakurzwelle) [ɔɔ-kah-
vay] FM
um [oom] around; at
um ... Uhr at ... o'clock
um zu in order to
umbringen [oombring-en] to kill
Umgebung f [oomgayboong]
surroundings; environment
Umgehungsstraße detour; by-
pass
Umkleidekabine f [oomklide-uh-
kabeen-uh] changing room
Umleitung f [oom-lytoong]
diversion
Umschlag m [oomshlahk]
envelope
Umstandskleid n [oomshtants-
klite] maternity dress
umsteigen [oom-shtygen] to
change (trains etc)
umstoßen [oom-shtohssen] to
knock over

umtauschen [oom-towshen] to
exchange
Umtausch gegen bar ist nicht
möglich goods cannot be
exchanged for cash
Umtausch nur gegen Quittung
goods may not be
exchanged without a receipt
umziehen: sich umziehen [zish
oomtsee-en] to change
(clothes)
unabhängig [oonap-heng-ish]
independent
unangenehm [oon-angenaym]
unpleasant
unbedeutend [oon-bedoytent]
unimportant
unbefugt unauthorized
unbekannt [oon-bekannt]
unknown
und [oont] and
Unebenheiten uneven surface
Unentschieden n [oon-
entsheeden] draw
Unfall m [oonfal] accident
Unfallgefahr accident black
spot
Unfallrettung f [oonfal-rettoong]
ambulance, emergency
service
Unfallstation f [oonfal-shtats-
yohn] casualty department
ungefähr [oon-gefair]
approximately
ungeschickt [oon-geshickt]
clumsy
unglaublich [oon-glowplish]
incredible
Unglück n [oon-glɔɔck] disaster;

accident; unhappiness

unglücklich [**oo**n-gl**oo**cklish]
unhappy; unfortunate

ungültig [**oo**n-g**oo**ltish] invalid

unhöflich [**oo**n-hurflish]
impolite, rude

Unkosten pl [**oo**n-kosten]
overheads

unmöbliert [**oo**n-mur-bleert]
unfurnished

unmöglich [**oo**n-m**ur**klish]
impossible

uns [**oo**nss] us

unschuldig [**oo**n-shooldish]
innocent

unser [**oo**nzer], unsere
[**oo**nzer-uh] our

unsicher [**oo**n-zisher] unsafe;
unsure

Unsinn m [**oo**nzinn] nonsense

unten [**oo**nten] down; at the
bottom; downstairs

unter [**oo**nter] below, under;
underneath; among

Unterbodenwäsche f
[**oo**nter**boh**den-vesh-uh]
underbody cleaning

unterbrechen [**oo**nterbreshen] to
interrupt

Unterführung f [**oo**nterf**oo**roong]
underpass

Untergeschoß n [**oo**nter-geshoss]
basement

Unterhaltung f [**oo**nterh**a**ltoong]
entertainment; conversation

Unterhemd n [**oo**nter-hemt] vest,
(US) undershirt

Unterkunft f [**oo**nterkoonft]
accommodation

Unternehmen n [**oo**nterna**ay**men]
company; undertaking

Unterricht m [**oo**nter-risht]
lessons

untersagt prohibited

Unterschied m [**oo**ntersheet]
difference

unterschreiben [**oo**ntershr**y**ben]
to sign

Unterschrift f [**oo**ntershrift]
signature

untersuchen [**oo**nter-z**OO**KHen] to
examine

Untersuchung f [**oo**nter-
z**OO**KHoong] examination;
check-up

Untertasse f [**oo**nter-tass-uh]
saucer

Untertitel m [**oo**nterteetel]
subtitle

Unterwäsche f [**oo**nter-vesh-uh]
underwear

untreu [**oo**ntroy] unfaithful

unverbleit [**oo**nfairblite]
unleaded

unverkäufliches Muster not for
sale, sample only

unverschämt [**oo**nfairsh**ay**mt]
outrageous

Unverschämtheit f [**oo**n-
fairsh**ay**mt-hite] cheek, nerve

unwichtig [**oo**nvishtish]
unimportant

uralt [**OO**r-alt] ancient

Urlaub m [**OO**rlowp] holiday,
vacation

Urlauber m [**OO**r-lowber],
Urlauberin f holidaymaker

Urteil n [**OO**rtile] sentence;

judgement
usw. (und so weiter) etc

V

vakuumverpackt vacuum-
packed
Vater m [fahter] father
Vati m [vahtee] dad
Ventil n [venteel] valve
Ventilator m [ventilahtor] fan
Verabredung f [fair-ap-raydoong]
appointment
verantwortlich [fair-antvortlish]
responsible
verärgert [fair-airgert] angry
Verband m [fairbant] bandage;
association
verbergen [fairbairgen] to hide
verbessern [fairbessern] to
improve
Verbindung f [fairbindoong]
connection
verbleit [fairblite] leaded
verboten [fairbohten]
forbidden, prohibited
Verbrauch m [fairbrowKH] use;
consumption
zum baldigen Verbrauch
bestimmt will not keep
Verbraucher m [fairbrowKHer],
Verbraucherin f consumer
Verbrecher m [fairbresher],
Verbrecherin f criminal
verbrennen: sich verbrennen
[zish fairbrennen] to burn
oneself
Verbrennung f [fairbrennoong]
burn

verdammt (noch mal)!
[fairdammt (noKH mahl)]
bloody hell!
verdienen [fairdeenen] to earn;
to deserve
Verein m [fair-ine] club
Vereinigte Staaten f [fair-ine-isht-
uh shtahten] United States
Vereinigtes Königreich n [fair-
ine-ishtess kurnish-rysh]
United Kingdom
Verengte Fahrbahn road
narrows
Verengte Fahrstreifen road
narrows
Verfallsdatum n [fairfals-dahtoom]
best before date
Vergaser m [fairgahzer]
carburettor
vergessen [fairgessen] to forget
Vergewaltigung f [fairgeval-
tigoong] rape
vergleichen [fair-glyshen] to
compare
Vergnügen n [fairg-noogen]
pleasure
vergriffen unavailable, out of
stock
Vergrößerung f [fair-grursseroong]
enlargement
verhaften [fairhaften] to arrest
verheiratet [fair-hyrahtet]
married
verhindern [fairhindern] to
prevent
Verhütungsmittel n [fair-
hootoongs-mittel]
contraceptive
Verkauf m [fairkowf] sale

verkaufen [fairk**ow**fen] to sell

zu verkaufen [ts00] for sale

Verkauf nur gegen bar cash
sales only

verkaufsoffener Samstag open
on Saturday; Saturday
opening

Verkehr m [fairk**air**] traffic

verkehren [fairk**air**en] to run

verkehrt alle ... Minuten runs
every ... minutes

Verkehrspolizei f [fairk**air**s-
poleetsd traffic police

Verkehrspolizist m [fairk**air**s-
politsist] traffic policeman

Verkehrsunfall m [fairk**air**s-
oonfal] traffic accident

Verkehrszeichen n [fairk**air**s-
tsyshen] roadsign

verlangen [fairl**a**ngen] to ask for

Verlängerungsschnur f
[fairl**e**ngeroongs-shn00r]
extension lead

verlassen [fairl**a**ssen] to leave

verleihen: zu verleihen [ts00 fair-
l**r**en] for hire, to rent

verletzt [fairl**e**tst] injured

verliebt [fairl**ee**pt] in love

verlieren [fairl**ee**ren] to lose

verlobt [fairl**oh**pt] engaged

Verlobte m/f [fairl**oh**pt-uh]
fiancé; fiancée

Verlobung f [fairl**oh**boong]
engagement

Verlust m [fairl**oo**st] loss

vermeiden [fairm**y**den] to avoid

vermieten: zu vermieten [ts00
fairm**ee**ten] for hire/to rent;
to let

Vermieter m [fairm**ee**ter]
landlord

Vermieterin f [fairm**ee**terin]
landlady

vermissen [fairm**i**ssen] to miss

Vermittlung f [fairm**i**ttloong]
operator

vernünftig [fairn**oo**nftish]
sensible

verpassen [fairp**a**ssen] to miss

verriegeln [fair-r**ee**geln] to bolt

verrückt [fair-r**oo**ckt] mad

verschieden [fairsh**ee**den]
different

verschlafen [fairshl**ah**fen] to
oversleep

verschlucken [fairshl**oo**cken] to
swallow

Verschluß m [fairshl**oo**ss]
shutter

verschmutzt [fairshm**oo**tst]
polluted

verschwinden [fairshv**i**nden] to
disappear

verschwinden Sie! go away!

Versicherung f [fairz**i**sheroong]
insurance

Versicherungspolice f
[fairz**i**sheroongs-pol**ee**ss-uh]
insurance policy

verspätet [fairshp**ay**tet] late,
delayed

Verspätung f [fairshp**ay**toong]
delay

versprechen [fairshp**re**shen] to
promise

verstauchen [fairsht**ow**KHen] to
sprain

verstehen [fairsht**ay**-en] to

understand
ich verstehe nicht [fairshtay-uh nisht] I don't understand
verstopft [fairshtopft] blocked; constipated
Versuch m [fairzOOKH] attempt
versuchen [fairzOOKHen] to try
Verteiler m [fairtyler] distributor
Vertrag m [fairtrahk] contract; treaty
Vertreter m [fairtrayter], **Vertreterin** f representative; agent; sales rep
verwählen: sich verwählen [zish fairvaylen] to dial the wrong number
verwitwet [fairvitvet] widowed
Verzeihung! [fair-tsʀoong] I'm sorry; excuse me
Verzogen nach ... moved to ...
Verzögerung f [fairtsurgeroong] delay
verzollen [fairtsollen] to declare
Vetter m [fetter] cousin
viel [feel] much, a lot (of)
viele [feel-uh] many
vielen Dank [feelen] thanks a lot
viel Glück! [feel glOOck] good luck!
viel Glück zum Geburtstag [tsoom geboortstahk] happy birthday
vielleicht [feelysht] maybe
vier [feer] four
Viertel n [feertel] quarter; district
Vierwaldstätter See m [veervalt-shtetter zay] Lake Lucerne
vierzehn [feer-tsayn] fourteen

vierzig [feertsish] forty
Visitenkarte f [veezeeten-kart-uh] card; business card
Visum n [veezoom] visa
Vogel m [fohgel] bird
Volk: das Volk [follk] the people
voll [fol] full; crowded
voll belegt full, no vacancies
vollklimatisiert fully air-conditioned
Vollnarkose f [fol-narkohz-uh] general anaesthetic
Vollpension f [fol-pangz-yohn] full board
volltanken [foltanken] to fill up
vom Umtausch ausgeschlossen cannot be exchanged
von [fon] of; by
von ... bis ... from ... to ...
von ... nach ... from ... to ...
vor [for] before; in front of
vor ... Tagen ... days ago
vor dem Frühstück before breakfast
vor Kindern schützen keep out of reach of children
vor dem Schlafengehen before going to bed
Vorausbuchung unbedingt erforderlich reserved seats only
voraus: im voraus [vorowss] in advance
vorbei [forby] over
vorbei an ... past ...
Vorderrad n [forder-raht] front wheel
Vorderseite f [forder-zite-uh] front

Vorfahr m [forfahr] ancestor
Vorfahrt f [forfahrt] right of way
Vorfahrt beachten give way
Vorfahrt gewähren give way
Vorfahrtsstraße f [forfahrts-
shtrahss-uh] major road
(vehicles having right of way)
vorgestern [forgestern] the day
before yesterday
Vorhang m [forhang] curtain
vorher [forhair] before
Vorhersage f [forhairzahg-uh]
forecast
Vorliebe f [forleeb-uh] liking
Vormittag m [formittahk] (late)
morning
vorn [forn] at the front
Vorname m [fornahm-uh]
Christian name, first name
Vorprogramm n [for-programm]
supporting programme
Vorschlag m [forshlahk]
proposal, suggestion
vorschlagen [forshlahgen] to
propose
Vorsicht f [forzisht] caution;
take care
Vorsicht bissiger Hund beware
of the dog
vorsichtig [forzishtish] careful
vorsichtig fahren drive carefully
Vorsicht Stufe! mind the step!
Vorstadt f [forshtatt] suburbs
vorstellen [forshtellen] to
introduce
Vorstellung f [forshtelloong]
performance
nächste Vorstellung um ... next
performance at ...

Vorteil m [fortile] advantage
Vorurteil n [for-oortile] prejudice
Vorwahl f [forvahl] dialling code
Vorwahlnummer f [forvahl-
noommer] dialling code
vorziehen [fortsee-en] to prefer

W

wach [vaKH] awake
wachsen [vaksen] to grow
wagen [vahgen] to dare
Wagen m car; coach; carriage
Wagenheber m [vahgen-hayber]
jack
Wagenstandanzeiger order of
carriages
Wahl f [vahl] choice; election
wählen [vaylen] to choose; to
elect; to dial
Wahlkampf m [vahlkampf]
election campaign
Wahnsinn m [vahnzinn]
madness
Wahnsinn! fantastic!
wahr [vahr] true
während [vairent] during; while
Wahrheit f [vahr-hite] truth
wahrscheinlich [varshinelish]
probable; probably
Währung f [vairoong] currency
Wald m [valt] forest
Waliser m [valeezer] Welshman
Waliserin f [valeezerin]
Welshwoman
walisisch [valeezish] Welsh
Wand f [vant] wall
wandern [vandern] to hike, to
walk

Wanderweg m [**va**ndervayk]
walk, route; trail

wann [van] when

war [var] was

waren [**va**hren] were

Waren fpl goods

Warenaufzug m [**va**hren-
owftsook] service lift

Warenhaus n [**va**hren-howss]
department store

warm [varm] warm; hot

warst [varst], wart [vart] were

warten [**va**rten] to wait

Wartesaal m [**va**rt-uh-zahl]
waiting room

Wartezimmer n [**va**rt-uh-tsimmer]
waiting room

warum? [va**room**] why?

was? [vass] what?

Waschbecken n [**va**shbecken]
washbasin

Wäsche f [**ve**sh-uh] washing;
laundry

waschen [**va**shen] to wash
sich waschen to wash
(oneself)

Wäscherei f [**ve**sher-ɾ] laundry

Waschlappen m [**va**shlappen]
flannel; coward

Waschmaschine f [**va**shmasheen-
uh] washing mashine

Waschpulver n [**va**shpoolver]
washing powder

Waschraum m [**va**shrowm] wash
room

Waschsalon m [**va**sh-zalong]
launderette, laundromat

Waschstraße f [**va**sh-shtrahss-uh]
car wash

Waschzeit washing time

Wasser n [**va**sser] water

wasserdicht [**va**sserdisht]
waterproof

Wasserfall m [**va**sser-fal]
waterfall

Wasserhahn m [**va**sser-hahn] tap,
faucet

Wasserkessel m [**va**sser-kessel]
kettle

wasserlöslich soluble in water

Wasserski n [**va**sser shee]
waterskiing

Wassersport m [**va**sser-shport]
water sports

Waterkant f [**va**hterkant] North
German name for the North
German coastal area

Watte f [**va**tt-uh] cotton wool,
absorbent cotton

wechselhaft [**ve**kselhaft]
changeable

Wechselkurs m [**ve**ksel-koors]
exchange rate

wechseln [**ve**kseln] to change

Wechselstube f [**ve**ksel-shtoob-
uh] bureau de change

wecken [**ve**cken] to wake up

Wecker m [**ve**cker] alarm clock

weder ... noch [**va**yder – no**KH**]
neither ... nor ...

Weg m [vayk] path

wegen [**va**ygen] because of

Wegen Krankheit vorübergehend
geschlossen temporarily
closed due to illness

Wegen Umbauarbeiten
geschlossen closed for
alterations

weggehen [vek-gay-en] to go away

wegnehmen [vek-naymen] to take away

Wegweiser m [vayk-vyzer] signpost

wegwerfen [vek-vairfen] to throw away

weh tun: es tut weh [ess toot vay] it hurts

weiblich [vipe-lish] female

weich [vysh] soft

Weihnachten n [vynaKHten] Christmas

weil [vile] because

Weile f [vile-uh] while

weinen [vynen] to cry

Weinhandlung f [vine-hantloong] wine shop

Weinprobe f [vine-prohb-uh] wine-tasting

Weinstraße f [vine-shtrahss-uh] route through wine-growing areas

Weinstube f [vine-shtoob-uh] wine bar (traditional style)

weiß [vice] know; knows; white

weißt [vysst] know

weit [vite] far; wide
  weit entfernt far away

weiter [vyter] further

Weitzone f [vite-tsohn-uh] long-distance zone

welche? [velsh-uh] which?

Welle f [vell-uh] wave

Welt f [velt] world

wenden [venden] to turn
  sich wenden an to contact

wenig [vaynish] little; few

weniger [vayniger] less

wenn [venn] if

wenn vom Arzt nicht anders verordnet unless otherwise prescribed by your doctor

wer? [vair] who?

Werbung f [vairboong] advertising; publicity

werde [vaird-uh] will; become

werden [vairden] to become; will

werdet [vairdet] will; become

werfen [vairfen] to throw

Werkstatt f [vairkshtatt] auto repairs

Werktag m [vairktahk] weekday

Werkzeug n [vairk-tsoyk] tool

wert [vairt] worth

Wert m [vairt] value

Wertmünzen tokens

Wertsachen fpl [vairtzaKHen] valuables

Wespe f [vesp-uh] wasp

Wessi m [vessee] West German

Weste f [vest-uh] waistcoat

Westen m [vesten] west

westliche Stadtteile city west

westlich von [vestlish fon] west of

Wette f [vett-uh] bet

wetten [vetten] to bet

Wetter n [vetter] weather

Wetterbericht m [vetter-berisht] weather forecast

Wettervorhersage f [vetter-forhair-zahguh] weather forecast

wichtig [vishtish] important

wider [veeder] against

widerlich [veederlish] disgusting

Widerrechtlich abgestellte Fahrzeuge werden kostenpflichtig abgeschleppt illegally parked vehicles will be removed at the owner's expense

widersprechen [veeder-shpreshen] to contradict

widerwärtig [veeder-vairtish] obnoxious

wie? [vee] how?

wie [vee] like
   wie bitte? pardon (me)?, what did you say?
   wie geht es Ihnen? [gayt ess eenen] how are you?
   wie geht's? how are things?

wieder [veeder] again

wiederholen [veeder-hohlen] to repeat

Wiederhören: auf Wiederhören [owf veeder-hur-ren] goodbye (said on the phone)

wiegen [veegen] to weigh

Wien [veen] Vienna

wieviel? [veefeel] how much?

wie viele? [vee feel-uh] how many?

Wildleder n [viltlayder] suede

will [vill] want to; wants to

willkommen! [villkommen] welcome!

willst [villst] want to

Wimperntusche f [vimpern-toosh-uh] mascara

Windel f [vindel] nappy, diaper

windig [vindish] windy

Windschutzscheibe f [vintshoots-shibe-uh] windscreen

Winterfahrplan m [vinterfahrplahn] winter timetable/schedule

Winterschlußverkauf winter sales

wir [veer] we

wir müssen draußen bleiben sorry, no dogs

wir sind umgezogen we have moved

wird [veert] will; becomes

wirklich [veerklish] really

wirst [veerst] will; become

Wirt m [veert] landlord; host

Wirtin f [veertin] landlady; hostess

Wirtschaft f [veert-shafft] pub; economy

Wirtshaus n [veerts-howss] inn; pub

wissen [vissen] to know

wißt [vist] know

Witwe f [vitv-uh] widow

Witwer m [vitver] widower

Witz m [vits] joke

wo? [vo] where?

woanders [vo-anderss] elsewhere

Woche f [voKH-uh] week

Wochenende n [voKHen-end-uh] weekend

Wochenkarte f [voKHenkart-uh] weekly ticket

Woge f [vohg-uh] wave

woher? [vo-hair] where from?

wohin? [vo-hin] where to?

Wohnblock m [vohnblock] block

of flats, apartment block

wohnen [**voh**nen] to live; to stay

Wohnmobil n [**voh**n-mobeel] caravan, (US) trailer

Wohnort m [**voh**n-ort] place of residence

Wohnung f [**voh**noong] flat, apartment

Wohnwagen m [**voh**nvahgen] caravan, (US) trailer

Wohnzimmer n [**voh**n-tsimmer] living room

Wolke f [v**o**lk-uh] cloud

Wolle f [v**o**ll-uh] wool

wollen [v**o**llen] to want
    wollen Sie ...? do you want ...?

womit [vo-m**i**t] with which; with what

worauf [vo-r**ow**f] (up)on which

worden [v**o**rden] been

worin [vo-r**i**n] in which

Wort n [vort] word

Wörterbuch n [v**ur**terbOOKH] dictionary

wovon [vo-f**o**n] from which; from what

wozu? [vo-ts**OO**] what for?

Wunde f [v**oo**nd-uh] wound

wunderbar [v**oo**nderbar] wonderful

Wunsch m [voonsh] wish

wünschen [v**OO**nshen] to wish

wurde [v**oo**rd-uh] was; became

würde [v**OO**rd-uh] would

wurden [v**oo**rden], wurdest, wurdet were; became

würzen [v**OO**rtsten] to season

würzig [v**OO**rtsish] spicy

wußte [v**oo**sst-uh], wußten, wußtest knew

Wut f [voot] fury

wütend [v**OO**tent] furious

Z

zäh [tsay] tough

Zahl f [tsahl] number

zahlbar [ts**ah**lbar] payable

zahlen [ts**ah**len] to pay

Zahlung f [ts**ah**loong] payment

Zahn m [tsahn] tooth

Zahnarzt m [ts**ah**n-artst], Zahnärztin f [ts**ah**n-airtstin] dentist

Zahnbelag m [ts**ah**n-belahk] plaque

Zahnersatz m [ts**ah**n-airzats] dentures

Zahnklinik f [ts**ah**n-kleenik] dental clinic

Zahnpasta f [ts**ah**n-pastah] toothpaste

Zahnschmerzen mpl [ts**ah**n-shmairtsen] toothache

Zange f [ts**a**ng-uh] pliers

Zapfsäule f [ts**a**pf-zoyl-uh] petrol/gas pump

Zaun m [tsown] fence

z.B. (zum Beispiel) eg

ZDF (Zweites Deutsches Fernsehen) [tset-day-**e**ff] Second German Television Channel

Zebrastreifen m [ts**ay**brah-shtryfen] zebra crossing

Zehe f [ts**ay**-uh] toe

zehn [tsayn] ten

Zehnmarkschein m [tsayn-mark-shine] ten-mark note/bill

Zeichen n [tsyshen] sign

zeichnen [tsyshnen] to draw

zeigen [tsygen] to show; to point

Zeit f [tsite] time

Zeitansage f [tsite-anzahg-uh] speaking clock

Zeitschrift f [tsite-shrift] magazine

Zeitung f [tsytoong] newspaper

Zelt n [tselt] tent

Zelten verboten no camping

Zeltplatz m [tseltplats] campsite

Zentimeter m [tsentimayter] centimetre

Zentner m [tsentner] 50 kilos

Zentralheizung f [tsentrahl-hytsoong] central heating

Zentrum n [tsentroom] centre

zerbrechen [tsairbreshen] to break

zerstören [tsairshtur-ren] to destroy

Zettel m [tsettel] piece of paper

Zeuge m [tsoyg-uh], Zeugin f witness

Ziege f [tseeg-uh] goat

ziehen [tsee-en] to pull

Ziel n [tseel] aim; destination

ziemlich [tseemlish] rather

Zigarre f [tsigarr-uh] cigar

Zimmer n [tsimmer] room

Zimmer frei room(s) to let/rent, vacancies

Zimmermädchen n [tsimmer-maytshen] chambermaid

Zimmernachweis m [tsimmer-naKHvice] accommodation service

Zimmerservice m [tsimmer-'service'] room service

Zimmer zu vermieten rooms to let/rent

Zinsen pl [tsinzen] interest

Zinssatz m [tsinss-zats] interest rate

Zoll m [tsol] Customs

Zollbeamte m [tsoll-buh-amt-uh], Zollbeamtin f customs officer

zollfrei [tsolfry] duty-free

zollfreie Waren fpl [tsolfry-uh vahren] duty-free goods

Zone 30 zone with 30 km/h speed limit

zu [tsoo] to; too; shut

zubereiten [tsoo-beryten] to prepare

Zuckergehalt sugar content

zufrieden [tsoofreeden] pleased

Zug m [tsook] train; draught

zu den Zügen to the trains

Zugabe f [tsoogahb-uh] encore

zugelassen für ... Personen carries ... persons

zuhören [tsoo-hur-ren] to listen

Zukunft f [tsookoonft] future

zum [tsoom] to the

zum Ochsen The Ox (pub etc name)

zunächst [tsoonaykst] first, firstly

Zunahme f [tsoonahm-uh] increase

Zuname m [tsoonahm-uh] surname

Zündkerze f [tsoont-kairts-uh] spark plug

Zündung f [tsoondoong] ignition

zunehmen [tsoonaymen] to increase; to put on weight

Zunge f [tsoong-uh] tongue

zur [tsoor] to the

zurück [tsoorook] back

zurückgeben [tsoorook-gayben] to give back

zurückkehren [tsoorook-kairen] to go back, to return

zurückkommen [tsoorook-kommen] to come back

zusammen [tsoozammen] together

Zusammenstoß m [tsoozammen-shtohss] crash

Zuschauer m [tsooshower], Zuschauerin f spectator

Zuschlag m [tsooshlahk] supplement

zuschlagpflichtig [tsooshlahk-pflishtish] supplement payable

zustimmen [tsooshtimmen] to agree

Zutaten fpl [tsootahten] ingredients

Zutreffendes ankreuzen cross where applicable

Zutritt für Unbefugte verboten no admission to unauthorized persons

zuviel [tsoofeel] too much

Zuwiderhandlung wird strafrechtlich verfolgt we will prosecute

zwanzig [tsvantsish] twenty

Zwanzigmarkschein m [tsvantsish-mark-shine] twenty-mark note/bill

Zweck m [tsveck] purpose

zwei [tsvy] two

Zweibettzimmer n [tsvybett-tsimmer] twin room

Zweig m [tsvike] branch

Zweigstelle f [tsvike-shtell-uh] branch

Zweimal täglich einzunehmen to be taken twice a day

zweite(r,s) [tsvite-uh, -er, -ess] second

zweite Klasse f [tsvite-uh klass-uh] second class

zweiter Stock m [tsvyter shtock] second floor, (US) third floor

zweite Wahl seconds

Zwillinge mpl [tsvilling-uh] twins

zwischen [tsvishen] between

Zwischenlandung f [tsvishen-landoong] intermediate stop; stopover

Zwischenmahlzeit f [tsvishen-mahltsite] snack between meals

zwölf [tsvurlf] twelve

z.Zt. (zur Zeit) at the moment

Menu Reader:

Food

Aal [ahl] eel

Aalsuppe [**ah**lzoop-uh] eel soup

Ananas [**a**nanass] pineapple

angemacht mit prepared with

Äpfel [**e**pfel] apples

Äpfel im Schlafrock [shl**ah**frock] baked apples in puff pastry

Apfelkompott stewed apples

Apfelkuchen [-k**OO**KHen] apple pie

Apfelmeerrettich [-mayr-rettish] horseradish with apple

Apfelmus [-m**OO**ss] apple purée

Apfelrotkohl red cabbage cooked with apples

Apfelsinen [apfelz**ee**nen] oranges

Apfelstrudel apple strudel

Apfeltasche [-tash-uh] apple turnover

Aprikosen [aprik**oh**zen] apricot

Arme Ritter [**a**rm-uh] bread soaked in milk and egg then fried

aromatisiert aromatic

Artischocken artichokes

Artischockenherz [-hairts] artichoke heart

Aspik [asp**ee**k] aspic

Auberginen [ohbair**J**eenen] aubergines, eggplants

Auflauf [**ow**f-lowf] (baked) pudding or omelette

Aufschnitt [**ow**f-shnitt] sliced cold meats, cold cuts

Austern [**ow**stern] oysters

Bachforelle [ba**KH**-forell-uh] river trout

backen to bake

Backobst [**ba**ckohpst] dried fruit

Backofen oven

Backpflaumen [-pflowmen] prunes

Baiser [bezz**ay**] meringue

Balkansalat [b**a**lkahn-zal**a**ht] cabbage and pepper salad

Bananen [ban**ah**nen] bananas

Bandnudeln [bantn**oo**deln] ribbon noodles

Basilikum basil

Bauernauflauf [b**ow**ern-owflowf] bacon and potato omelette

Bauernfrühstück [-fr**oo**sht**oo**k] bacon and potato omelette

Bauernomelett [-omlet] bacon and potato omelette

Baumkuchen [b**ow**mk**OO**KHen] cylindrical, layered cake

Béchamelkartoffeln sliced potatoes in creamy sauce

Béchamelsoße [-z**oh**ss-uh] creamy sauce with onions and ham

Beilagen [b**y**lahgen] side dishes; side salads, vegetables

belegtes Brot [bel**ay**ktess broht] sandwich

Berliner (Ballen) [bairl**ee**ner (bal-en)] jam doughnut with icing

bestreut mit sprinkled with

Bienenstich [b**ee**nen-shtish] honey and almond tart

Bierschinken [b**ee**r-shinken] ham sausage

Biersuppe [b**ee**rzoop-uh] beer soup

Birnen [beernen] pears

Biskuit [biskweet] sponge

Biskuitrolle [biskweet-rol-uh] Swiss roll

Bismarckheringe [-hairing-uh] filleted pickled herrings

Blätterteig [blettertike] puff pastry

Blattsalat [-zalaht] green salad

Blattspinat [-shpinaht] leaf spinach

blau [blow] boiled, au bleu

Blaufelchen [blow-faylshen] blue Lake Constance trout

Blaukraut [blowkrowt] red cabbage

Blumenkohl [bloomenkohl] cauliflower

Blumenkohlsuppe [-zoop-uh] cauliflower soup

blutig [blootish] rare

Blutwurst [bloot-voorst] black pudding, blood sausage

Bockwurst large frankfurter

Bohnen beans

Bohneneintopf [-ine-topf] bean stew

Bohnensalat [-zalaht] bean salad

Bohnensuppe [-zoop-uh] bean soup

Bonbon [bongbong] sweet

Bouillon [boolyong] clear soup

Bouletten meat balls

Braten [brahten] roast meat

braten to fry

Bratensoße [-zohss-uh] gravy

Brathähnchen [braht-haynshen] roast chicken

Bratheringe [-hairing-uh] (pickled) fried herrings (served cold)

Bratkartoffeln fried potatoes

Bratwurst [-voorst] grilled pork sausage

Brezel [braytsel] pretzel

Brombeeren [brombairen] blackberries

Brot [broht] bread

Brötchen [brurtshen] roll

Brotsuppe [brohtzoop-uh] bread soup

Brühwurst [broovoorst] large frankfurter

Brunnenkresse [broonnen-kress-uh] watercress

Bückling [bookling] smoked red herring

bunte Platte [boont-uh plat-uh] mixed platter

Burgundersoße [boorgoonder-zohss-uh] Burgundy wine sauce

Butterbrezel [bootter-braytsel] butter pretzel

Buttercremetorte [bootterkraym-tort-uh] cream cake

Champignoncremesuppe [-kraym-zoop-uh] cream of mushroom soup

Champignons [shampinyongs] mushrooms

Champignonsoße [-zohss-uh] mushroom sauce

Chicorée [shikoray] chicory

Chinakohl [sheena-kohl] Chinese leaf

Chips crisps, potato chips

Cordon bleu veal cordon bleu

Curryreis [-rice] curried rice

Currywurst [-voorst] curried pork sausage

Dampfnudeln [-noodeln] sweet yeast dumpling

dazu reichen wir ... served with ...

deutsches Beefsteak [doytshess] mince patty

dicke Bohnen [dick-uh] broad beans

Dillsoße [-zohss-uh] dill sauce

durchgebraten [doorsh-gebrahten] well-done

durchwachsen [doorsh-vacksen] with fat

durchwachsener Speck [shpeck] streaky bacon

Edelpilzkäse [aydelpilts-kayz-uh] blue cheese

Ei [ī] egg

Eier [ī-er] eggs

Eierauflauf [-owf-lowf] omelette

Eierkuchen [-kookhen] pancake

Eierpfannkuchen pancake

Eierspeise [-shpize-uh] egg dish

eingelegt [ine-gelaykt] pickled

eingelegte Bratheringe pickled herrings

eingemacht [ine-gemakht] preserved

ein paar ... some ...

Eintopf [ine-topf] stew

Eintopfgericht [-gerisht] stew

Eis [ice] ice; ice cream

Eis am Stiel [shteel] ice lolly

Eisbecher [-besher] sundae

Eisbein [-bine] knuckles of pork

Eisbergsalat [-bairk-zalaht] iceberg lettuce

Eisschokolade [-shockolahd-uh] iced chocolate

Eissplittertorte [-shplitter-tort-uh] ice chip cake

Endiviensalat [endeev-yen-zalaht] endive salad

englisch [eng-lish] rare

Ente [ent-uh] duck

Entenbraten [entenbrahten] roast duck

entgrätet boned

Entrecote sirloin steak

Erbsen [airpsen] peas

Erbsensuppe [-zoop-uh] pea soup

Erdäpfel [airt-epfel] potatoes

Erdbeeren [airtbairen] strawberries

Erdbeertorte [-tort-uh] strawberry gâteau

Erdnüsse [airtnooss-uh] peanuts

Essig vinegar

falscher Hase [fal-sher hahz-uh] meat loaf

Fasan [fazahn] pheasant

Faschierte Laibchen [fasheert-uh lipe-shen] rissoles

Faschiertes [fasheertess] minced meat

Feldsalat [feltzalaht] lamb's lettuce

Fenchel fennel

Filet [fillay] fillet (steak)

Fisch [fish] fish

Fischfilet fish fillet

Fischfrikadellen fishcakes

Fischgerichte fish dishes

Fischstäbchen [-shtaypshen] fish
fingers

Flädlesuppe [flaydl-uh-zoop-uh]
soup with strips of pasta

flambiert flambé

Fleisch [flysh] meat

Fleischbrühe [-broo-uh] bouillon

Fleischkäse [-kayz-uh] meat loaf

Fleischklößchen [-klurss-shen]
meat ball(s)

Fleischpastete [-pastayt-uh]
meat vol-au-vent

Fleischsalat [-zalaht] diced meat
salad with mayonnaise

Fleischtomate [-tomaht-uh] beef
tomato

Fleisch- und Wurstwaren meats
and sausages

Fleischwurst [-voorst] pork
sausage

Flugente [flook-ent-uh] wild
duck

Folienkartoffel [fohl-yen-] baked
potato

Fond [font] meat juices

Forelle [forell-uh] trout

Forelle blau [blow] trout au bleu

Forelle Müllerin (Art) [moollerin]
trout coated with
breadcrumbs and served
with butter and lemon

Frikadelle [frickadell-uh] rissole

frisch gepreßt freshly squeezed

Frischwurst [-voorst] fresh
sausage

fritiert [friteert] (deep-)fried

Froschschenkel [frosh-shenkel]
frogs' legs

Frühlingsgemüse [froolings-
gemooz-uh] spring vegetables

Frühlingsrolle [-rol-uh] spring
roll

Gabelrollmops [gahbel-] rolled
pickled herring, rollmops

Gans [ganss] goose

Gänsebraten [genz-uh-brahten]
roast goose

Gänseleber [-layber] goose liver

Gänseleberpastete [-pastayt-uh]
goose liver pâté

gar cooked

garniert [garneert] garnished

Gebäck [gebeck] pastries, cakes

gebacken fried

gebeizt [gebytst] marinaded

gebraten [gebrahten] roast

gebunden [geboonden]
thickened

gedämpft [gedempft] steamed

Gedeck set meal

gedünstet [gedoonstet] steamed

Geflügel [gefloogel] poultry

Geflügelleber [-layber] chicken
liver

Geflügelleberragout [-ragoo]
chicken liver ragout

Geflügelsalat [-zalaht] chicken/
poultry salad

gefüllt [gefoolt] stuffed

gefüllte Kalbsbrust [kalpsbroost]
veal roll

gegart cooked

gegrillt grilled

gehackt minced; chopped

Gehacktes minced meat

gekocht [gekoKHt] boiled

gekochtes Ei [ī] boiled egg

Gelee [Jellay] jelly

gemischter Salat [gemishter zalaht] mixed salad

gemischtes Eis [ice] assorted ice creams

Gemüse [gemooz-uh] vegetable(s)

Gemüseplatte [plat-uh] assorted vegetables

Gemüsereis [-rice] rice with vegetables

Gemüsesalat [-zalaht] vegetable salad

Gemüsesuppe [-zoop-uh] vegetable soup

gepökelt [gepurkelt] salted, pickled

geräuchert [geroyshert] smoked

gerieben [gereeben] grated

Germknödel [gairm-k-nurdel] yeast dumplings

geschlagen [geshlahgen] whipped

geschmort [geshmohrt] braised, stewed

geschnetzelt [geshnetselt] .chopped

Geschnetzeltes strips of meat in thick sauce

Geselchtes [gezelshtess] salted and smoked meat

gespickt mit ... larded with ...

geschwenkt [geshvenkt] sautéd

Gewürze [gevoorts-uh] spices

Gewürzgurken [-goorken] gherkins

Goldbarsch [goltbarsh] type of perch

Götterspeise [gurttershpize-uh] jelly

gratiniert [gratineert] au gratin

Grießklößchen [greessklurs-shen] semolina dumplings

Grießsuppe [-zoop-uh] semolina soup

grüne Bohnen [groon-uh] French beans

grüne Nudeln [noodeln] green pasta

grüner Aal [ahl] fresh eel

Grünkohl (curly) kale

Gugelhupf [googel-hoopf] ring-shaped cake

Gulasch goulash

Gulaschsuppe [-zoop-uh] goulash soup

Gurke [goork-uh] cucumber; gherkin

Gurkensalat [-zalaht] cucumber salad

Hackepeter [hack-uh-payter] minced meat

Hackfleisch [-flysh] minced meat

Hähnchen [haynshen] chicken

Hähnchenkeule [-koyl-uh] chicken leg

Haifischflossensuppe [hyfishflossen-zoop-uh] shark-fin soup

halbes Hähnchen [haynshen] half chicken

Hammelbraten [-brahten] roast mutton

Hammelfleisch [-flysh] mutton

Hammelkeule [-koyl-uh] leg of
mutton

Hammelrücken [-roocken] saddle
of mutton

Handkäse [hant-kayz-uh] very
strong-smelling cheese

hartgekochtes Ei [hartgekoKHtess
ī] hard-boiled egg

Hartkäse [-kayz-uh] hard cheese

Haschee [hashay] hash

Haselnüsse [hahzelnooss-uh]
hazelnuts

Hasenbraten [hahzenbrahten]
roast hare

Hasenkeule [-koyl-uh] haunch of
hare

Hasenpfeffer jugged hare

Hauptgerichte main dishes

Hauptspeisen main courses

Hausfrauenart [howssfrowenart]
home-made style

hausgemacht [howss-gemaKHt]
homemade

Hausmacher (Art) [howssmaKHer]
home-made style

Hausmarke [howss-mark-uh]
own brand

Hecht [hesht] pike

Hechtsuppe [-zoop-uh] pike
soup

Heidelbeeren [hydelbairen]
bilberries

Heilbutt [hile-boott] halibut

Heringssalat [hairings-zalaht]
herring salad

Heringsstipp [-shtip] herring
salad

Heringstopf pickled herrings

Herz [hairts] heart

Himbeeren [himbairen]
raspberries

Himmel und Erde [oont aird-uh]
potato and apple purée with
liver sausage

Hirn [heern] brains

Hirschbraten [heershbrahten]
roast venison

Hirschmedaillons [-medah-yongs]
small venison fillets

Holsteiner Schnitzel [holshtyner
shnitsel] breaded veal cutlet
with vegetables, topped with
a fried egg

Honig [hohnish] honey

Honigkuchen [-kooKHen]
honeycake

Honigmelone [-melohn-uh]
honey melon

Hoppelpoppel bacon and
potato omelette

Hüfte [hooft-uh] haunch

Huhn [hoon] chicken

Hühnerbrühe [hooner-broo-uh]
chicken broth

Hühnersuppe [-zoop-uh] chicken
soup

Hülsenfrüchte [hoolzenfroosht-uh]
peas and beans, pulses

Hummer [hoommer] lobster

Imbiß [imbiss] snack

inbegriffen included

Inklusivpreis all-inclusive price

Jagdwurst [yahkt-voorst] ham
sausage with garlic

Jägerschnitzel [yaygershnitsel]
pork with mushrooms

junge Erbsen [yoong-uh airpzen]
spring peas

Kabeljau [kahbelyow] cod

Kaiserschmarren [kyzershmarren]
sugared pancakes with
raisins

Kalbfleisch [kalpflysh] veal

Kalbsbraten [-brahten] roast veal

Kalbsbries [-breess] sweetbread

Kalbsfrikassee veal fricassee

Kalbshaxe leg of veal

Kalbsmedaillons [-medah-yongs]
small veal fillets

Kalbsnierenbraten [-neeren-
brahten] roast veal with
kidney

Kalbsschnitzel [-shnitsel] veal
cutlet

kalte Platte cold meal

kalter Braten [brahten] cold
meat

kaltes Bufett cold buffet

kalte Speisen cold dishes

Kaltschale [kaltshahl-uh] cold
sweet fruit soup

kalt servieren serve cold

Kaninchen [kaneenshen] rabbit

Kaninchenbraten [-brahten] roast
rabbit

Kapern [kahpern] capers

Karbonade [karbonahd-uh]
carbonade, beef and onion
stew cooked in beer

Karfiol [karf-yohl] cauliflower

Karotten carrots

Karpfen carp

Karpfen blau [blow] carp au
bleu

Kartoffel potato

Kartoffelbrei [-bry] potato purée

Kartoffelklöße [-klurss-uh] potato
dumplings

Kartoffelknödel [-k-nurdel]
potato dumplings

Kartoffeln potatoes

Kartoffelpuffer [-pooffer] potato
fritters

Kartoffelpüree [-pooray] potato
purée

Kartoffelsalat [-zalaht] potato
salad

Kartoffelsuppe [-zoop-uh] potato
soup

Käse [kayz-uh] cheese

Käsebrötchen [-brurtshen]
cheese roll

Käsegebäck [-gebeck] cheese
savouries

Käsekuchen [-kooкнen]
cheesecake

Käseplatte [-plat-uh] selection
of cheeses, cheeseboard

Käse-Sahne-Torte [-zahn-uh-tort-
uh] cream cheesecake

Käsesalat [-zalaht] cheese salad

Käseschnitzel [-shnitsel]
escalopes with cheese

Käsesoße [-zohss-uh] cheese
sauce

Käsespätzle [-shpetz-luh] home-
made noodles with cheese

Kasseler Rippenspeer [rippen-
shpair] salted ribs of pork

Kasserolle [kasserol-uh]
casserole

Kassler smoked and braised
pork chops

Kastanien [kast**ah**n-yen] chestnuts

Katenleberwurst [k**ah**tenlayber-voorst] smoked liver sausage

Katenrauchwurst [-rowKH-voorst] smoked sausage

Keule [k**oy**l-uh] leg, haunch

Kieler Sprotten [k**ee**ler shpr**o**tten] smoked sprats

Kinderteller children's portion

Kirschen [k**ee**rshen] cherries

klare Brühe [kl**ah**r-uh br**oo**-uh] clear soup

Klößchensuppe [kl**u**rss-shen-zoop-uh] clear soup with dumplings

Klöße [kl**u**rss-uh] dumplings

Knäckebrot [k-n**e**ck-uh-broht] crispbread

Knacker frankfurter(s)

Knackwurst [-voorst] frankfurter

Knoblauch [k-n**oh**b-lowKH] garlic

Knoblauchbrot [-broht] garlic bread

Knochen [k-n**o**KHen] bone

Knochenschinken [-shinken] ham on the bone

Knödel [k-n**ur**del] dumplings

kochen [k**o**KHen] to cook; to boil

Kohl cabbage

Kohlrabi [-r**ah**bee] kohlrabi (type of cabbage)

Kohlrouladen [-r**oo**l**ah**den] stuffed cabbage leaves

Kohl und Pinkel cabbage, potatoes, sausage and smoked meat

Kompott stewed fruit

Konfitüre [konfit**oo**r-uh] jam

Königinpastete [k**u**rnigin-past**ay**t-uh] chicken vol-au-vent

Königsberger Klopse [k**u**rniksbairger kl**o**ps-uh] meatballs in caper sauce

Königskuchen [k**u**rniks-k**oo**KHen] type of fruit cake

Kopfsalat [k**o**pfzalaht] lettuce

Kotelett [k**o**tlet] chop

Krabben shrimps, prawns

Krabbencocktail prawn cocktail

Kraftbrühe [kr**a**ftbr**oo**-uh] beef consommé, beef tea

Krapfen jam doughnut with icing

Kräuter [kr**oy**ter] herbs

Kräuterbutter [-bootter] herb butter

Kräuterkäse [-k**ay**z-uh] cheese flavoured with herbs

Kräutersoße [-z**oh**ss-uh] herb sauce

Krautsalat [kr**ow**tzalaht] coleslaw

Krautwickel [-vickel] stuffed cabbage leaves

Krebs [kr**ay**ps] crayfish

Kren [kr**ay**n] horseradish

Kresse [kr**e**ss-uh] cress

Kroketten croquettes

Kruste crust

Küche [k**oo**sh-uh] cooking; cuisine; kitchen

Kuchen [k**oo**KHen] cake; pie

Kümmel [k**oo**mel] caraway

Kümmelbraten [-br**ah**ten] roast with caraway seeds

Kürbis [k**oo**rbiss] pumpkin

Labskaus [**l**apskowss] meat, fish and potato stew

Lachs [lacks] salmon

Lachsersatz [-airz**a**ts] sliced and salted pollack

Lachsforelle [-for**e**ll-uh] sea trout

Lachsschinken [-**s**hinken] smoked rolled filet of ham

Lakritz liquorice

Lamm Lamb

Lammrücken [-r**oo**ken] saddle of lamb

Languste [lang**oo**st-uh] crayfish

Lauch [lowKH] leek

Lauchsuppe [-zoop-uh] leek soup

Leber [l**ay**ber] liver

Leberkäse [-kayz-uh] baked pork and beef loaf

Leberklöße [-klurss-uh] liver dumplings

Leberknödel [-k-nurdel] liver dumplings

Leberknödelsuppe [-zoop-uh] liver dumpling soup

Leberpastete [-past**ay**t-uh] liver pâté

Leberwurst [-voorst] liver sausage

Lebkuchen [l**ay**p-k**oo**KHen] type of gingerbread biscuit

legiert thickened

Leipziger Allerlei [l**i**pe-tsiger **a**l-er-ly] mixed vegetables

Lendensteak loin steak

Linseneintopf [l**i**nzen-inetopf] lentil stew

Linsensuppe [-zoop-uh] lentil soup

Lutscher [l**oo**tsher] lollipop

mager [m**a**hger] lean

Majoran [m**a**hyo-rahn] marjoram

Makrele [makr**a**yl-uh] mackerel

Makronen [makr**oh**nen] macaroons

Mandarine [mandar**ee**n-uh] tangerine

Mandeln almonds

Margarine [margar**ee**n-uh] margarine

Marille [mar**i**ll-uh] apricot

Marinade [mareen**a**hd-uh] marinade

mariniert marinaded, pickled

Markklößchen [-klurss-shen] marrow dumplings

Marmelade [marmel**a**hd-uh] jam

Marmorkuchen [m**a**rmor-k**oo**KHen] marble cake

Maronen [mar**oh**nen] sweet chestnuts

Matjesfilet [m**a**tyess-fill**ay**] fillet of herring

Matjes(hering) [-**h**airing] young herring

Maultaschen [m**ow**l-tashen] pasta filled with meat, vegetables or cheese

Medaillons [m**a**ydah-yongs] small fillets

Meeresfische [m**a**iress-fish-uh] seafish

Meeresfrüchte [-fr**oo**sht-uh]

seafood

Meerrettich [m**ai**r-rettish]
horseradish

Meerrettichsoße [-zohss-uh]
horseradish sauce

Mehl [mayl] flour

Mehlspeise [-shpize-uh] sweet
dish, flummery

Melone [mel**oh**n-uh] melon

Menü set menu

Miesmuscheln [m**ee**ss-moosheln]
mussels

Milch [milsh] milk

Milchreis [-rice] rice pudding

Mirabelle [meerab**e**ll-uh] small
yellow plum

Mischbrot [m**i**shbroht] rye and
wheat bread

Mohnkuchen [m**oh**nk**OO**KHen]
poppyseed cake

Mohnstrudel poppy-seed
strudel

Möhren [m**ur**-ren] carrots

Mohrrüben [m**oh**r-r**oo**ben]
carrots

Mus [m**OO**ss] purée

Muscheln [m**oo**sheln] mussels

Muskat(nuß) [m**oo**sk**ah**t(nooss)]
nutmeg

nach Art des Hauses [h**ow**zess]
à la maison

nach Hausfrauenart [h**ow**ss-
frowenart] home-made

nach Jahreszeit depending on
season

Nachspeisen [n**a**KH-shpyzen]
desserts

Nachtisch [n**a**KHtish] dessert

Napfkuchen [n**a**pf-k**OO**KHen] ring-
shaped poundcake

natur [nat**oo**r] plain

nicht gar underdone

Nierenragout [n**ee**ren-rag**OO**]
kidney ragout

Nudeln [n**OO**deln] pasta

Nudelsalat [-zal**ah**t] noodle
salad

Nudelsuppe [-zoop-uh] noodle
soup

Nuß [nooss] nut

Nüsse [n**OO**ss-uh] nuts

Obst [ohpst] fruit

Obstsalat [-zal**ah**t] fruit salad

Ochsenschwanzsuppe [**o**ksen-
shvants-zoop-uh] oxtail soup

ohne Knochen filleted

Öl [url] oil

Oliven [ol**ee**ven] olives

Olivenöl olive oil

Omelett [oml**e**t] omelette

Orangen [oron-Jen] oranges

Originalrezept original recipe

Palatschinken [pallatsh**i**nken]
stuffed pancakes

Pampelmuse [pampel-m**OO**z-uh]
grapefruit

paniert [pan**ee**rt] with
breadcrumbs

Paprikarahmschnitzel [p**a**preekah-
r**ah**mshnitsel] cutlet in
creamy sauce with paprika

Paprikasalat [-zal**ah**t] pepper
salad

Paprikaschote [-shoht-uh]
pepper

Paradeiser [parad**y**zer] tomatoes

Parmesankäse [parmez**ah**nkayz-uh] Parmesan cheese

Pastete [past**ay**t-uh] vol-au-vent; pâté

Pellkartoffeln potatoes boiled in their jackets

Petersilie [payterz**ee**l-yuh] parsley

Petersilienkartoffeln potatoes with parsley

Pfannengerichte fried dishes

Pfannkuchen [-k**OO**KHen] pancake

Pfeffer pepper

Pfefferminz peppermint

Pfeffernüsse [-n**OO**ss-uh] gingerbread biscuits

Pfefferrahmsoße [-rahmzohss-uh] peppered creamy sauce

Pfifferlinge [pf**i**fferling-uh] chanterelles

Pfirsiche [pf**ee**rzish-uh] peaches

Pflaumen [pfl**ow**men] plums

Pflaumenkuchen [-k**OO**KHen] plum tart

Pflaumenmus [-m**oo**ss] plum jam

Pichelsteiner Topf [p**i**shelshtyner] vegetable stew with diced beef

Pilze [p**i**lts-uh] mushrooms

Pilzsoße [p**i**lts-zohss-uh] mushroom sauce

Pilzsuppe [-z**oo**p-uh] mushroom soup

Platte [pl**a**t-uh] selection

Plätzchen [pl**e**ts-shen] biscuit

pochiert [posh**ee**rt] poached

Pökelfleisch [p**u**rkelflysh] salted meat

Pommes frites [pom frit] chips, French fries

Porree [p**o**rray] leek

Potthast [p**o**t-hast] braised beef with sauce

Poularde [pool**ar**d-uh] young chicken

Preiselbeeren [pr**y**zel-bairen] cranberries

Preßkopf [pr**e**sskopf] brawn

Prinzeßbohnen [prints**e**ss-] unsliced runner beans

Pumpernickel black rye bread

Püree [p**oo**ray] (potato) purée

püriert [p**oo**reert] puréed

Putenschenkel [p**OO**tenshenkel] turkey leg

Putenschnitzel [-shnitsel] turkey escalope

Puter [p**OO**ter] turkey

Quark [kvark] type of low-fat cream cheese, quark

Quarkspeise [-shp**i**ze-uh] dish made with low-fat cream cheese

Radieschen [rad**ee**ss-shen] radishes

Rahm (sour) cream

Rahmschnitzel [-shnitsel] cutlet in creamy sauce

Räucheraal [r**oy**sher-ahl] smoked eel

Räucherhering [-hairing] kipper, smoked herring

Räucherlachs [-lacks] smoked salmon

Räucherspeck smoked bacon

Rauchfleisch [rowKH-flysh] smoked meat

Rehbraten [ray-brahten] roast venison

Rehkeule [-koyl-uh] haunch of venison

Rehrücken [-rœken] saddle of venison

Reibekuchen [ribe-uh-kOOKHen] potato waffles

Reis [rice] rice

Reisauflauf [-owf-lowf] rice pudding

Reisbrei [rice-bry] creamed rice

Reisfleisch [-flysh] meat with rice and tomatoes

Reisrand [-rant] with rice

Reissalat [-zalaht] rice salad

Reissuppe [-zoop-uh] rice soup

Remoulade [remOOlahd-uh] remoulade (mayonnaise and herb dressing)

Renke [renk-uh] whitefish

Rettich [rettish] radish

Rhabarber [rabarber] rhubarb

rheinischer Sauerbraten [rynisher zowerbrahten] braised beef

Rinderbraten [rinder-brahten] pot roast

Rinderfilet [-fillay] fillet steak

Rinderleber [-layber] beef liver

Rinderlende [-lend-uh] beef tenderloin

Rinderrouladen [-rOOlahden] stuffed beef rolls

Rinderschmorbraten [-shmohr-brahten] pot roast

Rinderzunge [-tsoong-uh] ox tongue

Rindfleisch [rintflysh] beef

Rindfleischsalat [-zalaht] beef salad

Rindfleischsuppe [-zoop-uh] beef broth

Rippchen [ripshen] spareribs

Rippe [ripp-uh] rib

Risi-Pisi [reezee-peezee] rice and peas

roh raw

Rohkostplatte [-plat-uh] selection of salads

Rollmops rolled-up pickled herring, rollmops

rosa rare to medium

Rosenkohl Brussels sprouts

Rosinen [rohzeenen] raisins

Rostbraten [-brahten] roast

Rostbratwurst [-braht-voorst] barbecued sausage

Rösti [rurshtee] fried potatoes and onions

Röstkartoffeln [rurst-] fried potatoes

Rotbarsch [rohtbarsh] type of perch

rote Bete [roht-uh bayt-uh] beetroot, red beet

rote Grütze [roht-uh grOOts-uh] red fruit jelly

Rotkohl [roht-] red cabbage

Rotkraut [-krowt] red cabbage

Roulade [rOOlahd-uh] beef olive

Rühreier [rOOr-ī-er] scrambled eggs

Rührei mit Speck scrambled eggs and bacon

Russische Eier [rOOssish-uh ī-er] egg mayonnaise

Sachertorte [zaKHertort-uh] rich chocolate cake

Sahne [zahn-uh] cream

Sahnesoße [-zohss-uh] cream sauce

Sahnetorte [-tort-uh] cream gateau

Salat [zalaht] salad; lettuce

Salate salads

Salatplatte [-plat-uh] selection of salads

Salatsoße [-zohss-uh] salad dressing

Salatteller side salad; selection of salads

Salz [zalts] salt

Salzburger Nockerln [zaltsboorger] sweet soufflés

Salzheringe [-hairing-uh] salted herrings

Salzkartoffeln boiled potatoes

Sandkuchen [zantkooKHen] type of Madeira cake

Sauerbraten [zowerbrahten] marinaded potroast

Sauerkraut [zowerkrowt] white cabbage, finely chopped and pickled

Sauerrahm [-rahm] sour cream

Schafskäse [shahfs-kayz-uh] sheep's milk cheese

Schaschlik [shashlik] (shish-) kebab

Schattenmorellen morello cherries

Schellfisch haddock

Schildkrötensuppe [shiltkrurten-zoop-uh] real turtle soup

Schillerlocken [shiller-] smoked haddock rolls

Schinken [shinken] ham

Schinkenbrötchen [-brurtshen] ham roll

Schinkenröllchen [-rurlshen] rolled ham

Schinkenspeck [-shpeck] bacon

Schinkenwurst [-voorst] ham sausage

Schlachtplatte [shlaKHtplat-uh] selection of fresh sausages

Schlagobers [shlahk-obers] whipped cream

Schlagsahne [-zahn-uh] whipped cream

Schlei [shly] tench

Schmorbraten [shmohrbrahten] pot roast

Schnecken [shnecken] snails

Schnittlauch [shnitt-lowKH] chives

Schnitzel [shnitsel] cutlet

Schokolade [shokolahd-uh] chocolate

Scholle [sholl-uh] plaice

Schollenfilet [-fillay] fillet of plaice

Schulterstück [shoolter-shtoock] slice of shoulder

Schwarzbrot [shvartsbroht] dark rye bread

Schwarzwälder Kirschtorte [shvartsvelder keershtort-uh] Black Forest cherry gateau

Schwarzwurzeln [-voortseln] salsifies

Schweinebauch [shvine-uh-bowKH] belly of pork

MENU READER: FOOD

Schweinebraten [-brahten] roast
pork

Schweinefilet [-fillay] fillet of
pork

Schweinefleisch [-flysh] pork

Schweinekotelett [-kotlet] pork
chop

Schweineleber [-layber] pig's
liver

Schweinerippe [-ripp-uh] cured
pork chop

Schweinerollbraten [-rolbrahten]
rolled roast of pork

Schweineschmorbraten [-shmohr-
brahten] roast pork

Schweineschnitzel [-shnitsel]
pork fillet

Schweinshaxe [shvine-ss-hacks-
uh] knuckle of pork

Seelachs [zaylacks] pollack

Seezunge [-tsoong-uh] sole

Sellerie [zelleree] celery

selten [zelten] rare

Semmel [zemmel] bread roll

Semmelknödel [-k-nurdel] bread
dumplings

Senf [zenf] mustard

Senfsahnesoße [-zahn-uh-zohss-
uh] mustard and cream
sauce

Senfsoße mustard sauce

serbisches Reisfleisch
[zairbishess rice-flysh] diced
pork, onions, tomatoes and
rice

Sohle [zohl-uh] sole

Soleier [zohl-ī-er] pickled eggs

Soße [zohss-uh] sauce; gravy

Spanferkel [shpahn-fairkel]
suckling pig

Spargel [shpargel] asparagus

Spargelcremesuppe [-kraym-zoop-
uh] cream of asparagus soup

Spätzle [shpets-luh] home-made
noodles

Speckkartoffeln [shpeck-]
potatoes with bacon

Speckknödel [-k-nurdel] bacon
dumplings

Specksoße [-zohss-uh] bacon
sauce

Speckstreifen [-shrtyfen] strips
of bacon

Speisekarte [shpize-uh-kart-uh]
menu

Spezialität des Hauses our
speciality

Spiegeleier [shpeegel-ī-er] fried
eggs

Spieß: am Spieß [shpeess] on
the spit

Spießbraten [shpeess-brahten]
joint roasted on a spit

Spinat [shpinaht] spinach

Spitzkohl [shpits-] white
cabbage

Sprotten [shprotten] sprats

Stachelbeeren [shtaKHel-bairen]
gooseberries

Stangenspargel [shtangen-
shpargel] asparagus spears

Stangen(weiß)brot [shtangen-
(vice-)broht] French bread

Steinbutt [shtine-boott] turbot

Steinpilze [-pilts-uh] type of
mushroom

Stollen [shtollen] type of fruit
loaf

Strammer Max [shtrammer] ham
and fried egg on bread

Streuselkuchen [shtroyzel-
kOOKHen] sponge cake with
crumble topping

Sülze [zOOlts-uh] brawn

Suppe [zoop-uh] soup

Suppen soups

Suppengrün [zOOpengrOOn]
mixed herbs and vegetables
(in soup)

Süßigkeiten [zOOssish-kyten]
sweets

Süßspeisen [zOOss-shpyzen]
sweet dishes

Süßwasserfische [zOOss-vasser-
fish-uh] freshwater fish

Szegediner Gulasch
[shegaydeener] goulash with
pickled cabbage

Tafelspitz [tahfel-shpits] soured
boiled rump

Tagesgericht [tahgess-gerisht]
dish of the day

Tageskarte [-kart-uh] menu of
the day; set menu

Tagessuppe [-zoop-uh] soup of
the day

Tatar [tatahr] raw mince with
spices

Taube [towb-uh] pigeon

Teigmantel [tike-mantel] pastry
covering

Teigwaren [-vahren] pasta

Thunfisch [tOOnfish] tuna

Tintenfisch [-fish] squid

Tomate [tomahtuh] tomato

Tomatensalat [-zalaht] tomato
salad

Tomatensuppe [-zoop-uh]
tomato soup

Topfen quark

Törtchen [turtshen] tart(s)

Torte [tort-uh] gateau

tournierte Butter shaped butter
segments

Trauben [trowben] grapes

Truthahn [trOOt-] turkey

überbacken [OOberbacken] au
gratin

Ungarisches Gulasch
[OOngahrishess] Hungarian
goulash

Vanilleeis [vanill-uh-ice] vanilla
ice cream

Vanillesoße [-zohss-uh] vanilla
sauce

vegetarisch [vegaytahrish]
vegetarian

verlorene Eier [fairlohren-uh i-er]
poached eggs

Vollkornbrot [follkornbroht] dark
rye bread

vom Grill grilled

vom Kalb veal

vom Lamm lamb

vom Rind beef

vom Rost grilled

vom Schwein pork

vorbereiten to prepare

Vorspeisen [forshpyzen] hors
d'œuvres, starters

Waffeln [vaffeln] waffles

Waldmeister [valtmyster]
woodruff

Waldorfsalat [valdorf-zal**aht**] salad with celery, apples and walnuts

Wassermelone [va**sser-melohn**-uh] water melon

Weichkäse [v**y**sh-kayz-uh] soft cheese

Weinbergschnecken [v**ine**-bairk-shnecken] snails

Weincreme [v**ine**-kraym] pudding with wine

Weinkraut [-krowt] sauerkraut

Weinschaumcreme [-showm-kraym] creamed pudding with wine

Weinsoße [-zohss-uh] wine sauce

Weintrauben [-trowben] grapes

Weißbrot [v**ice**-broht] white bread

Weißkohl white cabbage

Weißkraut [-krowt] white cabbage

Weißwurst [-voorst] veal sausage

Wiener Schnitzel [v**ee**ner shn**i**tsel] veal in breadcrumbs

Wiener Würstchen [v**oo**rstshen] frankfurter(s)

Wild [vilt] game

Wildbret [-brayt] venison

Wildgerichte venison dishes

Wildschweinkeule [v**i**ltshvine-koyl-uh] haunch of wild boar

Wildschweinsteak wild boar steak

Windbeutel [v**i**ntboytel] cream puff

Wirsing [v**ee**rzing] savoy

cabbage

Wurst [voorst] sausage

Wurstbrötchen [-brurtshen] roll with sausage meat

Würstchen [v**oo**rstshen] frankfurter(s)

Wurstplatte [v**oo**rst-plat-uh] selection of sausages

Wurstsülze [-z**oo**lts-uh] sausage brawn

Würzfleisch [-flysh] spicy meat

Zander [ts**a**nder] pike-perch, zander

Zartbitterschokolade [tsartbitter-shokol**ah**d-uh] plain chocolate

Ziegenkäse [ts**ee**gen-kayz-uh] goat's cheese

Zigeunerschnitzel [tsig**oy**ner-shnitsel] veal or pork with peppers and relishes

Zitrone [tsitr**oh**n-uh] lemon

Zitronencreme [-kraym] lemon cream

Zucchini [tsook**ee**nee] courgettes, zucchini

Zucker [ts**oo**cker] sugar

Zuckererbsen [-airpsen] mange-tout peas

Zunge [ts**oo**ng-uh] tongue

Zwiebel [tsv**ee**bel] onion

Zwiebelringe [-ring-uh] onion rings

Zwiebelrostbraten [-rostbrahten] steak with fried onions

Zwiebelsuppe [-zoop-uh] onion soup

Zwiebeltorte [-tort-uh] onion tart

Zwischengerichte entrées

Menu Reader:

Drink

---

alkoholfreies Bier [alkoh**ohl**fry-ess beer] alcohol-free beer

Alsterwasser [-vasser] shandy

Alt(bier) [**alt**(beer)] light brown beer, not sweet

Apfelsaft [**a**pfelzaft] apple juice

Apfelschorle [-shorl-uh] sparkling apple juice

Apfelwein [-vine] cider

Äppelwoi [**e**ppelvoy] cider

Auslese [**ow**sslayz-uh] wine selected from ripest bunches of grapes in top wine category

Ausschankwein [**ow**ss-shank-vine] wine by the glass

Bananenmilch [ban**ah**nen-milsh] banana milk shake

Beerenauslese [b**ai**ren-owsslayz-uh] wine from specially selected single grapes in top wine category

Berliner Weiße [bairl**ee**ner v**ice**-uh] fizzy beer

Bier [beer] beer

Bockbier [**bock**beer] strong beer

Bowle [b**oh**l-uh] punch

Buttermilch [b**oo**ttermilsh] buttermilk

Cidre [s**ee**dr-uh] cider

Doppelkorn grain schnapps

Eierlikör [**ī**er-likur] advocaat

Eiswein [**ice**-vine] wine made from grapes picked after frost

entkoffeiniert [entkoffay-een**ee**rt] decaffeinated

Erdbeermilch [**a**irtbair-milsh] strawberry milk shake

Erzeugerabfüllung estate bottled

Federweißer [**fay**der-vysser] new wine

Feuerzangenbowle [**foy**er-tsangen-bohl-uh] red wine punch with rum which has been flamed off

Flasche [fl**a**sh-uh] bottle

Flaschenwein [fl**a**shen-vine] bottled wine

fruchtig [fr**oo**KHtish] fruity

Fruchtsaft [fr**oo**KHtzaft] fruit juice

Gespritzter [geshpr**i**tster] wine and soda, spritzer

Getränke beverages

Glühwein [gl**oo**-vine] mulled wine

Grog hot water with rum and sugar

halbsüß [h**a**lp-z**oo**ss] semi-sweet

halbtrocken [h**a**lp-] medium dry

Hefeweizen [h**ay**f-uh-vytsen] fizzy beer made with yeast and wheat

Heidelbeergeist [h**y**delbair-gyst] blueberry brandy

heiße Zitrone [h**i**ce-uh tsitr**oh**n-uh] hot lemon

heiße Milch [h**i**ce-uh milsh] hot milk

Helles [h**e**lless] lager

herb [hairp] very dry

Himbeergeist [h**i**mbair-gyst]

raspberry brandy

Jahrgang [yahrgang] vintage

Kabinett light, usually dry, wine in top wine category

Kaffee [kaffay] coffee

Kaffee mit Milch [milsh] white coffee

Kakao [kakow] cocoa; hot chocolate

Kännchen (Kaffee) [kennshen (kaffay)] pot (of coffee)

Kellerei [keller-ī] (wine) producer's

Kir [keer] white wine with a dash of blackcurrant liqueur

Kir Royal [royahl] champagne with a dash of blackcurrant liqueur

koffeinfrei [koffay-een-fry] decaffeinated

Kognak [konyak] brandy

Korn type of schnapps

Kräuterlikör [kroyterlikur] herbal liqueur

Kräutertee [-tay] herbal tea

Krimsekt [krimzekt] Crimean champagne

Landwein [lantvine] country wine

Likör [likur] liqueur

Limo [leemo] lemonade

Limonade [limonahd-uh] lemonade

Liter [leeter] litre

Malzbier [maltsbeer] sweet stout

Maß [mahss] litre of beer

(Bavaria)

Milchmixgetränk [milshmix-getrenk] milkshake

Mineralwasser [minerahl-vasser] sparkling mineral water

mischen [mishen] to mix

Mokka mocha

Most [mosst] fruit wine

Nektar fruit squash

neuer Wein [noyer vine] new wine

Obstler [ohpstler] fruit schnapps

offener Wein [vine] wine by the glass

Orangensaft [oronJenzaft] orange juice

Pikkolo quarter bottle of champagne

Portwein [-vine] port

Pulverkaffee [poolver-kaffay] instant coffee

Qualitätswein b.A quality wine from a special wine-growing area

Qualitätswein m.P. top quality German wine

Radler(maß) [rahtler-mahss] shandy

Rosé(wein) [rohzay(vine)] rosé wine

Rotwein [rohtvine] red wine

Saft [zaft] juice

Schokolade [shokolahd-uh] chocolate

Schokomilch [shoko-milsh]